CHILDREN'S IMAGINATIVE PLAY

CHILDREN'S IMAGINATIVE PLAY

A Visit to Wonderland

Shlomo Ariel

Foreword by Brian Sutton-Smith

Child Psychology and Mental Health
Hiram E. Fitzgerald and Susanne Ayres Denham, Series Editors

PRAEGER

Westport, Connecticut
London

Library of Congress Cataloging-in-Publication Data

Ariel, Shlomo.
    Children's imaginative play : a visit to wonderland / Shlomo Ariel ; foreword by Brian
Sutton-Smith.
      p. cm. — (Child psychology and mental health, ISSN 1538–8883)
    Includes bibliographical references and index.
    ISBN 0–275–97757–9 (alk. paper)
    1. Play—Psychological aspects. I. Title. II. Series.
BF717.A75   2002
155.4'18—dc21   2002016949

British Library Cataloguing in Publication Data is available.

Library of Congress Catalog Card Number: 2002016949
ISBN: 0–275–97757–9
ISSN: 1538–8883

First published in 2002

Praeger Publishers, 88 Post Road West, Westport, CT 06881
An imprint of Greenwood Publishing Group, Inc.
www.praeger.com

Printed in the United States of America

The paper used in this book complies with the
Permanent Paper Standard issued by the National
Information Standards Organization (Z39.48–1984).

10 9 8 7 6 5 4 3 2 1

Contents

Series Foreword   vii

Foreword by Brian Sutton-Smith   ix

Preface   xiii

Introduction   1

1. What Is *Make-Believe Play*?   5

2. The Cryptic Codes of Make-Believe Play   15

3. Make-Believe Play as a Diplomatic Language   33

4. Mini-Legal Systems Regulating Sociodramatic Play   43

5. Make-Believe Play as an Emotional Moderator   57

6. Make-Believe Play and the Developing Child   71

7. Make-Believe Play in a Cross-Cultural Perspective   89

8. Applications of Make-Believe Play in Education   117

9. Play Therapy   127

Summary and Apologia   149

Appendix   153

References   185

Index   203

Series Foreword

The twentieth century closed with a decade devoted to the study of brain structure, function and development that in parallel with studies of the human genome has revealed the extraordinary plasticity of biobehavioral organization and development. The twenty-first century opens with a decade focusing on behavior, but the linkages between brain and behavior are as dynamic as the linkages between parents and children, and children and environment.

The Child Psychology and Mental Health series is designed to capture much of this dynamic interplay by advocating for strengthening the science of child development and linking that science to issues related to mental health, child care, parenting and public policy.

The series consists of individual monographs, each dealing with a subject that advances knowledge related to the interplay between normal developmental process and developmental psychopathology. The books are intended to reflect the diverse methodologies and content areas encompassed by an age period ranging from conception to late adolescence. Topics of contemporary interest include studies of socioemotional development, behavioral undercontrol, aggression, attachment disorders and substance abuse.

Investigators involved with prospective longitudinal studies, large epidemiologic cross-sectional samples, intensely followed clinical cases or those wishing to report a systematic sequence of connected experiments are invited to submit manuscripts. Investigators from all fields in social and behavioral sciences, neurobiological sciences, medical and clinical sciences and education are invited to submit manuscripts with implications for child and adolescent mental health.

Hiram E. Fitzgerald
Susanne Ayres Denham
Series Editors

Foreword

Children's imagination is one of the mysteries of the modern age. It is generally conceded to be a universal aspect of childhood, but just what it means is a matter of contradictory beliefs. On the negative side there are the Western industrial work ethic and puritanic attitudes that see play as a waste of time and its contributions to a useful life as being somewhat trivial. These views survive among those who currently don't want preschool class time or elementary school recess time to be wasted on play. They insist on more emphasis on the academic basics in the preschool and more on physical education in the recess period, which in itself they see only as a "lord of the flies" scene for violence and bullying.

Unfortunately, many moderns who do not sympathize with such ideological extremities nevertheless have little sympathy for the children's playground traditions. These often include quite a complex pastiche of male and female play genres that are more strikingly different from each other than modern sensitivities wish to admit. Each playground is often a fest of handclapping and jump rope rhymes and songs, riddles, tales and legends on the one hand; and on the other, teasing, jokes, gross rhymes, pranks, ball games and play fighting. As well as this unrefined imaginative context, this is a political world in which children establish their own power hierarchies and loyalties, none of which are particularly attractive to those devoted to adult concepts of morality and socialization.

Friedrich Nietzsche was one of the few to argue that the child's fantasies of giants and lions and kings are primarily about power and what it means to exercise it. He says, "Innocence is the child, and forgetfulness, a new beginning, a game, a self-rolling wheel. A first movement. Aye for the game of creating which is at the same time a game of destroying."

Oddly this same turbulent view of child fantasy can be said to be implicit in the Freudian view of the child's fantasy life as a rearguard of pleasure-oriented compensation for the fallibilities of life's libidinal milestones. It is perhaps not surprising, therefore, that many academic social scientists have preferred to ignore this message of childhood emotional turbulence. Indeed much earlier in British literature, Charles Kingsley in *The Water Babies* defined the view that childhood was a stage which had to be sacrificed if adult maturity was to be attained. He thought he was following Darwin in saying that children were passing through a more primitive stage that entitled them in theological terms to be sacrificed as sinners in order that in their maturity they might be united with God. Children, he said, were characterized by an inordinate desire for the things of this world, and this inherited disorder could be corrected only when they were taught how to will their extinction.

C.S. Lewis formulated the attitude this way: "To surrender a self-will inflamed and swollen with years of usurpation is a kind of death. We all remember this self-will as it was in childhood the bitter, prolonged rage at every thwarting, the burst of passionate tears, the black Satanic wish to kill or die rather than to give in. Hence the older type of nurse or parent was quite right in thinking that the first step in education is to 'break the child's will.' And if, now that we are grown up, we do not howl and stamp quite so much, that is because our elders began the process of killing our self-will in the nursery."

These moralizing attitudes are answered ironically by Mark Twain in *The Adventures of Huckleberry Finn*, when he says "persons attempting to find a motive in this narrative will be prosecuted; persons attempting to find a moral in it will be banished; persons attempting to find a plot will be shot." And in *Alice's Adventures in Wonderland*, Charles Dodgson (Lewis Carroll) takes up the similar irony that instead of childhood having to be gotten over its imagining, it becomes rather the redemption of adulthood, not its loss, which was also a theme throughout the poetry of William Wordsworth.

Contrary to much of this "negative" viewing of the so-called Wonderland of Play, since about 1750 the concept of the imagination took its place as a central concept in the Enlightenment notions of rationality. Philosopher Immanuel Kant contended that without imagination there could be no hypotheses in science. Furthermore in many secular quarters the imagination even took on the humanistic importance once occupied by the concept of the soul.

This very positive attitude to the imagination was echoed in the preschool nineteenth-century pedagogies of F.W.A. Froebel, and these still continue to be a fundamental tenet within the U.S. National Association for the Education of Young Children, despite the rising tide of antiplayground play mentioned earlier. Even so, a victory is not entirely there because in general even in most positive contemporary research on childhood there is a narrow search for the character of play's rationality. For example, those who are the most imaginative are said to be more humorous, happier, smiling, empathic, less aggressive—all of which is nice to know. But very little mention is made about the darker side of the imagination which is so dominant in video games for children, as well as children's free fantasy play, in their own freely told stories (see Sutton-Smith, 1981 in the References at the end of this book), and in their multifarious playground folk play just mentioned.

The incongruity of these dark imaginative childhood phenomena are paralleled by the dark play in adult festivals, carnivals, roasts, tricksters, clowns, fools and jokesters which have been much written about by folklorists and anthropologists. But what is so "rationalizing" about most modern research on children's imaginations is not only that the darker side and social context of power are neglected, there is also a very intensive concern with children as conspicuous experiential consumers (self-esteem, flow, autonomy, etc.) rather than as groups of children making up their own beliefs. The focus is also upon what it is that adults should do to encourage the appropriate socialization of the child's imaginary qualities in order to develop such rationalities as literacy, or cognition or self-awareness.

There is thus throughout modern developmental psychology a thinly disguised rationalistic and moralistic concern with the way parents socialize their children into higher levels of complexity. This is almost always the narrow major focus in the modern supposed science of development.

And this brings us to the present work on *Children's Imaginative Play* by Shlomo Ariel. This book is a transforming work that does for this kind of play what the classics by Robert Fagen did for *Animal Play Behavior* (1981), and Mihail Spariosu did for the philosophical history of play in *Dionysius Reborn: Play and the Aesthetic Dimension in Modern Philosophical and Scientific Discourse* (1989), and perhaps even what Johan Huizinga did for play history in *Homo Ludens: A Study of the Play Element in Culture* (1949). Each of these in-depth studies provided a coherence and breadth to the material on play that had not existed before, and in so doing transcended the prior subject matter, lifting the subject of play to an ever more central position in the understanding of human existence. And so it is with Shlomo Ariel's new work. All prior works so commendably cited by him throughout the book are nevertheless transcended.

As a beginning in this work, all the phases of imaginative play are phrased with a semiotic systemics that has not hitherto been available in former otherwise enterprising studies. What we receive is a study of play as a complex semiotic system, which then is used to examine the realm of play as an arena of power struggles within which we discover the intensity of the negotiations that are undertaken to both enter and maintain the field of playing. There is an exciting account of the child-engendered mini-legal system governing laws of participation, of leadership, of possession, of sanctions and of legal negotiations.

For the first time in this field, Ariel has arrived at a way of discussing the quite different ways of imagining that are tolerated in different cultures with different kinds of power fields. Like Nietzsche, he gives power the antecedent role in the understanding of the social workings of the human imagination. What we learn however is that in modern urban society there is a proliferation of these legalities, whereas in some more traditional communities the preexisting hierarchy tends to predetermine all the moves.

Again, when the study moves to the meaning of play in individual terms, Ariel fulfills for the first time a point made by some prior scholars that the emotions are at the heart of the pleasures of play. His approach to the emotive regulations of play opens us to all of the sides of play, dark or light. He shows in these terms the children moving back and forth from more focal to more peripheral renderings of these themes, according to their levels of emotional comfort. Play becomes in itself a structural dialectic for the homeostatic management of personal and group feelings. Finally he reviews and revises most originally the developmental, educational and therapeutic literatures in these new terms.

It is a privilege to write the Foreword to a book that totally transforms this field of play study in such a novel and brilliant way.

NOTE

I want to thank my colleague Kevin James Sheehan for educating me about the Two Childhoods in terms of which to describe the children's literatures of England and the United States, from which most of the above quotations are derived (1995 Ph.D. dissertation, UMI no. 9534476). The rest of the quotes are to be found in chapters 8 and 9 in my own 1997 work (see References at the end of this book).

Brian Sutton-Smith

Preface

One winter afternoon, when my eldest son Gilad was five years old, I was sitting in a cozy armchair in our living room, reading a newspaper. Gilad and his friend Daliah were busy moving about, chatting vivaciously. Their faces were heavily painted with makeup. They were fancy-dressed with a whole assortment of colorful clothes which they took from my wife's wardrobe. They looked like witch doctors. I overheard parts of their chitchat. Gilad spoke with a funny tone of voice, expressing wonderment and fascination. "We are angels!" he called, "Fire angels! My hair is on fire! My wings are on fire! My belly is on fire! My tushie is on fire! Let's fly to that star over there!" And Daliah echoed him: "We are fire angels! Me too! It's our birthday! We are ten thousand years old! The fire does not burn us. It's a special kind of angels' fire!"

Then all of a sudden Gilad addressed me in his normal voice: "Daddy, can I light a match? Please, you'll hold the match and I'll hold the box!" And I said: "No, Gilad, you know mummy does not allow you to play with matches." But he continued begging: "Please, daddy, please, only this time." At that point Daliah began to yell in a panicky voice: "Fire angel! Let's fly away! The electricity monster is coming back!" Gilad addressed me again: "So give me a flashlight, OK daddy?" and I said: "OK!", impressed by the facility with which these kids could slip out of their world of wild imagination into the mundane reality around them and back.

This and many other similar episodes I had witnessed had aroused my curiosity with respect to children and their imaginative play. I began to watch my own and other children's make-believe games more attentively. Soon enough I became the laughingstock of my whole family, who saw me behaving like some kind of comical spy, hiding behind the door of my children's nursery room, writing feverishly in my notebook. I still don't know what Gilad's kindergarten teacher thought about his father, spending hours following the children and videotaping their play. The more I observed and listened, the more I was intrigued and fascinated. So much so, that at a certain stage I came to a decision to make the investigation of make-believe play one of my central pursuits.

The first opportunity to put this decision into practice came to me in the early 1970s, when I was invited to join the research team of the Study Center for Children's Activities of Oranim, The School of Education of the Kibbutz Movement. That project was motivated by the principle that the best approach to preschool education was active teachers' participation in the children's spontaneous play and creative activities. To become conversant with such activities, a cross-cultural ethnographic investigation of children's spontaneous individual and social behavior was conducted. Samples of play activities of children of various sociocultural communities, ranging from the Kibbutz communal nurseries to Bedouin tent camps in the Sinai Desert, were recorded in written protocols or videotaped and then systematically analyzed. I came to this task equipped with field techniques and analytic tools developed by anthropologists and linguists, acquired in my previous academic education. For me make-believe play was a kind of language, a rule-driven culturally transmitted system of heterogeneous signs and symbols through which children conduct their social interactions. This approach proved both fruitful and revealing.

I am still grateful to Gideon Levin, the director of the Study Center for Children's Activities, a man of vision and an innovator in the field of education, for having invited me to join that exciting and important project. I also owe a debt of gratitude to my colleagues in this research team, Matia Kam and Irene Sever.

Another opportunity came to my door in 1979, when I was invited by Jerome L. Singer and Dorothy Singer, leading investigators of make-believe play, to join their research team at Yale University. Professor Singer let me dig in his treasures—cardboard boxes full of reprints of journal articles and dissertations about play. From these and from my informal conversations with him I learned to look at make-believe play through the lenses of cognitive, developmental and clinical psychology. I began to appreciate the role of make-believe play as an emotional pacifier, a mechanism by which children regulate and balance their level of emotional arousal. I also became keenly aware of the central contribution of make-believe play to the child's cognitive and socioemotional development. I am still thankful to Jerome and Dorothy Singer for this formative year. I am also grateful to Jerome Singer for having agreed to devote time to reading the manuscript of this book and contribute valuable comments and suggestions.

Children's imaginative play was one of the attractions that lured me, like "The Pied Piper of Hamelin," to my current vocations—a clinical psychologist and a family therapist. Play therapy with individual children, groups of children and families seemed to me like an enthralling way of communicating with people and helping them overcome their difficulties. It would enable me to frequent the wonderful world of childhood. As a play therapist I would be able to bring together and put into practice everything I had learned about children and their play, and learn more.

This book is, in a way, a place in which all these avenues that have led me to that wonderland called children's imaginative play meet. It summarizes what I have learned about make-believe play all these years.

Beyond the persons mentioned above, I am greatly indebted to the following play scholars and clinicians, who have inspired and assisted me in various stages of my development as a play researcher and therapist: Brian Sutton-Smith, Greta Fein, Catherine Garvey, Artin Göncü, Cleo Gougoulis, Joop Hellendoorn, Galila Oren-Tabachnikov, Odeda Peled and Jean-Pierre Rossie. I owe a special debt of gratitude to Brian Sutton-Smith for having written the Foreword to this book. Jean-Pierre Rossie read the manuscript and offered important comments. I would like to thank him for his continuous attention. Cleo Gougoulis obtained English abstracts of all the Greek texts included in a book she co-edited (Gougoulis and Kouria, 2000).

Finally, my love and gratitude to my wife Ruttie for her support and encouragement and for her extremely useful comments on the manuscript.

Introduction

You are hereby invited to a very special journey, a journey to the wonderful world of children's make-believe. Such a journey does not require traveling far away. In fact, the make-believe world is very near. It is in the nursery room of our children, in their school, in our backyard, on our street. And yet, its gates are not widely open for everybody. For many adults, make-believe play is like a fascinating book on one's bookshelf which cannot be read because it is written in a language one cannot fully understand.

Everybody who has close contacts with young children—parents, teachers, caretakers, therapists—wants to understand them and achieve a meaningful rapport with them. Learning the language of imaginative play and its rules is a prerequisite for attaining this goal, because this is the main language through which young children express themselves and communicate with their peers. This book may be viewed as an introductory textbook for learning this language.

Every language is both individual and social, a medium into which we mold our private thoughts and feelings as well as a vehicle for communicating these thoughts and feelings to our fellows. The same applies to make-believe play. Learning the language of make-believe play involves becoming thoroughly familiar with both its personal expressive functions and its interpersonal, cultural and social-communicational functions.

We all want to enjoy our children's company. Deep understanding of their imaginative play will make the time spent with them more gratifying. Make-believe play is like good music: The better one understands it, the more pleasurable it becomes. I hope that an adult who has read this book will find watching the imaginative play of children or participating in it more enjoyable than before.

Another aspect of imaginative play discussed and illustrated in this book is its function as a major vehicle of learning and development. Children who play at home, in the street, on the playground or in the schoolyard acquire a great amount of information and many useful and important skills. They explore the cultural, social and material world in which they live. They ask themselves significant questions and attempt to find out the right answers or obtain them from their playmates. They exercise, rehearse and strengthen their physical and mental abilities.

Not all adults who take upon themselves the mission of raising and educating young children appreciate the great value of make-believe play as a vehicle of learning and as a propeller of development. In my many visits to nursery schools and kindergartens over the years I have encountered, over and over again, the following situation: The children are given a "free play time." They are engrossed in vivacious play activities, while the teachers and their assistants are sitting aside, resting, chatting, from time to time telling children to behave themselves. Afterward they assemble the children, have them sit around little tables and start "learning-activities time." Invariably, the learning done during this organized time is extremely meager and sterile compared with the rich, highly stimulating learning experiences the children have gone through during their free-play time.

Another purpose of this book is therefore to guide teachers and other caretakers toward instructive involvement in the play of the children under their care.

Sometimes we realize that our own child or a child under our care needs help, but we are at a loss trying to figure out what the trouble is and how help should be extended. Make-believe play can provide the key for detecting the child's sources of pain. It can help one find leads toward solutions. Yet another purpose of this book is to help teachers, parents and other adults working with children read and decipher signs of distress in a child's imaginative play. Furthermore, the question of how children use make-believe play to solve emotional and social difficulties, with or without the professional intervention of adults, is examined in this book in some detail.

To sum up, this book may be viewed as a general introduction to children's imaginative, make-believe play. This fascinating genre of human behavior is looked at from manifold angles in this book. It is viewed as a language for expressing and communicating thoughts, feelings and fantasies, a language that has its own characteristic vocabulary and rules of grammar and syntax. It is regarded as a product and as a vehicle of culture. The various functions of make-believe play are discussed in this book in some detail: its balancing, sublimational and cathartic powers with respect to the child's emotions; its culture-bound regulative role in children's social life; and its contributions to learning and development. All these are presented with a practical purpose in mind: to help adults understand children and establish a more rewarding and beneficial rapport with them.

The contents of this book are drawn from both the writer's own work and other people's work. The author has been engaged in children's imaginative play in many ways for many years—as a researcher, a child-and-family therapist, an educator, a field observer and a watchful parent. Much of what this book contains is a summary of his own ideas and insights, findings, observations and experiences. However, many concepts proposed by other specialists and research results reported in the literature since the early days of the twentieth century are also incorporated in the text.

The approach to make-believe play adopted in this work is interdisciplinary. This form of play has been studied by developmental psychologists, cognitive psychologists, social psychologists, clinical psychologists and psychiatrists, anthropologists and human ethologists, sociologists and linguists. Scholars and practitioners representing each of these fields have brought to the investigation of imaginative play their own special theoretical constructs, foci and research methods. All these are represented in this book.

The work presented in this book, being interdisciplinary, comprehensive and grounded in academic research, can be of interest to various groups of professionals and scholars, such as child psychologists and psychiatrists interested in play diagnosis and play therapy, educators, scholars and students interested in play research and child studies, linguists and semioticians, anthropologists specializing in socialization and children's culture, creators of children's theater, writers for children and producers of toys.

This book includes various techniques of formal analysis of diverse aspects of make-believe which can be applied in clinical and educational diagnosis and in research. It also contains narrative parts which can be beneficial for parents and other laypersons interested in children and their play. Notwithstanding the technical nature of parts of this book, efforts have been made to formulate its contents in a readable language, relatively free of scientific or professional jargon. The introduction of technical terms has been kept to a minimum. Highly specialized analytic techniques of interest mainly to researchers and other professionals have been placed in the Appendix rather than in the body of the text. The text is not interrupted by references to the literature, except where this is absolutely necessary. A Classified List of References is provided at the end of each chapter, arranged according to broad subject areas covered in each chapter.

1 What Is *Make-Believe Play*?

A DEFINITION OF *MAKE-BELIEVE PLAY*: IT'S ALL MENTAL

The term *make-believe play*, as it is used in this book, denotes a genre of play which has been designated by various other names, such as *imaginative play, fantasy play, symbolic play, pretend play, "as if" play, representational play* and *sociodramatic play*.

Many writers have referred to the concept of play in general and to that of make-believe play in particular as "illusive," "slippery" or "hard to define." To my mind, this verdict is unjustifiable. I believe that make-believe play can be defined exactly, in a way which clearly sets it apart from various different, superficially similar phenomena such as other forms of play, imitation, symbolization, pretending, fantasy, story-telling, drama, rituals and delusions. Moreover, as will be shown in many parts of this book, it is extremely important to define make-believe play in a formal, rigorous manner, because such a definition can throw light on many central characteristics and functions of this genre of play.

Imagine a little girl—let's call her Diligent—standing on a chair by the kitchen sink, washing dishes. What kind of activity is she engaged in? One possible answer is, plainly, "the activity of washing dishes." But this is not the only possibility. It is also likely that she is imitating her mother washing dishes. If this is so, her activity should be qualified not simply as "washing dishes," but rather as "imitation." There is however a third possibility: She is neither plainly washing dishes, nor imitating her mother. She is making believe that she is her own mother, washing dishes. If this is the case, her activity should be qualified as make-believe play.

Obviously, whatever the inner nature of Diligent's activity, whether it is just washing dishes, imitating or playing make-believe, she is doing exactly the same things, going through exactly the same motions. The differences between what makes her actions imitation, make-believe play or just washing dishes do not lie in their outward, observable features. These differences are to be looked for inside her own head. It is her mental attitude toward her own actions, her state of mind, that makes her activity into how it should be qualified. A definition of make-believe play must therefore identify and formulate those ingredients of the player's mental attitude which turn his or her activity into make-believe play.

Let us enter Diligent's head and try to see what is happening there when she is making believe she is her own mother washing dishes. Imagining myself to already be inside her head, I can see more or less articulate visual images popping into the darkness. One of these is the mental picture of Diligent's own mother, washing dishes. This particular image is now expanding, filling the whole space. The other images have disappeared. And now I can hear an extremely small voice, close to my ear. It reminds me of the voice of the looking-glass insect who spoke to Alice in the looking-glass train in Lewis Carroll's book *Through the Looking Glass*. I identify it as the voice of Diligent's unarticulated inner thoughts. What is the voice saying? I am listening very carefully. It is saying: "This picture is not inside my head. It is out here, in the real world. My real mother is actually washing dishes here at this very moment." Diligent is implicitly denying that the image of her mother inside her head is just a mental picture, a figment of her own inner mind. She is claiming that her real mother is actually present in the immediate external surroundings, washing dishes. In a way she is *animating* this mental picture, breathing life into it.

Still inside Diligent's head, I am straining my ears, listening very hard, expecting the tiny voice of her inner thoughts to speak again. Yes! I can hear it speaking, saying: "I am not being Diligent now. I have become my mother, washing dishes." In a way, Diligent has changed her usual identity. She is identifying herself with the mother image she has *animated*. She is not just *representing* her mother. She, as it were, has stopped being herself and has become her mother.

I keep listening. The tiny voice can be heard again. It is saying: "No! My mother is not really here now washing dishes, and I am not her, I'm me! I am just making believe. I am doing it just for the fun of it!"

What has my tour inside Diligent's head taught me about make-believe play? It has taught me that the silent mental activity underlying such play involves *animating* some mental image, *identifying* the player with it and *denying the seriousness* of both these mental operations.

Consider now another instance of simple make-believe play: A boy—let's call him Bonbon—is playing as if a little stone is a rabbit. Like Diligent, Bonbon is evoking a mental image, that of a rabbit. He is *animating* this image, telling himself that it is actually present in the external environment, as a concrete reality. He is singling out an object, a stone, and is *identifying* it as the animated rabbit. He is also disclaiming the seriousness of these two mental operations, the operation of *animating* and the operation of *identifying*.

What the latter observation tells us is that the object identified with the animated mental image should not necessarily be the player himself. It can be anything present in the immediate, visible or audible environment: the body of another player or of an incidental passer-by (identified, say, with an imagined monster), the sound of the siren of an ambulance heard in the distance (identified with the shriek of the monster), a toy or any object whatsoever.

Here is another instance of simple make-believe play: A little boy—let's call him Moxie—is saying to his playmate: "Let's play as if there's a lion here now." This boy is evoking a mental image, that of a lion. He is animating this mental image by declaring "There's a lion here now." He is also disclaiming the seriousness of this animation by saying "Let's play as if . . ." However, he is not identifying any object with the animated lion. His make-believe play is purely verbal.

Although in most of their make-believe games children do select some perceptible entities out of the immediate play environment and identify them with their animated mental images, they do not always do so. In some cases they make do with animating the mental image verbally. In most cases however they both verbalize their mental images and identify perceptible nonverbal entities with them.

The ground has now been prepared for defining the concept *make-believe play*.

A Definition of *Make-Believe Play*

Make-believe play is a kind of *mental activity* whose outward manifestations are verbal or nonverbal or both. This mental activity includes the following *mental operations*, performed simultaneously: *evoking* some *mental images* (e.g., mother washing dishes, rabbit, lion); *animating* these mental images, (e.g., implicitly or explicitly declaring them to be actually present in the immediate environment, not as mental images but as concrete entities in external, perceptible reality); *verbalizing* the mental operation of animating (e.g., saying "There's a lion here now"), or *identifying* some perceptible entity in the immediate play environment (e.g., the playing little girl herself, a stone) with it. [*identifying* means claiming that the entity in question is no longer what it usually is, but has actually been transformed into the animated mental image (e.g., the little girl has become her mother; the stone has become a rabbit)]; *disclaiming* the seriousness and validity of the above-mentioned mental operations (that is, *animating, verbalizing the animation* and *identifying* [e.g., Diligent is disclaiming the validity of her own inner statement "I am my own mother"; she does not really believe in its truth; she is playing as if she is, just for the fun of it; likewise, Bonbon is not seriously claiming that the stone is a rabbit]).

For convenience of reference, the main mental operations specified above will be labeled *animating verbally, animating by identifying* and *disclaiming seriousness*.

Some investigators of make-believe play (e.g., the great Swiss scholar Jean Piaget) have distinguished between its *signified* contents (our *animated mental images*) and the tangible *signifiers* by which these contents are expressed (the verbal or nonverbal entities *identified* with the animated mental image). Adopting this terminology, one would say that Diligent herself became a *nonverbal signifier* for the *signified* content "mother washing dishes." The little stone in Bonbon's play was the *nonverbal signifier* of the *signified* content "rabbit." The word "lion" in Moxie's play was the *verbal signifier* for the *signified* content "lion."

It should be stressed, however, that the terms *signifier* and *signified* apply not just to make-believe play but to all kinds of symbolic representation. For example, the word "apple" is a *signifier* for the *signified* object "apple." The Statue of Liberty is a *signifier* for the *signified* content "liberty." And so forth.

Children are fully aware of the fact that they perform these mental operations when they play. This awareness manifests itself by various verbal expressions accompanying their play, such as "Let's play as if this stick is a gun," "I'll be the pretend monster," or the like. This does not entail, of course, that they have the ability to analyze these mental operations or formulate them explicitly.

MAKE-BELIEVE PLAY AND ITS CLOSE RELATIVES

It has been stated above that make-believe play is akin to, and yet different from, phenomena such as other forms of play, imitation, symbolic representation, pretending, fantasy, story-telling, drama, delusions and rituals. The definition of make-believe play proposed above includes the conceptual tools required for making both the similarities and the distinctions between make-believe play and each of these other phenomena fully explicit.

Other Forms of Play

Jean Piaget and other students of children's play have classified play into the following three types: *practice play, games with rules* and *symbolic play* (our *make-believe play*).

Practice play is "functioning for pleasure," exercising sensorimotor or verbal skills to enjoy and reinforce competence. Examples of practice play are throwing objects just for the sake of throwing; hopping on a bed as if it was a trampoline and making up funny words. In practice play no mental images are necessarily evoked and the mental operations *animating verbally* and *animating by identifying* are not performed. When a child is throwing stones for pleasure the stones are just stones, the child is his own self and the throwing is nothing but throwing.

The make-believe play operation *disclaiming seriousness* bears some vague proximity to the fact that practice games are not performed for any purpose beyond the pleasure of functioning and are therefore "not serious." This however does not imply denying the seriousness of any mental claims. The child does not say to himself: "I am not really throwing these stones." He is saying to himself: "I am throwing these stones just for the fun of it."

Games with rules are social games such as marbles, races, ball games and table games. Most of these games are competitive. Like practice games, they are played mainly for the pleasure of exercising competence. As in the case of practice games, the mental operations of *animating verbally, animating by identification* and *disclaiming seriousness* are not usually performed while games with rules are being played.

Social make-believe play becomes relatively more structured as children grow up. Kindergarten and school-age children regulate and organize the forms and contents of their make-believe games by rules prescribing rights of participation, the play means used and the manners by which contents are chosen or created. Rules of this kind are discussed in detail in Chapter 4. One might rightly say that advanced make-believe games become games with rules. Such rules however are not an intrinsic property of make-believe play. The rules are a part of the social contexts in which the play is carried out. They are not a part of the play itself.

Imitation

Suppose Diligent is not playing make-believe, but is imitating her mother. What is going on inside her mind? Apparently, she, again, is retrieving, from long-term memory, a mental image of her mother washing dishes. And then she is repeating her mother's motions, as they are unfolding in this mental picture. Her actions become *signifiers* for her mother's actions as *signified*. It should be stressed however that the mental operation of *animating by identifying* is not performed at all while she is doing the imitation. She is not making-believe that her real mother is actually present in the immediate external play environment. Nor is she pretending to be her own mother instead of being herself. In her mind, she is remaining her own self and her mother is not there washing dishes at all. She is just acting like her mother.

Symbolic Representation

In symbolization, an entity is used as a symbol, a *signifier* for another entity, the *signified*. Unlike imitation, however, which is usually a transitory activity, symbolic representation is relatively stable and permanent. In symbolization, furthermore, the signifier is not necessarily similar to the signified. A word is a symbol for what it stands for. For example, the word "chair" is a symbol for the object "chair." The word "justice" is a symbol for the "idea of justice." Nonverbal actions can serve as symbols too. In many countries, for example, the gesture of describing the curved waistline of a female person's trunk with hand and arm movements is common among males. This gesture is a symbol for "an attractive woman." In some cultures a clenched fist is a symbol for "power." Pictures and objects are also often used as symbols. Road signs are symbols. The crown and the throne of a king or queen are symbols.

It has often been asserted that the signifiers of make-believe play are symbolic representations of their signified contents. Hence the term *symbolic play*, a synonym of *make-believe play*. It is not the presence of symbolic representation, however, that tells make-believe play apart from all other phenomena, but the activation of the mental operations *animating verbally* or *animating by identifying*, and *disclaiming seriousness*. None of these mental operations is necessarily performed in any kind of symbolic representation except make-believe play and drama (see below). Take for instance the "female-waistline" gesture mentioned above. A performer of this gesture just alludes to some features of a female person's body. He does not deny that his gesture is merely a movement of his hands and arms. He does not pretend that these movements have become the body of a real woman who has somehow popped out of his own mind. In other words, he neither *animates verbally* or *by identifying*, nor *disclaims seriousness*.

Pretending

Make believe play has been called also *pretend play*. The word "pretend" is ambiguous. It has at least two meanings: one is equivalent to "make-believe"; another is "put forward a false appearance with an intention to mislead and deceive." Pretending in the latter sense is not part and parcel of make-believe play. A player of make-believe has no intention to deceive or mislead anybody. The mental operation of *disclaiming seriousness* rules out any false pretenses. A boy who is telling his playmate "I am a monster" in the frame of a make-believe play, has no intention to lead his mate to believe that he is a real monster. He knows that *disclaiming seriousness* is shared by both of them, as a part of a tacit agreement that what they are doing together is make-believe play.

Fantasy and Imagination

Make-believe play has also been called (in the title of this book, for instance) *imaginative play* or *fantasy play*. These terms are justified for two reasons: First, the mental operations of *animating verbally* and *animating by identifying* activate the child's faculty of imagination. Diligent *imagines* that she is her own mother, washing dishes. Bonbon *imagines* that the little stone is a real rabbit. Second, most of the contents of children's make-believe play, at least in modern Western culture, are drawn from the realm of fantasy and imagination. The mental images animated in their play are usually borrowed from the world of fiction they meet in stories, children's books, the movies, television and computer games. Children often reorganize these materials in their own minds in highly creative, imaginative manners. The resulting contents are sometimes as way-out and bizarre as dreams. It should be stressed however that richness in fanciful contents is not an intrinsic characteristic of make-believe play. What Diligent is doing is definitely make-believe play. But beyond the fact that she is imagining herself to be her own mother, washing dishes, her play is rather concrete and unimaginative.

Storytelling

Children often make up realistic or fanciful stories. It is not always easy to distinguish between such a story and make-believe play. What renders it particularly difficult to mark these two kinds of activity as different is the fact the past tense often serves as an indicator of "make-believe time." A child is saying: "The monster kidnapped the baby" and what he has in mind is "I am making-believe that the monster is kidnapping the baby right now." Still, storytelling and make-believe play are quite definitely distinct phenomena. Verbal make-believe play is the product of the mental operation *animating verbally* and storytelling is not. In other words, in verbal make-believe play the player pretends that the events experienced within his own mind are actually happening in external reality at the time and place of playing. He verbalizes this claim, but denies its seriousness. In storytelling the child just relates these events, as happenings that came about there and then. Even if her story is fictional, she does not *disclaim seriousness*.

Drama

Theatrical shows are the closest relatives of make-believe play. When an actor playing Hamlet is "killing" the actor playing Polonius with a mock sword, the former is *animating* the mental image "Hamlet is killing Polonius with a sword." He materializes this animation by *identifying* himself with Hamlet, the other actor with Polonius and the mock sword with a real sword. He is also *disclaiming the seriousness* of these mental operations. Still, theatrical shows are not exactly instances of make-believe play. What are the differences then? Let us return to the actor playing Hamlet. Even though he does perform the trinity of operations defining make-believe play, he does not initiate them as private, spontaneous mental acts. The mental activity producing these operations is fully dictated by cultural conventions. In make-believe play, furthermore, the player's behavior is neither fully scripted by social usage, nor bound by a given text, as it is in theatrical shows. Finally, make-believe play is not usually performed for an audience.

Some recent investigators of make-believe play, notably R. Keith Sawyer, compare it to improvisational theater, a form of dramatic performance which has become common in Western urban centers since the 1950s. The most characteristic feature of improvisational drama is that it is nonscripted and spontaneous. The play acts are created by the actors on the spur of a moment. Often there is no audience. Indeed, improvisational theater may be viewed as a sub-genre of make-believe play, performed mainly by adults.

Delusions

Delusions bear some similarity to make-believe play. A person afflicted with psychosis who believes himself to be Jesus and behaves accordingly reminds one of a child playing make-believe. Delusions are not necessarily psychotic. In many societies all over the world, shamans and witch doctors perform healing ceremonies in which they act as if they have been transformed into animals, spirits or devils. Some anthropologists claim that these healers do not mislead their patients, but actually believe that their acts are genuine. There are also normal everyday delusions: the old geezer who believes himself to be a young Casanova; the scribbler who thinks of himself as the second Dostoyevsky, still to be discovered. In all these cases the person in question evokes and *animates* a certain mental image (Jesus, an animal spirit, Casanova, Dostoyevsky) by *identifying* himself or herself with it. In none of these cases, however, does the person *disclaim the seriousness* of these mental operations. On the contrary, he or she seriously believes in their validity.

Rituals

Some traditional rituals and ceremonies resemble make-believe play. For example, in some Polynesian societies the birth of a baby is accompanied by the following ritual: a group of women, bent to an arch-like posture, stand side by side, adjoining one another, forming a kind of tunnel which feigns the uterus. Another woman crawls through this tunnel. She represents the baby being born. Such a ritual is more akin to symbolic representation and imitation than to make-believe play. The whole act is a set of *signifiers* for the *signified* content "birth." The mental operation of *identifying* (claiming that the actors have actually been transformed into a uterus and a baby) is, apparently, missing.

Table 1.1 summarizes the distinctions among all the phenomena discussed above.

SUMMARY OF CHAPTER 1

This chapter presents an attempt to formally define the notion of "make-believe play." It is argued that make-believe play is a kind of mental activity rather than a genre of external behavior. Any overt behavior can become make-believe play if the relevant mental attitude toward it is implicitly or explicitly assumed by the player. This make-believe play attitude consists of the following simultaneous mental operations: *animating mental images verbally or by identifying* and *disclaiming seriousness*.

Animated mental images are the *signified contents* of make-believe play. Their

Table 1.1
The Distinctions among Phenomena Akin to Make-Believe Play

	animating	*identifying*	*disclaiming seriousness*	*other distinctions*
make-believe play	yes	yes	yes	spontaneous improvised; not performed for an audience; no intention to mislead; sociodramatic play is regulated by social rules; past tense refers to imagined time
improvised drama	yes	yes	yes	same as above; can be performed for an audience
traditional drama	yes	yes	yes	not spontaneous, prescribed, performed for an audience
practice play	no	no	no	practicing acquired skills for sheer pleasure of functioning
games with rules	no	no	no	rule-governed; usually competitive; leisure pastime
imitation	no	no	no	signifier copies signified; transitory
symbolization	no	no	no	signifier often arbitrary; relatively stable
pretending (in the sense of "false appearance")	yes	yes	yes	with intention to mislead
story-telling	no	no	yes	all tenses refer to imagined time
fantasy and imagination	not necessarily	not necessarily	yes	animating and identifying may be viewed as simple forms of imagining
delusions	yes	yes	no	psychotic or normal
rituals	no	no	no	elaborate symbolizations

verbal markers and the external, perceivable entities identified with them are their *signifiers*.

This definition makes it possible to draw clear boundaries between make-believe play and akin phenomena such as other forms of play, imitation, symbolization, pretending, fantasy, storytelling, drama, rituals and delusions.

This definition implies that the child engaged in make-believe play is already capable of rather complex and sophisticated cognitive processes.

The purpose of this attempt to define make-believe play has not been just engaging in intellectual gymnastics. This definition can lead to better understanding of the nature of the language of make-believe play and its cognitive, emotional and social functions and correlates. All these are discussed in the following chapters.

A CLASSIFIED LIST OF REFERENCES

Definitions of Make-Believe Play and Their Cognitive Substrata

Adams, 1978; Ariel, 1984; Auwaerter, 1986; Bateson, 1956; Bretherton, 1989; Curry and Arnaud, 1974; Evans, 1986; Fein, 1975; Forbes, Katz and Paul, 1986; Goldman, 1998; Golomb and Cornelius, 1977; Groos, 1901; Harris and Kavanaugh, 1993; Johnson and Christie, 1986; Kaarby, 1986; Leslie, 1987; Lillard, 1993a, 1993b; Loy, 1982; Mathews, 1977; Miller, 1974; Neubauer, 1987; Piaget, 1962; Schlosberg, 1947; Smith and Vollstedt, 1985; Sutton-Smith, 1997; Vaihinger, 1924.

Distinctions Between Make-Believe Play and Other Phenomena

Ariel, 1984; Eckler and Weininger, 1989.

The Use of the Past Tense in Pretend Play

Lodge, 1979.

Make-Believe Play as Improvisational Theater

Sawyer, 1996.

2 The Cryptic Codes of Make-Believe Play

MAKE-BELIEVE PLAY AS A SEMIOTIC SYSTEM

The term *semiotic system* refers to a system of signs and symbols. Make-believe play is a semiotic system. I have always been intrigued by its peculiarities and intricacies, and would like to share my thoughts about them. Some of the well-kept secrets of make-believe play as a semiotic system are hidden underneath its surface. To reveal them we shall have to excavate the surface and delve into its depths.

The Scope of the Term "Language"

In common parlance, a semiotic system is referred to by the word "language." The first thing that comes to mind when this word is sounded is tongues such as English, Hebrew or French. But people also use the term *"language"* to refer to other semiotic systems. They speak of the language of birds, body language, mute-and-deaf language, the language of theater, the language of motion pictures and so on. It is this wide sense of the term "language" that concerns us here. Make-believe play is a language, too, in this sense.

What is the range of application of the expression "the language of make-believe play"? Does it refer to make-believe play in general, or perhaps to the play of a specific child, of a particular group of children, of same-age children belonging to a distinct cultural community? The answer is: This expression refers to any of these. One can sample and analyze the language of make-believe play of a single specific child or of any group of children. Cross-cultural comparisons of the play patterns of children of different social groups can reveal common culture-bound rules. The regularities shared by all the groups researched will be considered the universal rules of the language of make-believe play in general.

In the current state of the art, one can say very little about the language of make-believe play in general. Only a few distinctive universal features of this language can be delineated. These are listed and illustrated below. The greater part of this and the following chapters will be devoted to analyzing particular texts, transcripts of videotaped observations of the spontaneous make-believe play of small groups of children.

Analyzing a Particular Make-Believe Play Text

The analysis of a particular text in any language, including the language of make-believe play, reminds me of a course in anatomy and physiology. The students learn how individual cells are aggregated into tissues and how the tissues are joined together to form functioning structures. The analysis proceeds from units to structures comprising these units and from concrete entities to abstract patterns. The procedure of analyzing a make-believe play text in this manner can be facilitatied by various heuristic techniques. Some such techniques are presented briefly below and are discussed and illustrated in detail in the Appendix.

ANALYSIS OF A DYADIC MAKE-BELIEVE PLAY TEXT

Let me illustrate my approach to the analysis of a make-believe play text by examining the following short excerpt of dyadic make-believe play:

Observation 1: Peace Forever

Avshalom (boy) and Sharon (girl), both eight years old now, are close Israeli friends who have been playing together regularly since they were four. They live in the same urban middle-class neighborhood. I have been following the development of their play partnership since the early days of their friendship, videotaping the amusing, captivating children of their imagination.

The following play scene took place in Avshalom's bedroom, when he and Sharon were six years old. It is an extract of a longer play sequence, in which the two children pretended to be two "naughty boys" who were fighting with each other and doing all kinds of forbidden things. A pretend father figure showed up a number of times during this sequence, reprimanding the children and threatening to punish them.

In the following observation protocol, my own speculations and interpretations are enclosed in square brackets.

Various plastic dolls representing human and semihuman figures of television adventure series such as Power Rangers, Ninja Turtles, Batman, and such were scattered on the carpet. Avshalom picked up a silvery plastic doll off the carpet. He sat down on the carpet, facing his bed, his legs underneath the bed. He placed the doll on his bed, holding it in a standing position.

Avshalom (speaking in a babyish voice, apparently "from his doll's mouth"): I am little.

Sharon (speaking in her ordinary voice): Why are you little?

Sharon picked up a black doll off the carpet. She placed it on Avshalom's bed, making it stand very close to Avshalom's silvery doll, facing it. She lay down on the carpet, most of her body, including her head, underneath Avshalom's bed. [Apparently this strange, uncomfortable posture was intended to convey the idea that she had become smaller than Avshalom. The two children seemed to express the notion of "size" both by varying the height of their own bodies and by representing their own selves by dolls of varying sizes.]

Sharon (in a babyish voice): And I am little too.

Avshalom: I've become smaller. Now I'm more little.

And then Avshalom hit Sharon's doll with his doll, producing an *ek* sound with his throat. [Seemingly, Avshalom and Sharon began competing for "littleness." When Avshalom "had become little" Sharon "contracted" to a smaller size and then Avshalom became "more little." He, apparently, did not want Sharon to compete with him for size. This made him angry. That is why he hit Sharon's doll with his own doll.]

Sharon moved her beaten doll away from Avshalom's, who was moving to a lying position, pushing his body into under the bed [to mark his having become "more little"?]. Then Avshalom suddenly stood up.

Avshalom (assuming the voice of an angry, scolding adult): Children! Stop with these pities! ["pities"? What did he mean by this word?]

Sharon (from underneath the bed, in a babyish voice): We don't want to!

Avshalom let go of the doll held in his hand. He gripped Sharon's head.

Avshalom (adult voice, scolding): Don't be cheeky!

Sharon (in a babyish voice): Don't hold us with your hands like that!

Avshalom picked up his silvery doll from the bed and threw it forcefully on the bed.

Avshalom (assuming a derisive adult voice): Like that?!

Sharon: Ouch!

Avshalom sat down on the bed. He held his silvery doll with both his hands, directing it toward Sharon.

Avshalom (speaking in an "adult" voice full of scorn, his whole body shaking with disdain): Are you trying to pity me, as if you are poor little toys?

He sealed these words with a punch on the silvery doll's face. ["pity" again. Did he mean "trying to make me pity you"?]

Sharon: I . . .

Avshalom slapped the black doll in Sharon's hand forcefully. The doll was tossed in the air, landing on the floor behind the bed.

Avshalom (speaking in an angry "adult" voice): Now you'll have to fetch your toy by yourself! [This seemed to be an out-of-play expression, addressing the real Sharon.]

Avshalom got up, looking at Sharon's doll behind the bed. Then he is threw his silvery doll on the bed.

Avshalom: You too!
Sharon: Ouch!

Avshalom picked up his silvery doll. Sharon went to fetch her black doll.

Sharon: I can go by myself.

Sharon returned with her black doll. Avshalom was half lying on the bed. Sharon bent over him, very close to him.

Sharon: It has not been worthwhile for us to fight all the time.

Avhsalom rolled his body away from Sharon. He placed his silvery doll on the bed, so that his body was between Sharon and his doll.

Avshalom: (childish voice): Daddy, believe us, we are really little!

Sharon moved over, placing her doll close to Avshalom's, facing his.

Avshalom (in a friendly, "fatherly" voice): I really can't find you. I am really pitying.

Sharon (speaking in her ordinary voice, her doll facing Avhsalom's): If we make peace and become good friends again, this will set everything right. Hold my little finger and I'll hold yours.

Sharon made Avshalom's doll and her's hold hands.

Sharon (chanting): Peace Peace forever
                            At odds at odds Never!

Avshalom joined her chanting. [Holding the little fingers and chanting this verse, a free translation of the Hebrew Sholem Sholem LeOlam, Brogez Brogez Af Paam, is a common traditional "becoming friends again" ceremony in Israeli children's culture.] Avshalom and Sharon repeated this verse, but Avshalom drew his doll away from Sharon's. She made her doll follow his and drew closer to his.

Avshalom stood up on the bed. Holding the silvery doll, he began dancing rhythmically and singing with a tune he was improvising:

Avshalom: You should not enjoy beating
                     It's not nice! It's not nice!

Sharon, sitting on the bed, was trying to sing together with him.

In the end you'll get into trouble
With your parents
And you'll become little!
So listen to us, we are right!
So listen to us, we are right!
So listen to us
Listen, listen listen
To us, us us!
We are speaking truth!
Truth
And that's the end of the song.

Avshalom placed his doll next to Sharon's.

Sharon (in a babyish voice): Peace is between us and we'll become big, become big!
Avshalom: You are right, but we have nothing with which we can become big.

Sharon raised her body, sitting opposite him

Sharon: We'll make peace . . . We'll try . . . It's been a pleasure to meet you, it's been a pleasure.

Sharon drew her doll very close to Avshalom's.

Avshalom (pulling his doll away from hers): But this is not working.

Sharon: But you should try to do everything to grow! (She raised her doll high in the air): Grow! Grow! Like that.

Avshalom: It's not working.

After having videotaped this scene, I was puzzled by some parts of it. I was particularly intrigued by the expression "pitying." It seemed to denote something different from the usual, adult sense of this word. I therefore decided to show the videotaped play to Avshalom and Sharon and ask for their own interpretations. The two enjoyed seeing themselves playing very much. They kept giggling and exclaiming excitedly. Here are some of their comments, verbatim, in literal translation into English:

Sharon: This was a story about two children; there was a cake with guests and they threw the cake on the floor and messed up the room and daddy punished them.

Avshalom: And as a punishment they became little because they were naughty, like Pinocchio's nose that grew longer when he was lying.

Sharon: But the daddy thought they only pretended to be little.

Avshalom: Like a clown in a cemetery. When you are in an important event and then you play as if you are little. Is that nice?

Shlomo: Did they pretend to be little because they wanted their daddy to pity them and not punish them?

Avshalom: "Pitying" here is something different, it is like pretending to be something else when you do bad things and he is pitying you and is not punishing you.

Sharon: But he did not believe them and did not want to pity them and he thought you are trying to make a fool of me as if you are doing imaginary things.

The story, as seen from the children's viewpoint, now began to make sense: Two naughty children misbehaved at a party, embarrasing their father in front of the guests, like clowns in a cemetery. They were punished by some magical power that made them little. Their father however did not believe them. He thought they were just pretending to be little [not responsible for their misdeeds, like babies?] to escape punishment. They wanted him to "pity" them but he would not.

I could not sidestep the impression that this text contained much more than that. It appeared to be patterned on a number of levels. One level was the choice of signifiers. Avshalom and Sharon did not choose signifiers randomly. They seemed to share a relatively small repertoire of signifiers, which were organized along a few dimensions such as using one's own body versus using dolls to represent differences of size and age, varying the height of one's body for the same purpose, changing distance between dolls to express different degrees of cordiality, altering the quality of voice (adult, baby-like, derisive) to symbolize difference of age and types of interpersonal messages, and so on.

Another level was the choice of signified contents. These were not selected fortuitously either. As in the case of signifiers, the signified contents shared by Avshalom and Sharon were grouped around a few basic dimensions, such as size, age, parent/son, parental anger versus "pitying," parental believing versus suspecting, ability versus inability to grow up, quarelling versus making peace.

A third level was the players' interpersonal relations as manifested in their play behavior. The competition "who's smaller" has already been mentioned above. Another salient feature of their play relationship had to do with interpersonal distance. Sharon was striving for closeness and cordiality. Avshalom on the other hand kept drawing away from her and exhibited a great deal of aggression.

Another aspect of Avshalom and Sharon's play which seems to be systematically patterned rather than random is structure—that is, the ways in which signifiers, signified contents and meta-play verbal and nonverbal expressions were sequenced and combined together. The above-mentioned pursuer-avoider relationship between Avshalom and Sharon can be formulated as a structural rule:

• When Sharon comes close to Avshalom, the latter draws away.

Avshalom and Sharon's interchanges concerning "littleness" can also be defined by two rules:

• If the figure in Sharon's play becomes smaller than Avshalom's, his figure becomes even smaller.
• If Sharon's figure urges Avshalom's to become bigger, his figure claims that he cannot.

Furthermore, the above play scene has a clear plot structure:

• Children figures have become little.
• Children figures are competing for littleness.
• Father figure is scolding children figures for their "pities."
• Children figures are responding by being cheeky.
• Father figure is reacting with aggressive, violent punishing.
• Sharon's figure is calling for making peace and reconciliation.
• Father figure and children figures are reconciling.
• Sharon's figure sees this as an opportunity to become big again.
• Avshalom's figure declares that he is unable to become big.

To sum up, the play signifiers and signifieds and the meta-play verbal and nonverbal expressions in this play scene are systematically patterned in the following two ways: (1) They can be classified into a small number of *categories* on clearly defined dimensions. (2) These categories are combined or sequenced according to specific *syntactic rules*.

The categories and syntactic rules specified above have been arrived at by using inference and intuition. This cannot always be the case, however. In most cases, dimensions and rules underlying a make-believe play text cannot be reached by sheer intuition and inference, although activating these mental faculties is indispensable in any scientific endeavor. Some such dimensions and rules are covert, hidden underneath the surface. They are so abstract, so far removed in character and shape from the actual observed data, that special heuristic techniques are needed for them to be unearthed and made accessible. A number of such techniques have been borrowed from semiotics (the science of signs and symbols), general linguistics and anthropological linguistics. They have been modified and elaborated, to be adapted to being used in analyzing make-believe play texts. Following is a succinct description of each of the main techniques. For readers who would like to gain a thorough knowledge and understanding of these techniques or apply them in their research or in their work with children, a fuller presentation is offered in the Appendix. There, these techniques are illustrated with respect to another observation representing the make-believe play of Avshalom and Sharon. As readers of the Appendix will see, the similarity in structure and content between that observation and "Peace Forever" is striking. Other applications of these analytic techniques are discussed and illustrated in Chapters 3 and 5.

1. *Analysis of observed play behavior by expressive media across time units.* A videotaped or written observation of play is divided into equal time units. The recorded behavior on each time unit is analyzed into expressive media features: verbal-vocal, spatial, motional and tactile. Take for instance the beginning of the above observation, "Peace Forever": "Avshalom picked up a silvery plastic doll off the carpet. He sat down on the carpet, facing his bed, his legs underneath the bed. He placed the doll on his bed, holding it in a standing position."

Avshalom (speaking in a babyish voice, apparently "from his doll's mouth"): I'm little . . .

This part of the observation can be divided into two time units, each of about one minute in length:

Unit 1

Spatial—Avshalom on the carpet

Motional-tactile—Avshalom bending, picking up silvery plastic doll off the carpet

Unit 2

Spatial—Avshalom sitting on carpet, facing bed, legs underneath bed. Doll on bed, standing

Motional-tactile—Avshalom holding doll

Verbal-vocal—Avshalom: I'm little; babyish voice (as doll)

The results of this analysis are arranged in a tabular form (see Appendix table 1).

2. *Classifying features into minimal signifier-signified units.* The spatial, motional, tactile and vocal-linguistic features analyzed by the above techniques are classified into minimal signifier-signified units, the basic semiotic building blocks of the play text. For example the aggregate of features [doll + player sitting or lying + babyish voice] seem to constitute together a single semiotic unit signifying "littleness."

3. *Revealing dimensions underlying signfier-signified units by Context-Dependent Componential Analysis. Componential Analysis* is a technique developed by anthropological linguists as a method for revealing and describing semantic systems—that is, covert interrelations among meanings of words in various "exotic" languages (see Hammel, 1965). *Context-Dependent Componential Analysis* (CDCA) is my own elaboration of this technique. With the aid of CDCA the contextualized uses of both signfiying features (e.g., size, height, quality of voice) and signified contents (e.g., "age," "punishment") are systematically categorized into sets defined by dimensions and subdimensions. The final result of each such analysis is a map exhibiting the hierarchical relations among the various signifying or signified (semantic) dimensions and subdimensions. Such a map constitutes a partial description of the deep, covert structure underlying a make-believe play text. Furthermore, it facilitates the further discovery and formulation of more rules representing hidden patterns lying underneath the surface of a make-believe play text.

4. *Describing structures and their uses, their creators' presuppositions and purposes.* A structure is a combination of minimal signifier-signified units. Not every such combination is a structure, however. For a combination of units to be considered a structure, the signified contents of the units must be interrelated, adding up together to a significant whole. Take for instance the following excerpt of "Peace Forever": "Avshalom: I've become smaller. Now I'm more little." And then Avshalom hit Sharon's doll with his doll, producing an *ek* sound with his throat. Avshalom was moving to a lying position, pushing his body into under the bed. The whole of this excerpt represents a single structure, conveying the idea of Avshalom's competing with Sharon for "littleness" and his being angry at her for "daring" to compete with him.

Most structures have well-defined context-dependent interpersonal *uses.* In order to describe the use of a structure one has, as it were, to read the mind of the creator of the structure, to guess his *presuppositions* and *purposes* with respect to his mate. An external observer who cannot probe the players' minds has no choice but to infer their purposes and presuppositions from the context. Searching the context of the above structure, for instance, can lead the observer to the conclusion that Avshalom produced this structure *on the presupposition* that Sharon had entered into what he considered an illegitimate competition with him. His *purposes* were to prevent her from winning and express his anger at her "insolence."

The same concepts, *presupposition* and *purpose*, can be employed in describing the use of out-of-play structures that say something about the play.

Examining the sequence of presuppositions and purposes of each player can reveal the players' *interpersonal goals* with respect to one another and their *plan* or *strategy* for reaching these goals. See the Appendix and Chapters 3 and 4 for further discussions.

DISTINCTIVE FEATURES OF THE LANGUAGE OF MAKE-BELIEVE PLAY

The language of make-believe play has peculiar characteristics, which set it apart from many other languages. Following is a discussion of some of these characteristics.

Observation 2: The Kittens Are Being Born

John, Suzette and Anna, five years old, are playing in Anna's room. All three are lying on the carpet, assuming a fetal posture. They are all covered with a blanket.

John: Let's pretend we are being born now.

The three children mew like kittens, and crawl out of the blanket.

Anna (in a high-pitched mewing voice): Mommy-cat, what's all that?

Nobody says anything.

Anna (straightening up, speaking in her normal voice): Who's gonna be mommy-cat?
John: Suzette.
Anna: Mommy-cat, what's all that?
Suzette (in a mature cat-like voice): Mew, mew! It's the world.

Suzette points at John.

Suzette: This is daddy-cat, and all this is our pen.
John (in a high-pitched mewing voice): I am not daddy-cat, I'm a baby kitten!
Suzette: No. Let's pretend now is next year and you are already daddy-cat. And let's pretend here is the kittens' school.

To set up this scene, John, Anna and Suzette made use of different kinds of signifiers: Ordinary everyday speech and vocal effects such as mewing (linguistic and vocal signifiers), body postures and movements such as a fetal position and crawling (motional and spatial signifiers) and objects such as a blanket (tactile signifiers). All these were interwoven into a harmonious fabric having a definite thematic structure. Although the signifiers themselves were commonplace, they were used in unusual, peculiar manners, characteristic of make-believe play. Here are some of the distinctive features of these uses:

1. *Ad hoc combinations of different signifiers.* The child creates a new structure, an innovative combination of different kinds of signifiers. Each such original combination signifies a specific content. For instance, in "The Kittens Are Being Born," the linguistic expression "We are being born," the high-pitched mewing (vocal), the blanket (an object) and the crawling out of it (motional-spatial-tactile) form together an improvised structure, an ad hoc combination signifying the birth of the kittens.

In this respect, the language of make-believe play is different from many other languages, such as spoken languages like English or French and the language of music. In the latter, most of the minimal units and their combinations into grammatical and syntactic structures are not created ad lib, but are stored in the users' minds as parts of a standardized repertoire—the vocabulary and grammatical forms of English, the notes, scales and rhythms of the Western musical tradition, and so forth.

As claimed above, however, some such ad hoc combinations can get stabilized. They are stored in the minds of specific children or particular groups of children as complex units, idioms that can be drawn from their pool and used over and over again.

2. *Attributing unconventional signified to signifiers.* In "The Kittens Are Being Born" the blanket does not signify a blanket. It signifies the location of the unborn kittens—the mother-cat's belly. The crawling out of the blanket signifies the birth. The room signifies "a pen."

The great Swiss linguist Ferdinand de Saussure coined the term *arbitrariness of the signifier.* This means that some kinds of signifiers can refer arbitrarily to any signifieds. This arbitrariness is due to the operation of *identifying,* included in the formal definition of the concept "make-believe play" discussed in Chapter 1. This operation turns anything into anything else.

Again, this property of the language of make-believe play sets it apart from other kinds of languages. In the language of road signs, for instance, the signifiers are not arbitrary but conventional.

3. *Transformations.* The player can readily replace the signified content of a signifier by another signified content. In "The Kittens Are Being Born," Suzette turned herself into a newborn kitten and immediately afterward into a mommy-cat. The room signified "a pen" but soon was turned into "the kittens' school." This peculiarity is shared by the language of dreams, for instance, but not by spoken languages such as English or French.

4. *Going in and out of the play.* Children enter their play and slip out of it

with great facility. When they step out they employ normal verbal and nonverbal expressions. When they come back their modes of expression become playful again. Anna, for instance, was inside the play. She was crawling and speaking in a high-pitched voice. She said: "Mommy-cat, what's all that?" But then, having realized that no player was "mommy-cat," she stepped out of the play, straightened up and spoke in her normal voice. When she asked "Who's gonna be mommy-cat?" she did not speak as a kitten but as Anna. John said "Suzette" and then Anna, satisfied that the role of "mommy-cat" had been filled, slipped back into the play. Her body reassumed the crawling position. Her voice became kitten-like again. She repeated her question "Mommy-cat, what's all that?" The latter utterance was asked inside the play. Anna asked it not as Anna but as a newborn kitten.

Sometimes the very same expression is simultaneously inside and outside the play. For example, John, speaking in a high-pitched mewing voice, said "I am not daddy-cat, I'm a baby kitten!" John's voice attested to the fact that he spoke inside the play, as a kitten. His words, however, expressing his refusal to play the part which Suzette wanted him to play, indicated that he said what he did out of the play, as John. Another example is found in "Peace Forever": "Avshalom (speaking in an angry "adult" voice): 'Now you'll have to fetch your toy by yourself!' " Avshalom spoke as "daddy," inside the play, but he spoke about "your toy," the signifier, and this seems to indicate that his words were uttered outside the play. Another interesting expression which seems to be relevant here is Avshalom's: "Are you trying to pity me as if you are poor little toys?" This expression is definitely inside the play, but the fact that Avshalom refers to the imaginary children as pretending to be little toys suggests that he stepped out of the play for awhile and spoke about the signfiers, toys, rather than about the signifieds, the children.

Children distinguish quite well between in-play and out-of-play expressions. Often play discourse includes expressions such as "I am speaking out of the play" or "This is not a part of the play."

In sociodramatic make-believe play, out-of-play expressions have extremely important functions. Thanks to these expressions the improvised drama created conjointly by the children can continue to unroll without getting stuck. Staying with the theater analogy, these expressions serve as both the stage instructions written into the play by the playwright and the directives issued by the producer, the director and the stage designer.

Various investigators of make-believe play attempted to classify out-of-play verbalizations into types, according to their functions with respect to the play. Goldman, for instance, proposed a typology of such verbalizations in his 1998 book. Here is a paraphrase of this typology, with my own examples:

Underscorings: Statements in which the child explains his or her playmates' play acts. Example: Ben is stirring a mixture of sand and water in a bowl, saying: "I am preparing porridge for the baby."

Prompts: Instructions on what to say and do in the play, given by players to other players.

Example: Jill is "a dog" and Mary is "a cat." Jill is prompting Mary to run away: "Run away! Why don't you run away?!"

Explicit fantasy proposals: Proposals to develop previous play contents or introduce new contents. Examples: In "The Kittens Are Being Born":

> John: Let's pretend we are being born now.
> Suzette: No. Let's pretend now is next year and you are already daddy-cat. And let's pretend here is the kittens' school.

Performative evaluations: Players evaluate or criticize various aspects of the play's signified contents or the means (signifiers) by which these contents have been expressed. Example:

> Joel: The giant lives with us.
> Daniel: That's impossible. Giants can't live in a people's house. They're too big.

Negotiations: Discussions in which various aspects of the play are being planned and organized: roles, props, actions and settings. Examples: Role negotiations in "The Kittens Are Being Born":

> Anna: Who's gonna be mommy-cat?
> John: Suzette.
> John: I am not daddy-cat, I'm a baby kitten!
> Suzette: No. Let's pretend now is next year and you are already daddy-cat.

Props, actions and settings negotiations. Example: Simon and Nicole are approaching the blocks corner in the kindergarten. Pat and Vicky are playing there.

> Pat: You can't play here. We are building a palace here.
> Simon: We have to build a castle before the black knights come!

5. *The language of make-believe play as a theater of the absurd*. Let us look at the sentence "We are being born now." It is easily identified as a make-believe play sentence. A real baby cannot report in real time about his being born. The same applies to the sentence "Let's pretend now is next year." In any other context except make-believe play this sentence will sound absurd. Such seemingly senseless expressions occur quite often in children's make-believe play. Additional examples are found in the next observation:

Observation 3: The Pirate and the Shark

David: Let's pretend the pirate killed the shark.

David is "shooting" at Jonathan with a stick signifying a gun, producing a *tsh* sound with his voice.

Jonathan: No, he didn't kill him. The shark wasn't here. He was there, far away.
David: Let's pretend there is here now. So now he did kill him.

David is "shooting" again.

Jonathan: No! It was an air-shark. He could not kill him.

The sentence "There is here now" is analogous to the sentence "Now is next year," and equally absurd.

Another kind of irrationality is illustrated in the sentence "Let's pretend the pirate killed the shark." David ("the pirate") said this to Jonathan ("the shark") and only afterward feigned the act of shooting. One would expect David to have said something like "Let's pretend the pirate is going to kill the shark," but he preferred to use the past tense rather than the present or future tense. Another illogical expression is the compound "air-shark."

All these paradoxical uses except the last one can be explained by the special nature of make-believe play, described by the formal definition proposed in Chapter 1. According to this definition, the playing child *animates* an entity born in her mind, *verbalizes* this entity or *identifies* some real, concrete element of the external environment with it, while being aware that both the animating and the identifying have not been done seriously. It follows from this definition that make-believe play is, by its very nature, two-faced. On the one hand the playing child creates a false identity between entities which belong to different worlds, the inner world and the outer world. On the other hand the child denies the existence of this identity. This duality is, of necessity, also a duality of time, place and character. The real time and place in which the play is being played (the real "now" of John, Anna and Suzette in Anna's room) are both identified and not identified with the imaginary time and place in which the play's plot takes place (the imagined "now" in which the kittens are being born in the pen). The child who embodies an imaginary character in his play (David who is playing "the pirate") both identifies and does not identify himself with this character. And if his playmate personifies another character (Jonathan, "the shark") he both identifies and does not identify his playmate with this character.

This duality of time, place and character explains the logic behind the illogical expressions listed above. In the sentence "We are being born now," the word "we" refers not to the playing children but to the imaginary kittens, and the words "are being born now" indicate not the present time but the imaginary time of the play's plot. If so, why didn't John say "They were born then"? Because the operations of *animating* and *identifying* cancel, as it were, the differences between the imaginary characters of the play ("they") and the players personifying them ("we"), between the imaginary time of the play ("then") and the real playing time ("now"). An analogous analysis can be applied to the expressions "Now is next year" and "There is here now."

Let us direct our attention to David's "Let's pretend the pirate killed the shark." The query regarding this sentence was the use of the past tense with respect to an action not yet performed. This query will evaporate, once it has been realized that the past tense refers not just to past time but also to imaginary or hypothetical time. "If everybody minded their own business," said the Duchess in *Alice's Adventures in Wonderland*, "the world would go round a deal faster than it does." And Alice said: "Which wouldn't be an advantage." The word "killed" in the sentence about the shark does not refer to past time, but to the imaginary time of the pretend killing. Such sentences detour around the basic duality of make-believe play. They constitute direct verbalizations of the imagined content of the play. They totally disregard the real time and place in which the play is being played, or the players personifying the imagined characters.

Although David personified the pirate and Jonathan the shark, the sentence "The pirate killed the shark," in distinction to "We are being born now" and "There is here now," said nothing about the playing children or the time and place of playing.

The expression "air-shark" is different from the other expressions, discussed above. Its distinction is not grounded in the operations of *animating* and *identifying*. Its absurdity is not a by-product of the very nature of make-believe play. It is an offshoot of the emotional and social regulative functions of play, to be discussed in Chapters 3 and 5. In "The Pirate and the Shark" Jonathan did his utmost to repel David's make-believe attacks, which nevertheless aroused unpleasant feelings in him. His last resort, after David had outmaneuvered all his previous tactics, was to make himself invulnerable, an air-shark.

Children often introduce absurd verbal and nonverbal structures into their play, whose function is to solve an emotional or an interpersonal problem. The compound "boatsy-submarine," a hybridization of a submarine and a boat, is mentioned in Chapter 5. It was created by a child to overcome his fear that an imaginary submarine he himself engendered would "drown." In Chapter 3 the compound "mommy-baby" is discussed. It was made up by a girl to solve an interpersonal problem, a power struggle between herself and her playmate. Assuming the self-contradictory role of mommy-baby seemed to this girl like a suitable compromise solution for this conflict.

SUMMARY OF CHAPTER 2

This chapter is devoted to make-believe play as a semiotic system, a language in the wide sense of this term. It proposes analytic tools and heuristic procedures for unearthing and describing the rules of this language. The distinctive features of this language, differentiating it from other languages, are discussed and illustrated subsequently.

The chapter begins with a presentation of some elementary concepts, terms and methods for analyzing and describing any language. The analysis and description include the following general steps:

- Identifying and describing minimal signifier-signified units and their combinations into structures.
- Identifying and describing the uses of structures—their creators' presuppositions and purposes.
- Distinguishing structures which say something about other structures and describing their uses.

- Classifying signifiers and signified into categories, and formulating rules constraining their combinations into structure and the uses of the structures.

The term "the language of make-believe play" is ambiguous. It can refer to make-believe play in general, to the play of a specific child, of a particular group of children, of children belonging to a distinct cultural community, and so forth. In this chapter the analytic steps listed above are illustrated only with respect to one observation of dyadic make-believe play, entitled "Peace Forever." Various heuristic and analytic techniques borrowed from the sciences of semiotics, linguistics and anthropology and adapted to our purposes can be systematically applied to such a play text. The following techniques are described succinctly in this chapter:

- analysis of observed play behavior by expressive media across time units;
- identifying minimal signifier-signified units;
- identifying and describing structures;
- inferring the context-dependent uses of structures (their creators' *purposes* and *presuppositions*);
- Context-Dependent Componential Analysis of signifying and signified units.

The same techniques are presented and illustrated in detail in the Appendix.
Applying these analytic devices to a play text serves three main purposes:

- corroborating prior intuitions about general patterns of form and meaning underlying the play text;
- revealing other such patterns;
- facilitating the formulation of rules.

This part of the chapter is followed by a discussion of the differential characteristics of the language of make-believe play. Its main distinctive features are

- ad hoc combinations of different signifiers;
- attributing unconventional signified to signifiers;
- transformations, in which the signified content of a signifier can be easily replaced by another signified content;
- going easily in and out of the play. When out of the play the players assume roles such as "playwright," "producer," "director," "stage designer," and so on.
- the use of verbal expressions which in other contexts would be considered absurd. This is explained by the basic duality of make-believe play, implied by its formal definition in Chapter 1.

A CLASSIFIED LIST OF REFERENCES

Analysis of Language and Other Symbolic Systems

Akmajian, Demers, Farmer and Harnish, 1995; Beaugrande, 1980; Cobley, Jansz and Appignanesi, 1997; Deely, 1982; Dinsmore, 1981; Fromkin and Rodman, 1998; de Saussure, 1972.

Componential Analysis

Ariel, 1994, 1999; Hammel, 1965.

Analysis of the Linguistic and Logical Peculiarities of Make-Believe Play

Ariel, 1984, 1992; Bateson, 1955; Fein, 1975; Lodge, 1979; Loy, 1982.

Make-Believe Play as a Semiotic System

Bretherton, 1989; Corsaro, 1983, 1992 ; Dixon and Shore, 1993; Duncan, 1988; Eckler and Weininger, 1989; Fein, 1979, 1989; Forbes and Yablick, 1984; Forbes, Katz and Paul, 1986; Galda and Pellegrini, 1985; Garvey, 1993; Garvey and Kramer, 1989; Gerstmyer, 1991; Giffin, 1984; Goldman, 1998; Golomb and Goodwin, 1987; Goencu, 1993; Hudson and Nelson, 1984; Kessel and Goencu, 1984; Leslie, 1987; A.K. Levy, 1984; Mathews, 1977; Maynard, 1985; McCune-Nicolich, 1981; Sachs, Goldman and Chaillé, 1985; Sawyer, 1996; Schwartz, 1991; Stromquist, 1984; Sutton-Smith, 1982b, 1984, 1989, 1997.

Techniques of Textual Analysis Applied to Make-Believe Play

Ariel, 1992; Goldman, 1998; Sawyer, 1996; Schwartz, 1991.

3   Make-Believe Play as a Diplomatic Language

THE REALM OF IMAGINATION AS AN ARENA OF POWER STRUGGLES

Make-believe play is a multipurpose instrument, remarkably flexible and sophisticated. One of its major functions is to enable children to manage their interpersonal differences and conflicts in a roundabout, "diplomatic" manner. The playing children transfer their conflicts into the imagined world of play. They pretend that the struggle is conducted not between their own selves but between imaginary figures in the fantasy world of their play.

Two six-year-olds, Billy and Timmy, play "forest animals." Billy is "the bear." He is standing on the floor. Timmy is "the monkey." He is sitting on a table, signifying "a tree." Billy says: "Let's pretend the bear told the monkey: 'you should climb off this tree.' " Timmy refuses. He does not want to get off the table. He says: "The monkey can't climb down the tree because the tree is too tall and the bear can't help him because bears can't climb trees." Actually, Timmy and Billy are contending, in the real world, for control. Billy is attempting to dominate Timmy, and Timmy is trying to shake him off his back. But this struggle is not being conducted overtly. The two want to continue being friends and enjoy playing. Therefore they transfer their encounter to the fantasy world of play.

Make-believe games of nursery school and older children include, quite often, long series of "diplomatic" exchanges of this kind. Each such series constitutes a kind of negotiation for proximity or control, replete with tactics and open or thinly disguised manipulations.

"PROXIMITY" AND "CONTROL" AS KEY CONCEPTS IN THE ANALYSIS OF INTERPERSONAL RELATIONS

The expressions "proximity" and "control" are highly significant in this juncture. They have not been chosen coincidentally. Numerous observations and investigations of humans and animals attest to the fact that relations among individuals and groups are primarily proximity and control relations having manifold manifestations. Both animal and human groups consist of rulers and subjects, leaders and followers, privileged and deprived. In most cases, a position of power can be achieved only after a bitter struggle, which is carried out by various means, ranging from brute force to all kinds of tactics and manipulations. The same applies to proximity relations. Both among animals and among humans there are various degrees of closeness between individuals and groups, from highly intimate relationships, as between lovers or between a mother and her baby, to total rejection and distancing, alienation, hostility and enmity. Very often, a desired degree of social proximity cannot be achieved without considerable exertion.

Children develop proximity and control relations among themselves since the time they begin having a mind of their own. Observe one-year-olds in a day nursery for an hour and you will witness scores of manifestations of such interactions. A boy is plucking a toy out of the hands of another boy. A girl is forcing another girl to sit down. A boy is trailing after a girl, seeking her company, but she is evading him. Two children are embracing and hugging each other. Two girls are feeding each other with a spoon. In this tender age, such interactions are usually short and simple. But as the children grow up, their control and proximity interactions become increasingly more durable and complex, and very often conducted in the "diplomatic" language of make-believe play.

What sets apart this application of make-believe play is not the very fact that play serves as a medium for negotiations about proximity and control, but the players' tacit mutual agreement to transfer these negotiations to the world of make-believe. Furthermore, the negotiation tactics employed by the children are unique to make-believe play and belong to its very special bag of tricks. Since in the make-believe realm children are at least partly free of the chains of reality and social conventions, they are at liberty to draw uncommonly rich, flexible and sophisticated devices from this bag. The following example includes a whole range of such devices.

Observation 4: Easy Riders

In one of my kindergarten visits, I sat on a little chair in the playground, waiting for some action to begin. It was a fine spring morning. Soon enough, two five-year-old girls, Dana and Ruttie, began playing. They approached a blue metal tube mounted on stands, which usually served as a kind of crawling tunnel. Dana approached the tube and called: "Ruttie! Let's get up on this horse!"

She mounted the tube and sat on it astride, moving her legs, alternately, slowly, forward and backward. I was immediately caught in her make-believe world, seeing in my mind's eye a rider on a slow-striding horse.

Ruttie ignored Dana's invitation to ride together. After a short while, Dana called "Halt!" and stopped moving her legs. She looked at Ruttie and made an inviting gesture with her arm and hand. Ruttie could not resist this gallant invitation. She mounted the "horse," but instead of sitting behind Dana, as might be expected, she sat astride in front of her, called out "Go!" and began moving her legs swiftly, as if galloping. And then she said: "Let's pretend the baby is in front and the mommy is behind."

This was very intriguing, the way Ruttie reversed well-established, customary scripts. Real mothers tell their real babies what to do and not the other way around. People who are invited to join a horse ride sit behind the rider, not in front of her, and certainly do not take over the horse leader's role. Why on earth should Ruttie invert the customary order of things in the real world? Apparently, the responses expected of her—to comply with Dana's invitation to join her for a horse ride, to behave like a baby, to be led—would not suit her goals. She wanted to be her own master, to be the leader herself perhaps. So, in order not to confront Dana directly and spoil the game, she at first ignored her suggestion to ride together and later feigned compliance, but manipulated the subsequent make-believe events to suit her own goals.

There were other surprises in store for me: Galloping, Ruttie continued speaking: "Let's pretend the mother allowed her baby to get lost, because she had a dog. When babies get lost the dog gets them back. Come on! You got home and told your baby: 'Cutie, you are allowed to get lost!' Are you gonna get off the horse then?" Dana cooperated. She climbed off the "horse" and said: "OK. I am going home."

This was amazing! Ruttie was now the monarch, the sole rider and horse leader. Dana was overthrown and effectively distanced. However, this coup d'etat was carried out inside the make-believe world and under a disguise of legitimacy. Dana was led to make-believe that Ruttie was still under her "parental" control. Apparently she took this idea seriously, as her next response was "I want you to work for me." But Ruttie had another plan. Instead of becoming Dana's employee, she said: "Mommy! Get me this bag. I need it! And this blanket too!"

Dana wanted Ruttie to work for her, but Ruttie inverted these roles and turned Dana into her employee instead. Dana complied. She began searching a box of junk articles for play placed near "the horse." She looked a little confused, apparently unable to find objects that could signify "a bag" and "a blanket." Ruttie had no time to waste on waiting. She climbed off "the horse," went to the junk case, drew a little box out of it and said: "Here's the bag." She placed "the bag" on the "horse's back," went back to the junk case and drew out a piece of cloth, which she placed on the "horse's back," saying "And here's the blanket." After a moment of hesitation, she added: "And now I need food." She found an old kettle in the junk case and filled it with little stones. After placing it on the "horse's back," she straddled the "horse," shouted "Go!" and began "galloping."

Suddenly the bag, the blanket and the food made sense to me. These were provisions for a solitary, long horse ride, in which the baby would get lost.

What could Dana do now? Ruttie outmanipulated all her attempts to keep her close to her and under her control. But she did not give in. She drew another rabbit out of her hat. She said: "Ruttie, let's pretend you are a baby-mommy. You are a queen, but you are a baby. And all this is your nursery." While saying this, Dana swept the whole playground with a grand arm gesture.

This looked like an heroic last battle, designed to maintain at least minimal control over Ruttie and prevent her from leaving a territory delimited by Dana and shared by her. Dana finally conceded that Ruttie had established a position of power and independence for herself. She declared Ruttie a mother and a queen. Still, she was reluctant to free Ruttie of her "babiness" completely. She accorded her therefore the dual status of "mommy-baby" and "a queen-baby." Moreover, she turned, with an arm-sweep, the whole playground, in a sense the whole imaginary play cosmos in which the play took place, into the nursery of this hybrid creature, mommy-baby queen-baby. If the nursery encompassed "all this," Ruttie would be free to ride wherever she desired. But in any location she would choose to be, she would still be confined within the bounds of the territory delimited by Dana.

But Ruttie rejected this move, too. Like an animal in a spacious reservation park, she was aware of being in captivity even though she was not locked up in a constricted cage. She said: "Let's pretend I didn't come to the nursery today" and increased the tempo of her leg movements ("galloping"). Even if "the nursery" included the whole play area, in Ruttie's make-believe world one had the power to decide "not to come" to it.

But Dana kept on trying. Previously Ruttie asked her to "get her things." This left Dana an opening to keep some kind of rapport with Ruttie, albeit in the role of a service-giver. She picked some pieces of plastic out of the junk case, held them out to Ruttie and said: "Darling, I brought you some food."

Ruttie ingored her. Dana said, now with a tinge of bitterness in her voice: "You should say 'Stop!' not just 'Go!' " But Ruttie continued ignoring her, and declared: "At last I've arrived at the village! That's wonderful! I've arrived at the village!"

Dana hastened to suggest: "Let's pretend we both lived together in that village." But Ruttie turned down this idea too. She said: "No, let's pretend you lived at home and this village is far far away and I lived in it alone."

Having witnessed this fascinating play scene, I began to imagine very methodical little puppeteers pulling strings inside the girls' heads. It was obvious to me that each of the girls was persistently striving toward specific proximity and control goals with respect to the other girl. Dana's goal was to keep Ruttie close to her, to control and supervise her. Ruttie's goal was the very opposite: to protect her own freedom, independence and separate personal space. I also realized that the clever, inventive, goal-oriented tactics concocted by the girls were not just improvisations thought up spontaneously, randomly, on the spur of a moment. All these tactics seemed to follow a general master plan, or strategy, consisting of ordered general principles for action as in a well-designed military operation or chess game I began attempting to explicate and formulate these strategies. To facilitate this endeavor, I began by conducting a step-by-step analysis of the "Easy Riders" text, as proposed in Chapter 2: dividing the text into minimal signifier-signified units, categorizing these units into types and subtypes, formulating the structures into which these units are combined, distinguishing between in-play and out-of-play structures, inferring the girls' purposes and presuppositions from the context, and so on. The results of this procedure follow.

TYPES OF CONCRETE IMAGES OF PROXIMITY AND CONTROL

Metaphors and concrete images are extremely common ways of expressing feelings and ideas. Our everyday language is replete with such expressive devices. We "blow off steam," "spill our guts" and "throw up our hands." Dreams and art speak almost exclusively in imagery, and so does make-believe play.

The notions "proximity" and "control" are abstract concepts pertaining to various aspects of interpersonal relations. Children translate these concepts into concrete make-believe play images such as "sitting in front on the horse," "getting off the horse" and "living in a distant village."

I read my own transcript of "Easy Riders" over and over again, and in my mind's eye the various concrete images of proximity and control began, little by little, to group themselves into organized troops, like soldiers in a parade. One troop included the images "horseback," "home," "nursery" and "village." I called this set of images *territories*, because in the girls' make-believe world these images were treated as private spaces into which one can invite or forbid a person to enter.

Then some groups of images ordered themselves by rank, representing three *degrees of participation in territories*. The *highest degree of territorial participation*, standing for the closest proximity, was indicated by the images "mount the horse together," "ride together" and "live together in the same village." A *medium degree of territorial participation* manifested itself by the images "stop the horse," "get off the horse," "go home," "work for," "bring (a bag, a blanket, food)," "queen-baby in nursery," "allow to get lost" and "the dog will bring back." These images portray situations in which the two characters in the make-believe play occupy different territories, but keep some kind of connection between them. For example, "the mommy" occupies the territory "home" and "the baby" the territory "horseback," but they are connected by the action of "bringing." The mommy brings things to the baby. The third, *low degree of territorial participation*, was realized by the images "galloping," "getting lost," "providing oneself, unaided, with supplies for a long journey" and "living alone in a distant village." These images depict situations in which the two characters occupy different and separate territories, which are cut off from each other.

All the above subgroups of images include concrete representations of *proximity*. But the make-believe play images in "Easy Riders" can be classified into another formation of categories: *Images of control*. One set of images of control represents *roles*. The images "mommy," "queen," "horse leader" and "employer" denote *controlling roles*, as against the images "baby," "back rider" and "employee," which denote *controlled roles*.

Another set of control images stands for *activities*. The images "sitting in front," "allowing," "getting the baby back home," "instruct to bring" and "employ" refer to *activities in which one is controlling*, as against the images "sitting behind," "being instructed to bring," "work for" and "be in the nursery," which indicate *activities in which one is controlled*.

There is a third set, however: *activities of independence*, in which the play character is neither controlling nor controlled, but independent. This set includes the images "galloping," "not coming to the nursery" and "living alone in a distant village."

To sum up, the concrete images of proximity and control in "Easy Riders" have been classified into the following types and subtypes:

proximity images—territories, degrees of territorial participation (high, medium and low)

control images—roles (controlling, controlled), activities (controlling, controlled, independent).

This classification helped me formulate the girls' strategies for achieving their respective proximity and control goals.

THE PLAYING CHILDREN AS MASTER STRATEGISTS

Here is the result of my attempt to formulate Dana's and Ruttie's plans for achieving their proximity or control goals.

Ruttie's plan is based on the following general principle: At first I should temporarily give Dana the semblance of cooperation, but later gradually assume a less and less cooperative attitude: I should take stronger and stronger measures to counteract Dana's moves and to achieve my goal.

More specifically: If Dana is in a *controlling role* or is engaged in a *controlling activity*, I'll assume a *controlled role* or enter into a *controlled activity*, but only for a short while. Afterward I should dethrone her, take over her *controlling role*, and engage myself in a *controlling activity*. Having accomplished that, I should gradually increase the distance between us, moving from *high* to *medium* and then to *low degree of territorial participation*. If, on the other hand, Dana is not in a *controlling role* or *activity*, why bother with power games? I should immediately strive toward a *low degree of territorial participation*.

Dana's plan is founded on the opposite principle: At first I should try to achieve my goal in its entirety, but if I meet stiff resistance I should gradually yield and make do with less and less.

More specifically: If Ruttie is in a *medium degree of territorial participation*, I should assume a *controlling role* or start a *controlling activity*, and invite her to enter my personal space, in order to achieve a *high degree of territorial participation*. If Ruttie resists being in a *controlled role* or being engaged in a *controlled activity*, I should sacrifice my *controlling role* or my *controlling activity*. I should even let her take over, but do everything in my capacity to prevent her from going from *high* to *medium* degree and from *medium* to *low degree of territorial participation*.

In the terms introduced in Chapter 2, these strategies are sets of syntactic rules, constraining the interrelations between the presuppostions and purposes the girls assigned to the in-play and out-of-play structures they produced.

TYPES OF "DIPLOMATIC MEANS" FOR ACHIEVING PROXIMITY OR CONTROL GOALS

"Easy Riders" is rich with "diplomatic" make-believe play tricks conjured up by the two girls to further their "political" interests:

- *A pair of opposites*—"mommy-baby." One member of the pair ("mommy") suits the proximity and control goals of Dana and the other ("baby") those of Ruttie.
- *Drawing a rabbit out of a hat*—"The mommy allows her baby to get lost, because she has a dog." Ruttie created, out of void, a dog, in order to soften Dana's resistance to her proximity goal.
- *Reversing*—Dana asked Ruttie to "work for her." Ruttie reversed this and made Dana work for her.
- *Swallowing*—"All this is your nursery." The image of the all-embracing nursery "swallowed" Ruttie's attempt to leave their connected (*medium degree*) territories.
- *Canceling*—"Let's pretend I didn't come to the nursery today." Ruttie canceled Dana's "All this is your nursery."

IN PRAISE OF THE METHODICAL LITTLE PUPPETEERS INSIDE THE GIRLS' HEADS

I was very proud of this analysis. It looked so rigorous, so elegant, so systematic. But then doubts began creeping into my mind. These little puppeteers inside the girls' heads, were they really that methodical? Wasn't that assuming too much? Maybe the contents of Dana's and Ruttie's play were just incidental responses to chance environmental stimuli? Maybe the play's plot was nothing but a random sequence of associations? Dana's eyes met, by chance, the metal tube mounted on stands. Its shape reminded her of a horse. So she introduced the horse image into her play. The presence of a horse summoned up the idea of a rider, which, in turn, evoked an association of a journey. The playground reminded Dana of a nursery; and so forth. This is incontestable, I thought. The choice of play contents is indeed influenced by environmental impressions or by previous contents already introduced into the play. Yet, the same environmental impressions and ready contents could have evoked numerous other associations. Why did the girls choose just the associations that they did out of all the other possibilities? Maybe the little puppeteers *were* highly methodical after all.

In Chapter 5 it is argued that the choice of play contents is motivated by the drive to balance the level of emotional arousal around emotionally loaded themes. In the present chapter it is claimed that the choice of contents is influenced also by the child's proximity and control goals. Both hypotheses seem to hold water. Moreover, these two motivations for choice of play contents seem to be interrelated. Suppose, for instance, that a child feels rejected and lonely. He attempts to balance this emotion by populating his make-believe play with contents of love, warmth and friendship. At the same time he tries to balance the very same emotions by choosing play contents designed to keep his playmates close. Another child feels restrained and restricted. She balances this emotion by creating a make-believe world in which she is free. Simultaneously, she attempts to balance the same emotion by inventing play contents aimed at preventing her playmates from controlling her.

My faith in the validity of the analysis presented above was heightened after I attempted to apply the same analytic tools to other videotaped samples of the make-believe play of the same two girls, Dana and Ruttie. These further analyses yielded similar types of concrete proximity and control images and similar strategic rules. I came to the conclusion that this analysis yielded a rather faithful description of some important parts of the vocabulary and syntactic rules of the language of make-believe play used by these two girls.

SUMMARY OF CHAPTER 3

This chapter examines one of the social functions of make-believe play—regulating the intensity of conflicts resulting from clashing proximity and control goals. It is argued that struggles to reach particular proximity and control goals are fundamental aspects of animal and human social life. In order to avoid open proximity and control conflicts which can disrupt friendship and cooperation, children transfer these conflicts to the realm of make-believe. Parameters of intimacy and power are translated into concrete images and metaphors, expressed by categories of make-believe play signifier-signified units. The production of structures consisting of such units is based on the players' *presuppositions* concerning the proximity and control *purposes* of their play-mates. The choice of structures is geared toward *purposes* fitting the players' ultimate proximity-control goals. In-play and out-of-play structures serving such purposes may be viewed as "diplomatic" tactics, having characteristic structural properties (*a pair of opposites, drawing a rabbit out of a hat, reversing, swallowing, canceling*, etc.). The use of such tactics by each player is subject to a master plan, a general strategy for overcoming the obstacles placed by the play-mates on the way to reaching one's proximity-control goals. Such strategies may be viewed as sets of syntactic rules regulating the choice of the players' make-believe play structures and their presuppositions and purposes.

A CLASSIFIED LIST OF REFERENCES

Proximity and Control as Fundamental Social Parameters

Ardrey, 1966; Ariel, 1999; Ariel, Carel and Tyano, 1984; Minuchin, 1974.

Channeling Conflicts to Play

Aldis, 1975; Ariel 1992, 1994; Aronson and Thorell, 1998; Asher and Coie, 1990; Auwaerter, 1986; Boggs, 1978; Conning, 1999; Doyle and Connolly, 1989; Garvey, 1974, 1979, 1993; Golomb and Goodwin, 1978; Gougoulis, 1999; Katz, Forbes, Yablick and Kelly, 1983; Kyratzis, 1992; Lein and Brenneis, 1978; Maynard, 1985; Takahama, 1995; Verba, 1993; Vespo and Caplan, 1993.

Social Functions of Play

Bakeman and Brownlee, 1980; Black, 1992; Cattanagh, 1998; Corsaro, 1985, 1992; Eifermann, 1971; Fantuzo, 1995; Fine, 1980, 1983; Furth and Kane, 1992; Garvey, 1974; Garvey and Kramer, 1989; Goencu, 1993; Gottfried and Caldwell, 1986; Howes, 1985; Howes, Unger and Matheson, 1992; Kane and Furth, 1993; Meckley, 1994; Parten, 1932; Riga, 2000; Singer and Singer, 1977, Verba, 1993; Vespo and Kaplan, 1993.

4 Mini-Legal Systems Regulating Sociodramatic Play

One of the most prevalent activities of children between the fourth and eighth years of their life is sociodramatic play—that is, social play in which groups of children improvise make-believe play conjointly. Sociodramatic play can be observed in kindergartens, schoolyards, playgrounds, backyards and other places in which children get together.

The first time I was properly introduced to sociodramatic play was back in the 1970s, in The Study Center for Children's Activities of Oranim, the School of Education of the Kibbutz Movement, Israel. The spontaneous play activities of kindergarten children of various cultural backgrounds were observed and analyzed by a multidisciplinary team of researchers. One of the members of the team was Irene Sever, an anthropologist. Her insights and penetrating observations had opened my eyes to the riches and sophistication of children's social life. Later Sever and I joined efforts in studying the sociodramatic play of children of various cultural communities.

Sever's area of specialization was systems of social control in general and indigenous legal systems in particular. Her initial observations had made her realize that kindergarten children would develop their own "mini-legal systems" through which they regulate their social relations and settle their conflicts and disputes. She set her mind to probing the nature of such mini-legal systems. Further observations conducted by her were focused on the children's out-of-play verbal discourse and nonverbal interchanges. Her protocols show that many of these interactions are constituted of negotiations around issues of proximity and control. As demonstrated in Chapter 3, children's in-play interactions consist very often of such negotiations. Sever's protocols show that the same applies to out-of-play interactions. Such out-of-play negotiations are aimed at settling conflicts about *rights of participation* (who is entitled to belong to a specific play group and participate in a particular sociodramatic play and who is not), *access to play territories* (who may be admitted into a predefined play area and who may not), *rights of possession* (who is allowed to play with a particular toy or play object and who is not) and *leadership* (who has the authority to accord or deny such rights? who is qualified to serve as the "playwright," "producer" or "director" of the sociodramatic play). Sever argued that in the course of such negotiations children often make reference to shared conventions or "laws." The common pool from which such laws are drawn is the children's own *mini-legal system.* Although children are aware of the rules and regulations imposed by their adult caretakers, their mini-legal systems are different from, and often contrary to, the former. They are the children's original creation.

THE CULTURAL SPECIFICITY OF MINI-LEGAL SYSTEMS

Mini legal systems are culturally specific. There are qualitative and quantitative cultural differences in the characteristics of mini-legal systems as well as in the nature of the interactions subsumed under them. These cultural differences are discussed in Chapter 7. All the examples in the present chapter are taken from the play of middle-class children of "modern Western" sociocultural background.

A SAMPLE OF LAWS

Here is a sample of laws found in children's mini-legal systems, with extracts of negotiations in which these laws are invoked. These examples have been taken from both Sever's protocols and my own observations of the sociodramatic play of various groups of children in Israel and other countries.

Leadership Laws

1. *Entitlement-for-leadership law.* Not all children are entitled to be in the position of a playgroup leader. Qualified are, primarily, children who are popular thanks to their social skills, personality, intelligence, imaginativeness, physical strength or other attributes.

Avi, Yossi and Oren play "Cops and Robbers" in the backyard of Avi's home.

Yossi: I'll be the cop and you'll be the robbers.

Oren: You don't decide about us

Yossi: Why?!

Oren: Because you don't know how to play such games.

2. *Seniority law*. The right of the child who initiated the playgroup to lead the group supersedes the right of a child who joined it later, even if the latter is more popular than the former. A child who has been a member of the playgroup for a longer time has a better chance to be accepted as the leader than a newcomer.

Mona, Sarah and Ada play as "a family of dogs" in the kindergarten's playground. Edna, "The Queen of the Kindergarten," approaches them, saying: "I'll be the mommy dog." Nobody challenges Edna's right to join the play. Mona, however, feels otherwise:

Mona: You can't be mommy dog. Sarah is already mommy dog.

Edna: So what? We can pretend that the little doggies had two mommies.

Mona: Edna, no, they have only one mommy.

Edna: Mona, you don't decide the play.

Mona: I do decide the play! I started this play! Sarah, tell her!

Sarah: Yes, Edna, Mona started this play.

3. *The leader's prerogatives law*. The playgroup's leader has the following prerogatives: (a) He or she has the right to play the most desirable and prestigious role in the sociodramatic play. (b) Although all the participants may express their wishes and preferences concerning their roles, the play scenario and all the other choices called for in planning and executing the play, the leader has the final say about all these. (c) The leader has also the final say about admitting outsiders to the playgroup or excluding them from it, although his or her decisions in this respect are constrained by the participation laws specified below.

Participation Laws

4. *The outsider law*. An outsider—that is, a child who has not been accepted as a participant in a playgroup engaged in a particular play activity—has no rights whatsoever with respect to the play group and its play.

Nitzan, Tomer and Gad play with "Pokemons" in their schoolyard. A fourth boy approaches them:

Ofer: Can I play with you?

Nitzan (the playgroup's leader): No.

Ofer: Why?

Nitzan: Because you are not our friend.

The children continue playing. Ofer is standing aside, watching them, disappointed and dejected. He is trying to continue being associated with them by making suggestions.

Ofer: Ash forgot to take Pikachu with him.

Nitzan: Ofer, You are not allowed to say anything.

Ofer: Why?

Nitzan: Because you're not playing with us.

5. *The freshman law.* A newly recruited member of a group should follow the lead of the group's leader and the other group members. He or she is not yet free to express his or her wishes and preferences concerning roles, the play scenario and all the other choices called for in planning and executing the play.

Rose and Angela play "Mommy and Baby" in the doll corner in their kindergarten. Jane asks to join them and they agree.

Rose: Let's pretend the mommy is taking the baby to the doctor.

Jane: No, she did not take him to the doctor, she took him to visit granny.

Rose: Jane, you can't tell the play because you just entered the play so you can't tell the play!

6. *The insider law.* A child may be admitted into a playgroup if he or she has a friend who is an insider, a member of the group. ("A friend" is a regular playmate.) An insider is allowed to invite a friend to join a particular sociodramatic play activity. If, however, the insider is not actively participating in a specific play activity, he or she is not permitted to invite a friend to join this activity.

Four kindergarten boys—John, Ben, Bob and Dan—play "building a house." These four children play together regularly; they constitute a playgroup. They load large play blocks on a toy truck. Afterward they unload the truck and erect a "construction." John is their leader. He plays the role of "the foreman," instructing the other children around. Ben gets tired of this play. He goes to the painting table and starts painting on a large sheet of paper. Another boy, Bill, approaches John, Bob and Dan. Bill is not a regular playmate of the latter.

Bill: Can I build with you?

John: No.

Bill: Why?

John: Because you don't play with us.

Bill: But Ben does play with you, and he's my friend.

John: But he's not playing with us now. He's painting.

7. *The loyalty law*. A participant in a specific play activity must not simultaneously participate in another play activity with another play group.

Mary, Sue and Jane play in the kitchen corner in their kindergarten, "cooking dinner." Jane is attracted to another playgroup, which plays "shopping" in another corner of the room. She keeps going away to the "shopping" group and back to Mary and Sue, until the following conversation takes place:

Mary: Jane, you can't play with us anymore.

Jane: Why?

Mary (pointing at the "shopping" group): Because you are playing with them.

Jane: But I'm going there to buy bread and meat and butter for our dinner.

Mary (insisting): No, if you want to play with us you should be with us, not with them.

Later a participant of the "shopping" group, calls out:

Laura: Jane, are you coming to shop with us?

Jane (calls back): No, I can't! I'm already playing with Mary and Sue!

Another participant of the "shopping group," Tanya, apparently the group's leader, tells Laura off for having attempted to breach the loyalty law:

Tanya: Laura, can't you see that she is with them, not with us?

The only way to bypass the loyalty law is to unite the two groups and merge their separate make-believe games into one. Jane continues negotiating with Mary, trying to persuade her to let her "shop" with the other group without losing her right to participate in Mary and Sue's "preparing dinner" play. Eventually Mary partly concedes. She offers to invite the whole "shopping" group to join the "preparing dinner" group and play a conjoint game:

Mary: They can buy the food for us and we can prepare dinner for all of them.

8. *The contribution law*. A child has a better chance to be accepted to a playgroup if he or she can make a significant contribution to the specific play activity, such as donate a valuable play object, offer a useful service, suggest a creative idea or play an interesting role.

John and Ben play "building a house" in the block corner.

Timmy (approaching them): Can I build with you?

John: No, there isn't room enough for too many builders here.

Ben: If you want to play with us you have to be the watchman. You watch the building when we go to fetch more blocks.

9. *The relevance law*. A child will have no right to participate in a play group if his or her participation has no relevance to the play activity—for example, if he or she has no role in the sociodramatic play.

Tomer, Gad and Ofer play with "Pokemons" in their schoolyard. Tomer and Gad pretend to be two Pokemons flying in the air to rescue their friend who was captured by "an evil Pokemon trainer." Ofer waves a flashlight held in his hand.

Gad: Ofer, what are you doing?

Ofer: I'm making light!

Gad: But we don't need light.

Ofer continues waving the flashlight.

Gad: Ofer, you are not in our play any more.

10. *The role title law*. A participant who plays a particular role in the sociodramatic play has possession rights with respect to this role. No other player is allowed to "steal" this role from him or her. Roles can be exchanged however by rotation.

Tomer, Gad and Nitzan play with "Pokemons." Tomer is Pikachu, Gad, Charmander and Nitzan, Mew.

Nitzan: I don't want to be Mew anymore. I want to be Pikachu.

Gad: But you can't be Pikachu, Tomer is Pikachu.

Nitzan: So let's swap. I'll be Pikachu and Tomer will be Mew.

11. *The gender segregation law*. Members of the other gender may not be accepted in a playgroup that is engaged in a play activity conceived by the children as gender-specific.

Four of the children mentioned above—John, Ben, Bob and Dan—play "building a house." Sue approaches them:

Sue: Can I play with you?

John: You can't play with us. There are very important boys' things here. Girls are not allowed to touch them.

Territory Laws

12. *The activity-territory law*. A playgroup may define a play territory—that is, a space serving as the site of a specific play activity—within a public area such as the kindergarten yard.

13. *The play territory's boundaries law*. A playgroup may define the bound-

aries of its play territory by physical markers such as play blocks or chairs or by a verbal declaration (e.g., "Everything under the table is ours").

14. *The presence law*. A participant of a playgroup is expected to be actually present in the area defined as the play territory. He or she must not play by "remote control."

Mary, Sue and Jane play in the kitchen corner. Jane has departed to watch another group of girls playing.

Jane (calling out loudly): Mary, is our baby sleeping well?

Mary: Jane, if you want to play with us you must be here with us, you can't be there and play with us!

15. *The suitability law*. The play territory may be divided into subterritories, each allocated for a particular activity type (e.g., "hunting," "sleeping," etc.). Participants must not play in the wrong subterritory (e.g., sleep in the area allocated for "hunting").

Possession Laws

16. *The primacy law*. This law refers to toys or any other play objects that are not the private property of any particular child, but are available to all the children to play with. This is the characteristic status of play objects and materials in kindergarten and other educational settings.

The first child who began playing with a toy or any other play object has a right to continue using it, until he or she has stopped playing with it, in which case the right of use is transferred to the first child who has got hold of it or has declared his or her intention to play with it.

"Stopped playing" is not the same as "stopped handling or manipulating" the play object. A child may be said to have stopped playing with an object only after this child herself no longer looks upon this object as having any active or passive role in her make-believe play. The primacy law is inapplicable if a child has appropriated a play object by force, preventing other children from getting hold of it.

John and Ben play "building a house" in the block corner. They are busy constructing. An empty toy truck previously used by them to transport blocks is placed by their side, apparently abandoned. Timmy, who is playing with another group, gets hold of the truck.

John: Timmy! Don't touch this truck! It's ours!

Timmy: But you are not playing with it!

John: But we found it first and we need it to get blocks.

17. *The temporary public appropriation law*. This law refers to a toy or any other play object that is the private property of a particular child (e.g., a doll

brought by a girl from home to the kindergarten). If the child who owns the play object is playing with this object in the framework of a particular play activity carried out by his or her playgroup, then the other members of the playgroup have the right to use this object in their play as long as the activity continues.

Another version of this law refers, again, to public rather than private play objects: If a child had brought a play object with her when she joined a play-group engaged in a particular activity, she may take this object with her when she decides to leave the group, when she is expelled from the group, or when the group breaks up.

Mary, Sue, Jane and Laura play "space travel" in their kindergarten yard. Laura is holding a little hand-held fan which she has brought from home.

Laura: Look what I got!

Jane: I know what it is. It's a fan. My mommy has it too.

Sue: It can be the dwarfs' spaceship.

Laura: But I brought it only to show it to you.

Mary: We can play with it and afterwards you can take it back home.

Laura consents. The girls play with the fan for a while, then:

Laura: OK, I'm going.

Mary gives her the fan without arguing and Laura departs.

18. *The role suitability law*. If a member of a playgroup needs an object for a particular role or activity (e.g., a child needs a toy gun for playing "a cop") he or she has priority with respect to the right to use this object.

19. *The territorial appropriation law*. Every play object lying within the boundaries of a group's play territory belongs to this group exclusively. If, however, an object within the boundaries is not actually used by the group as a part of a specific play activity, it may be claimed by another group under the primacy law.

Nitzan and Tomer play "whale fishing" in the kindergarten sandbox. There are various objects in the sand: plastic dolls representing people and animals, pieces of wood signifying "ships" and "guns" and a plastic pail. Gad, who has been playing with another group, comes and picks up a plastic rhinoceros from the sand.

Nitzan: Gad, don't touch it, its ours.

Gad: But we need it for our zoo.

Nitzan: We need it too.

Gad: But you can't have all the things. You can have some of the things!

Nitzan: All the things in the sandbox are ours. But you can take this pail if you want. It does not participate in our whale fishing.

20. *The possession transfer law*. A child has the right to use a particular play object if this object has been given to her willingly by another child who had possessed this object.

Mary, Sue and Jane play "cooking dinner" in the kitchen corner. Sue holds a toy clock.

Laura (who is playing with another group next to them, calls out): Hey, Sue, this clock is ours!

Sue: But Annie (a member of Laura's play group) gave it to me!

21. *The exchange law*. Play objects may be exchanged between individuals or groups.

Interrelations among Laws

The laws in a mini-legal system are not independent but interrelated in various ways. Some laws are subsumed under other laws. For example, *the territorial appropriation law* is subsumed under *the activity-territory law* and *the play territory's boundaries law*. A playgroup's claim to possess play objects lying within the boundaries of its play territory is derived from its right to delineate these boundaries. Other laws are, in certain conditions, incompatible. *The primacy law*, for instance, can in certain context clash with *the role suitability law*. Bob claims the right to use a particular play object under the primacy law. Tom argues, in accordance with the role suitability law, that he needs this object more than Bob. It is not easy to determine which of these two laws should overrule in this case.

Sanctions against Lawbreakers

Children who violate laws of a mini-legal system, by refusing to abide by them or by behaving illegally, are subjected to sanctions activated by their mates. Common sanctions are: being expelled from a particular play activity or, temporarily, from all the activities of a particular playgroup, terminating the status of being one's "friend" (a regular playmate) and reporting the violation to the adults in charge ("telling on"). Usually, before a sanction is implemented a warning is issued. Warnings are often expressed by routine figures of speech such as "I won't be your friend," "You won't play with us" and "I'll tell on you."

THE NATURE OF "LEGAL" NEGOTIATIONS

Verbal and nonverbal negotiations invoking the laws of mini-legal systems occur in situations of conflict: Two children contend for the leadership of a playgroup. A child attempts to be accepted in a playgroup but meets with refusal. One playgroup challenges the boundaries of a territory delineated by another group. Two children claim the right to use the same play object at the same time. The similarity to typical situations in which respectable adults go to law is striking.

Negotiations of this kind follow a characteristic format: A child (*the claimant*) performs a verbal or nonverbal act whose purpose is to gain ground in any of the above areas: leadership, playgroup participation, territory or possession of play objects. Another child, usually a playgroup leader (*the challenger*) challenges this act. The claimant evoks a mini-legal system law to support his or her claim. The challenger disputes the claimant's interpretation of this law or evokes another law that is supposed to override the former. The claimant tries to refute this claim, by invoking a different law, deriving corollaries beneficial to his or her case from certain laws, or offering a compromise. As a last resort the contestants invent their own arbitrary, ad hoc, laws. And so forth.

This exchange goes on until one of the sides yields. In some cases no side has the upper hand and the argument deteriorates to naked aggression. In all the stages of the negotiations, the two sides use both conventional figures of speech or nonverbal acts, drawn from the storehouse of "legal" terms and gestures available to the children, and expressions they construct on the spot. Examples of conventional nonverbal gestures are: getting hold of a play object to mark a claim for possession, putting an object in a particular place to delineate a play territory and climbing to the top of an object (e.g., a table) to indicate a position of dominance. Examples of conventional verbal figures of speech are "I found it first" or "I caught it first" and "It's mine" to declare possession rights; "You are not a friend" to reject a request to participate; and "You don't decide about us" to repel an attempt to assume a leadership position.

It takes a high degree of knowledge, resourcefulness and skill to be an effective junior negotiator. A competent negotiator, like a good lawyer, has to be a legal expert. Such a negotiator has to store many laws in memory and be able to retrieve the relevant laws in the appropriate situations. He or she should be aware of the above-mentioned complex interrelations among various laws in the mini-legal system and understand their implications with respect to negotiation tactics that can be contrived. He or she is able to draw situation-relevant inferences from each law and invoke pertinent precedents. Beyond these task-specific abilities, a competent young negotiator is required to possess advanced social and communication skills such as credibility, ability to interpret verbal and nonverbal messages correctly, creativity and inventiveness in interpersonal situations.

These high qualifications have far-reaching social and psychological consequences for individual children. Children who are relatively limited in these respects due to level of development, personality, emotional difficulties such as stubbornness or overvulnerability are liable to being rejected from playgroups and denied many other "legal" rights.

Here is an example of negotiations between competent negotiators:

Observation 5: The Magic Finger or the Sword?

Gal and Tamir play "Ninja fighters" in the fancy-dress corner of their kindergarten. This corner is furnished with a big box filled with various play objects, costumes, shoes, hats and masks, and a dressing table with a mirror and various make-up articles.

Gal and Tamir, holding toy Ninja swords, feign a Ninja duel, performing stylized gestures and producing swishing sounds with their mouths.

Avner, who had been working with finger paints at the painting table, approaches them. His forefinger is covered with black paint. He directs it at Gad and Tamir, making shooting sounds with his mouth.

Gal: Avner, you can't be with us.

Avner: Why?

Gal: Because you don't have a Ninja sword. You can't be a Ninja fighter if you have no sword. [the relevance law]

Avner: But I have a magic finger! And many other fighting tricks!

Gal: Ninja fighters must have swords. They can't fight with other weapons. [the relevance law]

Avner enters the fancy dress corner. He starts searching through the big box.

Gal: Avner, you can't find things in the box because you are not playing with us. [the play territory boundaries law; the territorial appropriation law; the outsider law]

Avner: But Tamir is my friend. Tamir, you are my friend, aren't you?

Avner continues searching the box. He draws out a wooden bowl and a red hood.

Tamir: Gal, Avner is my friend. [the insider law]

Avner: And I have a magic bowl and a war cloak too.

Gal: But I invented this game and I'm saying that he can't be a Ninja fighter with us. [the seniority law]

Avner: So let's pretend he helped us with magic weapons. [the contribution law]

Gal: But in The Ninjas 1 there are no magic weapons, only swords.

Avner: So let's do The Ninjas 2.

Gal: That's not the right way to play Ninja movies.

Avner: Gal, you don't decide about me.

Gal: But Avner, you've just come and you already want to decide? [the freshman law]

Avner: Everybody decides about his own weapons. [an ad hoc law]

Gal: No, that's not the right way to do Ninja movies.

Avner: Can't we do just a movie without a name?

Gal: OK, but then you'll be a different one that's fighting, so you'll need a different kind of weapon.

Avner: Let's pretend I was not real, I was just a hologram.

Gal: That's not fun! Holograms can't fight!

Avner: But why can't I fight with my magic finger?

Gal: But then I won't be able to say: You didn't hit me, you didn't hit me. A sword is long and a finger is short.

Avner: Gal, there's something you should know. We won't be against each other in this movie.

Gal: But even if you are going to fight with someone else you'll need a sword!

Avner: But I don't have a sword. Are you getting it? I don't have a sword.

Gal: You can use my sword then and give me your weapons, and then you can fight with Tamir. [the exchange law]

Avner: No, I need my weapons. [the primacy law; the role suitability law]

ADULTS' RULES AND CHILDREN'S LAWS

As mentioned above, children's mini-legal systems are different from, and often in conflict with, the rules and regulations imposed by adult caretakers such as parents and teachers. In the "modern Western," middle-class social milieus in which the observations reported in this chapter have been taken, adult care-takers usually attempt to lay down rules that are based on the values, or rather ideals, of equal rights, irrespective of age, social class, gender, physique and level of development, and on a pro-social, accepting attitude toward everybody. The children's mini-legal systems are often founded on the opposite values: Inequality in all the above-mentioned respects and segregation. This fundamental difference often gives rise to controversies between adult caretakers and children under their care.

Many adults are unaware of the fact that children have their own original and distinct rules and regulations. Since they do not understand the intricacies of the children's mini-legal system or the general principles on which it is based, they often misinterpret the children's arguments and squabbles as sheer stubbornness and misbehavior. Then they impose their own rules rather arbitrarily to the dismay and frustration of the children. The latter therefore often refrain from trying to enlist the aid of their adult caretakers when their "legal" argumentations jam, or steer away from the supervising eyes of these adults.

SUMMARY OF CHAPTER 4

This chapter is devoted to "mini-legal systems," sets of laws children develop in order to regulate their interactions and conflicts with respect to their social play activities in general and their sociodramatic play in particular. Twenty-one such laws are listed and illustrated by excerpts of "legal" interactions. These laws pertain to the right to participate in playgroup activities, leadership of play-groups, play territories and the right of use of play objects. All these are aspects of proximity and control. Chapter 3 covers struggles for proximity and control which are conducted mainly within the fantasy world of make-believe. The "legal" negotiations discussed in this chapter, on the other hand, are carried out mainly by verbal and nonverbal out-of-play expressions. There are considerable individual differences in the ability to conduct effective "legal" negotiations. Children who are weak in this respect are apt to be rejected or reduced to a low social status. Preschool educators and other caretakers often attempt to impose rules and regulations which are incompatible with the children's own laws on the children under their care. This reduces their chances of enlisting the children's full cooperation.

A CLASSIFIED LIST OF REFERENCES

Mini-Legal Systems

Ariel and Sever, 1980; Sever, 1980, 1984.

Play-Related Social Interactions

Asher and Coie, 1990; Auwaerter, 1986; Black, 1992; Bloch and Pellegrini, 1989; Cheska, 1981; Corsaro, 1985, 1992; Doyle and Connolly, 1989; Doyle, Doering, Tessler and de Lorimier, 1992; Duncan, 1988; Eifermann, 1970a, 1970b, 1971; Ellis and Scholtz, 1978; Evaldsson and Corsaro, 1998; Fine, 1980; Garvey, 1974, 1977, 1979, 1993; Garvey and Brendt, 1977; Garvey and Kramer, 1989; Golomb and Goodwin, 1987; Gottfried and Caldwell, 1986; Griffiths, 1935; Howes, Unger and Matheson, (1992); Katz, Forbes, Yablick and Kelly, 1983; Kyratzis, 1992; Lein and Brenneis, 1978; Lloyd and Goodwin, 1995; Maynard, 1985; Parten, 1932; Piaget, 1962; Riga, 2000; Russ and Grossman-McKee, 1990; Sachs, Goldman and Chaillé, 1985; Sawyer, 1996; Schultz, 1979; Schwartz, 1991; Sears, 1951; Singer, 1961, 1998; Singer and Singer, 1981, 1990; Sutton-Smith, 1966b; Takahama, 1995; Verba, 1993; West, 1988.

5 Make-Believe Play as an Emotional Moderator

A COMPLEX MECHANISM MEDIATES BETWEEN PLAY AND THE CHILD'S EMOTIONAL LIFE

There is an almost full consensus among play researchers that children's make-believe play flows from the child's emotional sources. The very engagement in this kind of play gives children pleasure and a great deal of emotional satisfaction. In the course of play children explore and express themes with which they are emotionally preoccupied. Playing pacifies them and provides them with ways out of their emotional entanglements.

Play therapy, the most widespread form of child psychotherapy, is based on these magic powers of make-believe play (see Chapter 9).

The links between make-believe play and the child's emotional life are intertwined into a complex, delicate mechanism. To fully understand these links, one is advised to become familiar with this mechanism. As a first step, let us see this mechanism in action.

Observation 6: The Soldier and the Submarine

I videotaped this observation in the playroom of the Department of Psychology of Tel Aviv University. The room was equipped with a sit-in sandbox and various toys and props.

Three children were playing: five-year-old Orie, his six-year-old sister Galya, and the latter's six-year-old friend Tamar. Galya and Tamar sat in the sandbox. They searched the sand and dug out various toys and playthings. Orie stood by the box. He picked up a big flashlight off the floor.

Orie (loudly, slowly, emphatically): A submarine with an enormous projector is going down into the sea.

He stuck the flashlight into the sand and began covering it with sand.

Orie: The submarine is looking for all kinds of colorful fishes. He loves to watch colorful fishes, the soldier.

Tamar, paying no attention to Orie, found a giraffe toy in the sand.

Tamar (addressing Galya): All of a sudden they saw a giraffe.
Galya: How come? It was a sea. I suppose it was drowning.

Orie got up hastily, moving quickly and incoherently. He snatched a toy soldier from a shelf placed over the sandbox. He threw it into the sandbox and then started moving it quickly toward the toy giraffe. He looked scared.

Orie (shouting): All of a sudden they saw a soldier, shouting "Help!" and starting to swim there!

When the toy soldier reached the toy giraffe, Orie stopped moving it. He turned the soldier upside down repeatedly, nervously, in the sand, making guttural choking sounds. And then he called out:

Orie: No more needed!

He took the soldier quickly out of the sand and threw it back onto the shelf. Then he addressed Galya and Tamar.

Orie: It was as if he stayed inside.

Galya picked up a blue plastic container off the floor and placed it on the sand. She put the toy giraffe inside it.

Galya: Let's pretend the giraffes were sailing in the boat.
Tamar: It was a floating zoo.
Galya: No, it was Noah's Ark.

Orie picked up a smaller, yellow, plastic container and placed it on the sand. He took the toy soldier off the shelf and put it inside the yellow container.

Orie: He finished sleeping. Now he is resting in the boat.

Galya and Tamar dug other toy animals out of the sand and put them inside the blue container.

Orie: It was a boatsy submarine.

Galya moved the blue container with the toy animals on the surface of the sand. Orie advanced his yellow container with the soldier in front of the blue container.

Orie: Let's pretend they chased him.

Orie got out of the sandbox, leaving the yellow container with the toy soldier in it on the sand. He looked for something on the floor. He found a doctor's medical box marked with a red Magen David (Star of David, the Israeli parallel of the Red Cross) and placed it on the sand.

Orie: Let's pretend there was a red Magen David submarine there.

He left the doctor's box on the sand and went back to his yellow container, moving it in front of Galya and Tamar's blue container.

Orie (loudly): They are shooting at him!

He made "shooting" noises with his lips. Then he took the toy soldier out of the yellow plastic container and threw it on the shelf.

INFORMAL ANALYSIS OF "THE SOLDIER AND THE SUBMARINE"—DETECTING THE EMOTIONAL REGULATION MECHANISM

Let us follow the course of Orie's play, with view to identifying and learning the mechanism associating the child's make-believe play with his emotional system.

Scene 1: Curiosity, Adventurousness, Courage, Aesthetic Interest

At the onset of the play episode, Orie created a scene in which a submarine with a huge projector, carrying a soldier, was delving into the sea. Apparently, Orie identified the soldier with himself. The submarine's mission was to look for all kinds of colorful fish. The atmosphere in this scene is permeated with adventure, boldness and aesthetic curiosity.

Scene 2: Panic, Tension, Unrest, Acting Out of Distress

The turning point occurred when Galya introduced the theme of drowning into the play. This seemed to have pushed Orie into a state of panic. He abandoned the search for colorful fish. He hurried to the shelf, took the toy soldier and cried: "All of a sudden they saw a soldier shouting 'Help!' " Was this a call to help the giraffe or himself? Perhaps both. Anyway, the soldier plunged into the water and began swimming toward the drowning giraffe. When he reached it, he began to struggle with it in order to draw it out of the water. In the course of this effort, however, he himself lost control over his own body and began suffocating. Since the soldier himself was in danger of drowning, Orie abandoned the effort to save the giraffe's life. Instead, he saved the life of the soldier. He took him quickly back to shore.

The mood accompanying this scene was scare, close to panic, tension and unrest. Orie, through the soldier, did an heroic act of plunging into the water to save the giraffe of the possibility of drowning. It seems, however, that this reaction was motivated more by fear than by noble sentiments. Soon enough the soldier escaped the battlefield in order to save his own skin.

Granted all that, Orie did not forget even for a moment that the entire drama took place only in the as-if world of the play. His verbal and nonverbal acts carried all the characteristics of in-play behavior. For instance, he did not shout "Help!" himself, but put this call in the mouth of the imaginary soldier. He did not choose his sister and her friend to serve as witnesses to the whole scene, but imaginary all-seeing "they."

Orie was not pleased with himself, having abandoned the drowning giraffe and escaped to the safety of the shore. He tried to clear himself of the guilt of cowardice by tactical moves characteristic of make-believe play. He declared "No more needed!" meaning "It is not necessary to save the life of the giraffe any longer. Its problem has somehow been already solved." Since, however, this solution did not seem to Orie sufficiently elegant, he added, addressing Galya and Tamar: "It was as if he stayed inside." That is to say, despite the incontestable fact that the soldier had already reached the safety of the shore (the shelf), Orie left him, by the word of his mouth, inside the water.

Scene 3: Rest, Gradual relaxation, Recovery

Orie, inspired by the creation of "a floating zoo" or "Noah's Ark" by Galya and Tamar, created a boat out of a yellow plastic container and began navigating it on the sand. He declared that the soldier "finished sleeping," moved it from the shelf to the boat and said: "Now he is resting in the boat." Afterward he explained that this was not really a boat but "a boatsy submarine," a kind of hybrid, being both a boat and a submarine.

Emotionally, this scene is characterized by a gradual diminution of the previous tension, and then repose, followed by recuperation, anticipating future adventures. After the soldier had slept on the shore, he was ready to return to sea, but not yet to swim or dive, acts still associated with the danger of drowning. All he could do was rest in the boat.

Having recovered in this way, the soldier's previous curiosity and adventurousness began awakening in him again. Therefore the serene boat started transforming into a submarine, going through an intermediate stage of being "a boatsy submarine."

Scene 4: New Dangers and Fears

Having calmed down and gained strength, Orie was ready for new contentions. He turned the peaceful situation, in which the soldier was resting in the "boatsy submarine" and all the animals were sailing in the "floating zoo" into a situation of a belligerent chase, in which the soldier was the one being chased.

Although Orie himself was the one who initiated this transformation, it aroused fears in him again. He left the sandbox and returned with a "Red Magen David submarine" which would extend medical care in case he is hurt. This move helped him feel secure enough to escalate the danger. He cried "They are shooting at him!" and produced shooting-like sounds. This imaginary hot pursuit aroused his fear again. He extricated the soldier quickly out of the danger zone and threw it again to the safe shore, the shelf.

What can one learn from this examination about the emotional mechanism of make-believe play?

First, one can see that the child brings signifiers and signifieds into his play, which illustrate and concretize his emotional concerns and core conflicts. In "The Soldier and the Submarine" Orie expressed his conflict between his curiosity and attraction to adventures on the one hand, and his fear of being exposed to dangers chanced by nature or human beings on the other.

Second, it is evident that the child develops his play plot so as to achieve a balance between extreme positions: situations in which he stretches himself emotionally up to the limits of his ability to bear the strain (drowning, a hot pursuit) and situations in which he lets himself relax and recuperate (escaping to the shore, sleeping on the shore, resting in the boat). Often, in the passage between the distressing situations and the moderate situations and back, the playing children mobilize their inventiveness and creative powers to make the transition as smooth as possible. They bridge over the two extremes by introducing entities and themes into the play, which can strike the observer as being senseless, odd, absurd (e.g., boatsy submarine, Red Magen David submarine, "It was as if he stayed inside"). From the viewpoint of the playing child, however, such productions make perfect sense and fit the natural course of the play plot. The final product is a zigzagging story line: peaks of tension followed by falling tension, back to heightened tension and so forth.

A PRINCIPLED PSYCHOLOGICAL EXPLANATION FOR
THE EMOTIONAL MECHANISM REGULATING PLAY

How can one explain the operation of this emotional-thematic system? Apparently, it is activated by a psychological mechanism whose application is much wider: the mechanism regulating the dynamic interactions between emotions and cognitions. One can fill a whole library with books and articles discussing various aspects of this mechanism (see the Classified Lists of References at the end of each chapter). Here is a summary of some of the most relevant aspects:

In a person's spontaneous mental life there is no such entity as a pure thought or pure emotion. What do exist are complex networks of associations among thoughts, feelings, sensations and emotions. These networks are organized, at least partially, around the person's *emotives*. An emotive is a theme with which a person is deeply preoccupied throughout her life or in a particular period of her life, a theme which arouses in her powerful emotions. For example, a person is troubled all her life with the thought that her mother has never loved her. This thought, whether well-founded or not, arouses in this person strong feelings of sadness, self-pity and anger. Another person is preoccupied in a particular period of his life with thoughts about difficulties in his business. These thoughts are accompanied with acute anxiety.

Judging by the admittedly limited sample presented in "The Soldier and the Submarine," Orie's main emotive seems to be "thoughts about his physical vulnerability, which arouse anxiety in him," or, in short, "anxiety with respect to his physical vulnerability." Attesting to the validity of this conclusion is the fact that Orie introduced this theme into his play over and over again, with accompanying manifestations of anxiety, while his sister and her friend remained calm.

Many emotives are not exclusive to a specific person, but are shared by many people of the same age or the same cultural background. The emotive "anxiety with respect to one's physical vulnerability," for instance, is very common among children, especially boys, of Orie's age. The emotive "guilt feelings associated with failure to implement religious commandments" is prevalent among orthodox Jews. And there are universal emotives, common to all or most human beings, such as fear of death.

Obviously, signifiers and signifieds associated with the child's emotives find their way into the child's make-believe play more than signifiers and signifieds which cannot be traced to the child's emotives. However, to fully understand the structure and functioning of the cognitive-emotional mechanism of make-believe play, one should go more deeply into the concept "emotive."

The emotionally loaded theme of an emotive ("doubt with respect to the mother's love," "physical vulnerability" or the like) is really only a general title designating an enormous, potentially infinite, field of private associations tied in the subjective mind of a particular person with the theme in question. Consider for instance the emotive "doubt with respect to the mother's love." A person whose emotive it is will respond with arousal of sadness, self-pity and rage whenever relevant childhood or adulthood memories emerge in her mind. Obviously, memories interpreted as direct manifestations of rejection on the side of the mother are relevant. But not all relevant stimuli are such direct manifestations. The same person can have similar emotional responses, for instance, after having seen her cat weaning her kittens by exposing her teeth and claws at them when they approached her udders. This person will be flooded with similar feelings when overhearing the song "Sometimes I Feel Like a Motherless Child." She will experience similar, though somewhat weaker, emotions after having heard her son complain that his teacher ignores him.

To sum up, some of the relevant stimuli are closer to the thematic focal point of an emotive. These are likely to arouse stronger emotions. Other relevant stimuli are farther removed from this focal point, closer to the margins of its association network. The latter will arouse weaker emotions.

We are beginning to get acquainted with the modes of functioning of the psychological mechanism regulating the interactions among cognitions and emotions. Our brain seems to give priority to handling materials associated with our emotives. To experience this, the readers are invited to perform the following exercise: Close your eyes. Relax. Let thoughts swarm in your mind. The leading thoughts and most of the thoughts following them are likely to be fragments of memories, visual or vocal images, words and suchlike, all drawn from the associative network of one or another of your emotives. These materials are likely to be closer to the focal points of your emotives than to their peripheries. The feelings aroused by this hot stuff can be so intense, that your mind is likely to prefer to distance itself from it. Then your thoughts will drift away to materials closer to the periphery of your emotives.

Summing up, the process of retrieving materials from memory and incorporating them in the free stream of consciousness are regulated by our emotives. These materials are taken from the center or the periphery of the associative network of each emotive.

Creative imagination is also regulated by our emotives. If one is asked to create original combinations of images, most of the resulting combinations will in all probability belong to the associative network of one of our emotives or another. A man was asked to invent a free combination of two images. He came up with the combination "a bottle gun" and immediately realized that this was related to his emotive "childhood memory of my father terrorizing the family when drunk."

Our emotives also regulate our auditory and visual perception. Take for instance a pregnant woman whose emotives are "joy and happiness with respect to the approaching motherhood" and "fear of birth." When she is strolling in a commercial street, her attention is directed selectively at pregnant women, women pushing baby carriages and stores selling products for babies. If she overhears a talk about birth pains and birth complications over the radio, she will probably switch to another station to keep away from anxiety-inducing materials belonging to the focal point of her emotive.

Our motivations for action are also influenced by our emotives. I used to know a man who, anticipating "The Year 2000 Bug," had been hoarding food and other supplies, filling the whole house with cans and boxes, to the extreme consternation of his wife and children. This man's hoarding activities were motivated by his emotive "fear of shortage in times of war and crisis." This emotive was related to his childhood war experiences.

In short, all the higher mental functions—memory, spontaneous thinking, creativity and imagination, attention, perception and motivation for action—are tuned and sensitized to the person's emotives. Materials closer to the focal point of an emotive have priority with respect to the right of access into all these channels. If, however, focal materials of an emotive arouse unbearable emotions, these materials lose their priority of access in favor of more peripheral materials. There are also extreme cases, in which the emotive materials are so troubling, that they are totally erased from one's conscious mind. These are the cases which psychodynamically oriented psychologists refer to as manifestations of "repression" and "denial."

The cognitive-affective mechanism described above may be seen as an homeostatic feedback system which regulates and balances the intensity of emotional arousal brought about by the contents associated with emotives. "A homeostatic feedback system" is a device functioning like a thermostat: It receives continuous feedback from its environment, and if the surrounding heat surpasses or comes below a preset level, the device switches itself out to maintain a balanced level of heat.

The connection between all these hypotheses and the emotional mechanism of make-believe play is immediate. The signified contents of the play are taken from the child's memory materials and their creative combinations. The selection of nonverbal signifiers requires allocation of attention, using the senses and activating one's perception. Therefore, all the above hypotheses apply to the choice of play signifiers and signifieds straightforwardly.

It follows that make-believe play is also a homeostatic mechanism regulating and balancing the level of emotional arousal with respect to the child's emotives. We saw such a system in action in Orie's play in "The Soldier and the Submarine." Orie's main emotive, materialized in this play text, is "fear of physical vulnerability." Most of the signified contents, which were taken from Orie's memory materials and their creative combinations, belong to the associative network of this emotive. Most of the signifiers, whose choice was the result of allocation of selective attention and activation of selective perception, belong to the very same associative network. Orie's first priority was to include signifiers and signifieds which are close to the center of the emotive in his play (e.g., drowning, hot pursuit). Since, however, those signifiers and signifieds had aroused a high level of fear in him, he felt the need to balance this emotional reaction. He first escaped to signifiers and signifieds lying out of the range of his emotive (e.g., sleeping on the shore). Afterward he returned for a while to signifiers and signifieds belonging to the periphery of his emotive (Red Magen

Table 5.1
Results of CDCA of Orie's Signifieds in "The Soldier and the Submarine"

Emotive: Fear of physical
Vulnerability

Degree of Vulnerability	highest	intermediate	lowest
Level of fear			
Danger zones	underneath water surface; on water surface, not inside a vessel	on water surface inside a vessel	on shore
Esthetic interest			colorful fish
Sailing vessels	a submarine a floating zoo	a boat a Red Magen David submarine Boatsy submarine	a submarine with an enormous projector
Type of danger	drowning suffocation being shot at	being chased	
Availability of help and protection	no help or protection	life saving Red Magen David submarine	
Level of energy	struggle	resting	sleeping
Direction of movement	vertical	horizontal	no movement

David submarine, boatsy submarine, a chase without shooting). Only after he calmed down did he let himself go back to signifiers and signifieds closer to the focal point of the emotive.

APPLYING CDCA TO "THE SOLDIER AND THE SUBMARINE"

The technique of Context-Dependent Componential Analysis, introduced in Chapter 2 and illustrated in detail in the Appendix, applied to a make-believe play text, can generate a map representing the cognitive-affective feedback mechanism underlying the text rather faithfully. Table 5.1 is such a map. It represents the results of an application of CDCA to "The Soldier and the Sub-marine." This map constitutes a description of that part of the associative net-work of the emotive "fear of physical vulnerability" represented in the play text. The signifieds belonging to this associative network are classified into compo-nents on the vertical dimension. These components are graded on the horizontal dimension into three levels of fear. The signifieds graded as belonging to the highest level of fear are closest to the center of the emotive. The signifieds attributed to the lowest level of fear are exterior to the associative network of the emotive, or are located in its periphery. The signifieds placed on the inter-mediate level of fear lie between the focal point of the associative network and its periphery. Some signifieds are placed on the borderline between levels of fears.

When Orie introduced signifieds belonging to the highest level of fear into his play, this generated intense fear in him. To calm himself down, the next signifiers he produced belonged to the lowest level of fear. Calmed down, he began to choose signifieds which belonged to the intermediate level of fear, and then, gradually, highest fear-level signifieds, and so on repeatedly.

Notice that a map like the one presented in Table 5.1 assigns each signified in Orie's play a different meaning than its customary meaning. The signified "shore" for instance is defined by this map as "a zone of minimal physical vulnerability and fear." The signified "a boat" has the meaning "a vessel of intermediate physical vulnerability and fear." The map assigns to each signified an interpretation according to its place in the associative network of Orie's emotive "fear of physical vulnerability."

THE VALIDITY OF THE CDCA OF "THE SOLDIER AND THE SUBMARINE"

A CDCA map such as Table 5.1 constitutes, or is, in a sense, a theory about the selection of signifieds in Orie's play. Like every theory, it is, in principle, falsifiable and replaceable by a better theory. Its validity can be tested by the following questions, among others:

1. Is it possible to construct a different CDCA map, which will describe Orie's choices of signifieds more adequately? Although I have not succeeded in constructing such a better map, this is something that is in principle possible to achieve.

2. What is the predictive power of this map? If this map has a significant predictive power, one should expect it to predict Orie's choices in further sam-ples of his make-believe play. One does not expect, of course, exactly the same signifieds as in the "The Soldier and the Submarine" to be replicated in these other samples. What does one expect, then? The first expectation is that a CDCA of additional samples of Orie's make-believe play will yield a map similar to the one presented in Table 5.1. Such an analysis of additional samples has

actually been carried out. It did generate similar maps for further play samples. These maps will not be presented here, for shortage of space.

The second expectation of a good test of predictive power of a theory is that it specify crucial properties shared by all samples of the observed behavior. The map in Table 5.1 informs its readers that the play sample "The Soldier and the Submarine" has the following properties:

1. *Constraints on co-occurrence* of signifieds belonging to different levels of fear. For example, signifieds belonging to a high level of fear are not played simultaneously with signifieds belonging to a low level of fear. (e.g., a struggle, assigned to "high level of fear," never happens on the shore, a zone of least danger and fear).

2. *Constraints on sequencing* of signifieds belonging to different levels of fear. Following the occurrence of signifieds belonging to a high level of fear (e.g., drowning), no other signifieds belonging to a high or intermediate level of fear (e.g. shooting, boat) will occur. Only signifieds belonging to the lowest level of fear will succeed highest fear level signified.

3. *Constraints on the location* of compounds of signifieds, in which signified contents belonging to different levels of fear are combined with each other (e.g., "boatsy submarine"). Such compounds will occur only on the borderline between one level of fear and another lying immediately above or below it.

4. *Constraints on accompanying out-of-play behavior.* Higher fear-level signifieds are accompanied in Orie's play by intense out-of-play behavior manifestations of stress: fast, unfocused movements, loud, panicky voice. Lower fear-level signifieds are accompanied by out-of-play behavioral display of tranquility.

If the map in Table 5.1 has a good predictive power, then the same constraints should equally apply to all other samples of Orie's play. Indeed, further samples of his play were found to be subject to the same constraints.

Here are some excerpts of another observation of Orie's make-believe play, recorded in the same month as "The Soldier and the Submarine." No systematic analysis of these excerpts will be attempted here, but please observe the similarity in Orie's use of signifiers and signified to manage his own emotional preoccupations:

Observation 7: The Naughty Teddy Bear and the Mixed-Up Rooster

Orie (addressing his playmate Gil): Gil, let's play as if my naughty teddy bear flew with his balloon and fell to the ground. He had a friend, the mixed-up rooster. You'll be the rooster.

Orie gives Gil a blue balloon. Gil blows it up. Afterward he gives it to Orie.

Orie: Lets pretend the rooster ran and pushed the teddy bear and he got entangled with the string and the balloon flew up with him.

Gil "flaps" his hands and Orie rotates the teddy bear, and then raises it in the air with the balloon attached to it.

Orie: The balloon went up in the air with the teddy bear, only that high (showing the height with his other hand), and then all the air went out of the balloon and the teddy bear fell to the ground.

Orie exhales to signify the air coming out of the balloon. He takes the teddy bear with the balloon down to the ground. He lays the teddy bear on his back.

Orie: He went to sleep. He is dreaming about the Land of Dwarfs. He is also tiny like all the dwarfs.

Almost everything found in the above analysis of "The Soldier and the Submarine" is present in "The Naughty Teddy Bear and the Mixed-Up Rooster" too: Orie's attraction to beautiful things (the balloon flight, a scene taken, apparently, from Winnie the Pooh), his adventurous character, his fear of being physically hurt and his manners of coping: avoiding too much risk ("only that high") and going to sleep in a safe place.

SUMMARY OF CHAPTER 5

This chapter is dedicated to the function of make-believe play as a cognitive-affective homeostatic feedback mechanism for regulating the child's level of emotional arousal. It is argued that all our cognitive information-processing systems—sense perception, memory, creative thinking, motivation for action—are monitored by our emotives. An emotive is a cognitive-affective structure, a set of associations centering around central emotionally loaded themes. Our perception is geared toward stimuli associated with the nuclei of our emotives. Memories associated with the centers of our emotives come to mind first. Creative thinking and action are motivated by emotive-related materials. Since make-believe play links memory and creative thinking (the sources of its animated signified contents), perception and action (the sources of its verbal and nonverbal signifiers), the choices made in play are directly influenced by the child's emotives. The child's first priority is to introduce signified contents and signifiers drawn from the core of his emotives into his play. If these materials, however, intensify his unpleasant feelings to an unbearable degree, he moves to signified contents and signifiers belonging to the periphery of his emotives. After he has calmed down he goes back to focal materials and the cycle repeats itself.

The technique of Context-Dependent Componential Analysis introduced in Chapter 2 can be used as a heuristic procedure for revealing and describing the child's central emotives and their structure of nuclear and peripheral associations.

A CLASSIFIED LIST OF REFERENCES

Regulative Mechnisms

Abramovitz, 1995; Ariel, 1987, 1997; Moray, 1963; Moustakas, 1955.

Theories of Emotions and Cognition

Blaney, 1986; S. Freud, 1959; Izard, 1991; Klinger, 1971; Piaget, 1962; Singer, 1973; Tomkins, 1962.

The Functions of Play as an Emotional-Regulative Mechanism

Amen and Renison, 1954; Ariel 1994, 1996, 1997; Axline 1947, 1964; Bach, 1945; Eisen, 1988; Erikson, 1940, 1972, 1977; Fein, 1978, 1980, 1984, 1986, 1989, 1995; Fein and Kinney, 1994; Fein and Rivkin, 1986; S. Freud, 1959; Gordon, 1993; Goerwitz and Wohlwill, 1987; Harper, 1991; Moustakas, 1955; Piaget, 1962; Russ and Grossman-McKee, 1990; Schultz, 1979; M.E. Scott, 1998; Sears, 1951; Singer, 1961, 1998; Singer and Singer, 1981; Sutton-Smith and Rosenberg, 1960; Warren, Oppenheim and Emde, 1997.

6 Make-Believe Play and the Developing Child

Make-believe play grows and develops with the growing and developing child. As the child is evolving and maturing mentally, socially and in motor skills, so is his make-believe play becoming more and more complex, well-organized, sophisticated and rich. There is a mutual fertilization between the child's general development and the development of her make-believe play.

When the child plays a make-believe game, she exercises and rehearses a whole assortment of skills required to make the play happen, and in this way reinforces and elaborates these skills. In sociodramatic make-believe play, multifold learning processes take place, of which the playing children are the agents. They are both the teachers and the pupils. All these contribute considerably to all aspects of the child's development.

THE DEVELOPMENTAL STAGES OF MAKE-BELIEVE PLAY

Let us trace the developmental course of make-believe play from its appearance in the second year of the child's life up to its gradual disappearance in midchildhood. In this survey, the interrelations between the development of play and the cognitive, psychomotor and social development of the child will be reviewed, highlighting the following developmental areas: sense perception and attention; motor skills; memory; creative thinking; reality testing; insight and self-awareness; organization and planning ability; knowledge and understanding of the world; egocentricity versus the ability to understand and consider the feelings, needs and wishes of others; the ability to understand and act according to common social codes and norms; the ability to achieve social goals, through the use of tactics and negotiations; and the ability to control one's emotional responses.

In each of these areas, make-believe play grows and evolves, with the child's maturation, in complexity, coherence, depth, sophistication, abstraction, objectivity and versatility. Let me demonstrate this in detail, with illustrative examples.

The Beginning of Make-Believe Play

Most play researchers trace the beginning of make-believe play to the onset of speech and language, that is, in the second year of the child's life. For example, Anna (13 months old) "drinks" out of an empty cup, laughing pleasurably. Dan (18 months old) places a play block shaped like an elongated tube on the floor, vertically, saying "candle" and laughing. Yael (20 months old) holds a plastic whistle resembling a microphone next to her mouth and starts singing.

Jean Piaget and other investigators saw the amused expression and the laughing accompanying such observed behaviors as a proof that these are genuine examples of early make-believe play. Keeping in mind the definition of make-believe play in Chapter 1, such outward behavioral manifestations may not be considered conclusive evidence for this claim. It is quite possible that Anna did not play as if she was drinking from the empty cup, but only imitated the act of drinking, and that her laugh only indicated that she found this imitation pleasurable. The same applies to the other examples discussed above and in the literature. It is impossible to determine categorically whether these examples are genuine instances of early make-believe play without reading these children's tender minds, a mission impossible.

Let us, for argument's sake, assume that these are authentic instances of make-believe play. If this is so, they constitute a fantastic developmental achievement for children so young. Let us examine this achievement in the light of the above-mentioned developmental parameters.

Some of these instances attest to a relatively very good capacity in the areas of sense perception and motor skills. Dan for instance showed ability to analyze some of the structural properties of a candle and to choose a signifier (a play block shaped like an elongated tube, placed vertically) representing these properties. This bears witness to visual perception, which is not automatic but analytic.

As to memory, the signified contents (drinking out of a cup, "inventing" a candle, etc.) are drawn from the child's long-term memory. That is, children so young are able to bring to the play not only entities they actually perceive in the course of the activity but also materials retrieved from their own long-term memory.

If these are really genuine examples of make-believe play, one should assume that the playing child *animates* a mental entity, *identifies* a real object or action with it but *denies the seriousness* of these two mental operations. If this is really so, children in the second year of their life already have a surprising capacity for insight and self-awareness, as well as an ability to monitor their own mental processes and distinguish between imagination and reality, truth and falsity. These play examples demonstrate that children of this age can already make false assertions deliberately, being fully aware of their untruth, without attempting to mislead. This ability requires sophistication of the kind found also in modes of expression such as humor and irony.

On the other hand, such early manifestations of make-believe play do not yet demonstrate highly developed creative thinking, or the availability of a rich store of knowledge of the world. The signifiers and signified mimic simple objects and actions of the immediate environment in which the child lives. This early make-believe play does not exhibit a high level of complexity, coherence, organization or planning. It consists of simple actions that are not driven by any deep underlying rules. These simple make-believe play acts are not yet social. The child does not create them together with other children, although he enjoys being watched by adults, who appear to be impressed.

The Middle Stage—The Third and Fourth Years

In the third and fourth years of the child's life one witnesses a great developmental leap forward in all the areas listed above. With the development of sense perception and motor skills, play signifiers become more complex. The child no longer creates only unidimensional signifiers such as a block signifying a candle, but also signifiers consisting of ad hoc combinations of words, sounds, movements and handy objects of the play environment. Such ad hoc combinations are discussed and illustrated in Observation 2 ("The Kittens Are Being Born") in Chapter 2. An example brought there is the improvised structure consisting of the linguistic expression "We are being born," a high pitched mewing (vocal), a blanket (an object) and the act of crawling out of it (motional-spatial-tactile) signifying the birth of the kittens.

The ability to create such ad hoc combinations evinces the child's facility in intersensory coordination and her adeptness at combining items into coherent structures. The invention of original, improvised combinations of signifying raw materials requires a relatively high level of creative thinking.

Three- and four-year-old children also begin to attribute unconventional signifieds to signifiers. Examples are provided in Chapter 2: In "The Kittens Are Being Born" the blanket does not signify a blanket. It signifies the location of the unborn kittens—the mother-cat's belly. The crawling out of the blanket signifies the birth. The room signifies "a pen." These signifiers attest to a higher level of development of perception and thinking than signifiers produced by younger children. The former do not mimic the signifieds but allude to them.

The similarity between the signifers and the signifieds cannot be visualized. To see this similarity one should use inference and associative thinking.

With the development of the child's memory capacity, power of imagination and life experience, the child's make-believe play becomes richer and more complex. Most of its signified contents, however, are still taken from the child's everyday experience. The playing children do not just duplicate daily episodes, but also transform these episodes to suit their emotional needs, using their imagination. These transformations often have a bizarre, dreamlike nature. Things change into other things, people and situations are transmuted and become unrecognizably different, defying all constraints of reality. These transformations do not seem to be subjected to a self-controlled, self-conscious creative imagination, but rather to the caprices of an egocentric mind seeking to fulfil its immediate wishes. The resulting play text is not a well-organized story, but a series of short, loosely structured episodes. Here is an observation, representing these characteristics:

Observation 8: Secrets

Almond, 3.5, is playing with her mother Rose in their home's living room. Various toys are scattered on the carpet. Almond picks up a plastic hammer which emits a click when hit against an object.

Almond: Look what I found! The hammer that makes noise!

Almond holds the hammer next to her ear.

Almond: He is telling me a secret.
Rose: What is he telling you?
Almond: Pop pop pop pop pop.
Rose: Only you understand his language.

Almond picks up a little doll representing a boy.

Almond: They called this little boy Kyarpash. Kyarpash played on the grass. He didn't know what to do. The dog wanted to eat him up. He ran away quickly with the mother. (Almond moves the doll toward some other dolls.) In the end he met dolls. Once he also met dolls from his yard. (Almond picks up a plastic ear.) But he didn't know what to do with the ear. He had no body. I forgot all the little children. They went away and I can't remember where they were.

Piaget (1962) reports the make-believe play of a four-year-old girl, who made up a creature she called *aseau*, a deliberate distortion of *oiseau* ("bird"). She herself played the role of *aseau*, transforming it rapidly into a kind of bird, a kind of dog, a person-like long-haired creature, a parental authority scolding the children and so forth.

These features of the play of three- to four-year-olds are determined by the child's characteristic developmental profile at this age-range. Although the child's memory span is much more spacious than a two-year-old's, and her attention and concentration powers are much greater, they are still rather limited. The child still cannot retrieve rich and long chunks of materials from long-term memory and turn them into play signifiers. Her attention wanders easily from one set of stimuli in the immediate environment to another. She turns each of these sets of stimuli into a play signifier and searches for appropriate signified contents to match them. When her attention wanders to another set of stimuli she abandons the previous signifier-signified and creates a new one, not necessarily related to the former. The child's thinking is not yet fully socialized. It is still egocentric and subjective, dictated by her immediate emotional needs rather than by an objective, detached examination of reality. Hence her play reflects her own rapidly changing needs and feelings and not her perception of the interests, feelings and needs of the other participants in the play.

Due to this egocentricity and the still-limited ability to coordinate thoughts and actions with other people, the child's play at this stage is either solitary or parallel. That is, even if two or more children play together, each of them produces his or her own signifiers and signifieds, without making any serious attempt to connect and relate them to the signifiers and signifieds of the other participants in any coherent, significant manner. Here is an example of such parallel play:

Observation 9: The Plane and the Washing Machine

Two four-year-old boys, Saul and Daniel, play in the blocks corner in their nursery school. Saul arranges big, oblong blocks on the floor, forming a rectangular shape. He sits inside the construction, making a rattling noise with his lips.

Saul: My plane is flying fast and fast and fast.

Daniel sits on one of the rear blocks of Saul's plane, his back to Saul. He presses the block with his forefinger.

Daniel: Now it's working. It's a washing machine.
Saul: Now I'm coming down.

Daniel picks up a block. He starts rotating it with his hand.

Daniel: I'm driving my car.

Saul kicks the block construction, scattering the blocks around.

Saul: What a silly plane I made.

Saul laughs. Daniel joins him, kicking the blocks. Both laugh.

The Latest Stage—Sociodramatic Play

From the fifth year of the child's life until the waning and eventual disappearance of make-believe play toward midchildhood, make-believe play reaches its full developmental capacity. This is precipitated by the child's maturation in many developmental areas.

Sense Perception and Attention

The child's longer attention span and wider perception range enable him to create longer and more complex ad hoc combinations of signifying raw materials. Ben (5.6) was playing "knights' war" in his nursery room with two of his mates. He began looking for suitable attire. His search took a long time, in which his attention was concentrated on this goal. He combed the whole apartment. He used a silvery plastic bag for a helmet, a black paper mask for a face shield, a wicker window shade for an armor plate, a silvery tray for a hand shield and a broom for a sword.

Since perception has grown more analytic, the child's choice of signifiers becomes original and inventive. The child can perceive and isolate nonobvious features of objects and materials, and bring them into play in signifying unexpected signified entities.

Sarah, five years old, employed a black gardening hose as signifier for "highway." Rami (5.3.) held a silvery candy box of which the lid was attached to the body by hinges. He began opening and closing the lid rhythmically and said: "I am knitting."

Since at this developmental stage perception and attention are less associative and fragmented and more organized, signifiers are not chosen at random. Their choice is regulated by deep underlying rules or principles of the kinds discussed in Chapter 2. The players strive for the signifiers to be well-motivated—that is, suitable for their signified contents and to the play plot.

Memory

Children at this developmental stage have a much wider memory capacity, which capacitates them to generate longer, more complex, multidimensional signified contents combined to coherent story lines and dramatic structures. Often playgroups continue playing the same story across different sessions separated by days or weeks, like television drama series. The choice of signifiers and signifieds is regulated by deep underlying rules, as shown in Chapters 2, 3 and 4.

Such full-fledged sociodramatic games are "The Shrunken People" not (Observation 13 in the Appendix) "Easy Riders" (Observation 4 in Chapter 3) and "The Soldier and the Submarine" (Observation 6 in Chapter 5). Here is another good example:

Observation 10: The Very Funny Truck

Two six-year-old boys, Ronen and Barak, were playing in Ronen's nursery room. Ronen was constructing a large figure with Lego pieces. Barak moved a toy truck across the room.

Ronen: Barak, look, I built an instrument with legs.

Ronen started making the Lego construction walk.

Ronen: It walked and walked and walked until it began to break apart.

Ronen began dismantling the Lego construction.

Barak: Let's pretend this was a garbage truck. They threw it into the garbage truck because it broke apart.

Ronen mounted the Lego construction on Barak's truck, with its two "legs" astride.

Ronen: Now the truck can walk with its legs.

The two boys were trying to make the truck "walk" with the "legs" of the Lego construction.

Ronen: This was a very funny truck. It could walk and then go with its engine and then walk and then go with its engine and then walk.
Barak: But its legs didn't carry him to where he wanted them to carry him.

Barak made the truck with the Lego construction bump against a Lego tower the two of them built previously.

Ronen: It collided with a tower and the tower became like an accordion, it went up and down like a spring and then it collapsed.

Barak made the tower collapse.

Ronen: But then the garbage truck and the instrument built a palace.

Ronen began making a different construction out of the Lego pieces of the toppled tower. Barak helped him.

Barak: The truck and the construction lived in the palace and they threw all the garbage to a garbage pile near the palace.

Creative thinking and problem solving

The improved capacity for creative thinking and inventiveness children possess at this developmental stage leads them to create, self-consciously, original play plots forging imaginary possible worlds. "The Very Funny Truck" is a good illustration of this developmental achievement.

Often, the sociodramatic play of children of these age groups offers them opportunities to encounter technical problems and use their creativity to solve them. On such occasions a good deal of incidental learning of rudimentary scientific laws and principles takes place.

Two five-year-old girls, Anna and Liat, made a see-saw for dolls out of a board of wood placed on a can. The see-saw went off balance and fell. The girls did not give up. They attempted to understand the causes for the failure and went on attempting to correct the errors and achieve good balance. In the course of this exchange they learned that they should find the center of gravity of the board in its midpoint and that the dolls should be of the same weight. Although they still lacked the exact language to formulate their findings, they could apply their discoveries to the problem in hand on the practical level.

A group of boys dug "a river" in the sand. Then they poured water into it from a pail, expecting the water to flow. It did not, and they tried to find out why. After some discussion they realized the cause of the failure: The surface of the ground was flat rather than sloping.

As demonstrated in Chapters 3 and 4, children of this developmental stage make up signifiers and signifieds intentionally for the purpose of solving emotional and interpersonal conflicts and difficulties. The generation of novel, original sequences of signifiers and signifieds is regulated and controlled by underlying rules of the kinds discussed in these chapters.

Insight, Introspection and Self-awareness

Children of this developmental stage already have a well-developed ability to look at their own thoughts, feelings and behavior from the outside, as it were. Thanks to this enhanced introspective ability, children have a high degree of control over the nature of their play. This is manifested in careful, purposeful, principled preplanning of the thematic contents and the structure of the sociodramatic play, as well as in continuous ongoing verbal and nonverbal monitoring of various aspects of it.

Organization and Planning

In this age range children have already acquired a considerably enhanced capacity to plan and organize their thinking and activities. This capacity contributes its share to some of the achievements already mentioned above. The playing children exhibit an impressive ability to preplan the plot of their sociodramatic play and to choose its settings, means and roles in advance. The planning and organization of the play is not subject to the whims, caprices and immediate subjective needs of the players. The course of the play is steered by objective considerations and controlled by abstract principles.

Both the capacity for introspection and the organization and planning ability of children of this developmental level are illustrated in the following, fuller version of "The Naughty Teddy Bear and the Mixed-Up Rooster" (Observation 7 in Chapter 5):

Observation 11: The Naughty Teddy Bear and the Mixed-Up Rooster (a fuller version)

Orie is playing with his friend Gil in Orie's nursery room. Orie holds a teddy bear.

Orie: This is my naughty teddy bear.

Orie hugs the teddy bear, and walks in a funny way.

Orie (singing): My little naughty teddy bear, naughty naughty teddy bear! Gil, let's play as if my naughty teddy bear flew with his balloon and fell to the ground. He had a friend, the mixed-up rooster. You'll be the rooster. The rooster pushed him and he was mixed up so he didn't know the balloon would fly up to the sky. OK?

Gil: OK. You got a balloon?

Orie: Why are you asking stupid questions, you mixed-up rooster? I've got many balloons, here in this box. Can you blow up this balloon?

Orie gives Gil a blue balloon. Gil blows it up. Afterward he gives it to Orie and starts waving his hands and calling "cockadoodledoo, cockadoodledoo." Orie ties one end of a string to the balloon and the other end to the teddy bear's hand.

Orie: Let's pretend the rooster ran and pushed the teddy bear and he got entangled with the string and the balloon flew up with him.

Gil runs toward the teddy bear. He pushes it with his hands.

Orie: No! The mixed-up rooster is waving its wings until the teddy bear is getting entangled!

Gil "flaps" his hands and Orie rotates the teddy bear, and then raises it in the air with the balloon attached to it.

Orie: The balloon went up in the air with the teddy bear, only that high (showing the height with his other hand), and then all the air went out of the balloon and the teddy bear fell to the ground.

Orie tries unsuccessfully to untie the string from the aperture of the balloon. He gives up.

Orie: The air is going out of the balloon and the teddy bear is falling down.

Orie exhales to signify the air coming out of the balloon. He takes the teddy bear with the balloon down to the ground. He lays the teddy bear on his back.

Orie: He went to sleep. He is dreaming about the Land of Dwarfs. He is also tiny like all the dwarfs. He thought it was nighttime but it was daytime.

Gil: His friend, the mixed-up rooster, mixed him up. At night he said: It's day time! And when it was day he said: It's night time! In the morning he told the teddy bear: Go to sleep! It's late at night!

Knowledge and Understanding of the World

Five-year-old children already possess a sizable store of information about the world in which they live. Their knowledge and understanding of material and social reality are much more advanced than younger children's. This is reflected in the thematic contents of their sociodramatic play. Whereas three- and four-year-olds bring mainly their mundane, everyday experience into their play—home and family life, cooking, shopping or the like—older children borrow materials from television and the movies, computer games, children's books and other secondary sources. They mix and remold these materials using their creative thinking and constructional abilities. Older children, furthermore, use the sociodramatic play arena to discuss abstract "scientific," philosophical and moral questions preoccupying them. This is amply reflected in the following observation:

Observation 12: The Power of Good and the Power of Evil

Itamar and Ofer, both seven years old, were playing on the sofa in the living room of Itamar's home. Itamar occupied the right corner of the sofa and Ofer the left corner.

Itamar: Let's play Koory and Mari.
Ofer: Mari was the good one, like last time.
Itamar: I was Koory, and Mefon, the commander of the Bad Ones, hypnotized me to kill Mari, even though he was my best friend.

Itamar wore a fixed stare, like a hypnotizer, stretching his two arms forward. His stare was directed at Ofer. Responding, Ofer attached the two palms of his hands to one another and then drew them apart abruptly.

Ofer (declaring ceremonially): Evil! Evaporate!

Itamar (whispering): It failed.

Itamar got up and started walking slowly toward Ofer, his arms stretched forward, like a sleepwalker. Ofer stopped him with the palms of his hands.

Ofer (with a slow, authoritative voice): Your heart. You can control it. You can decide who you are.

He stared directly into Itamar's eyes. Itamar bowed slightly toward Ofer, and then raised his still stretched arms, standing motionless.

Ofer: Do something.

Itamar ignored this command and turned his back on Ofer. He walked to the right corner of the sofa. He bent forward, bringing his face close to the sofa.

Itamar: I can see Mefon's face in the magic looking glass.

He straightened up, turning the front of his body toward Ofer, stretching his arms forward again. He was looking at Ofer like a sleepwalker.

Ofer: Are you again with The Evil? That's clear. You were told you had the right to decide who you are and you decided to be with The Evil.

Ofer took an apron placed on a bench near the sofa, and continued speaking with a formal, monotonic voice:

Ofer: Sometimes one has to kill people in order to do good, and sometimes one has to imprison them, and that is the right thing to do. And that's (raising his voice) what I'm doing.

And then he tied Itamar's wrists with the apron. Itamar did not object.

Ofer: You won't be able to free yourself! Koory, for the sake of your friend Mari, who was trustful, will you decide who you are? A member of the powers of good or a member of the powers of evil?

Itamar did not answer. He freed his hands of the apron and stretched his arms forward again, like a sleepwalker.

Itmar: My master!

Ofer: What do you mean?

Itamar: I am at your service. I was bad, but after I saw Mefon's wicked face in the magic looking glass I understood my heart and became good.

Ofer: I don't want you to be at my service. I want you to be free!

Itamar: But if I am free I'll feel bad.

Socialization

As children grow up, their level of socialization becomes higher and higher. This is manifested in various aspects of their play: They are engaged less in solitary or parallel play and more in conjoined, interactive sociodramatic play. Their play is coordinated and harmonized on all levels: Planning of plots, settings, means and roles, choice of signifiers and signifieds and ongoing monitoring of the play's progress. The coordinating efforts are carried out by continuous negotiations and other exchanges of verbal and nonverbal messages. The players improvise together like musicians in a jazz band, trying to attune themselves to each other. This often requires reading each other's minds, deciphering hidden messages lying behind the manifest ones. To achieve this children mobilize a pro-social attitude and a great deal of empathy and self-control. They take into account each other's emotional needs, wishes, ideas and goals, even when these are incompatible and conflicting, as in "Easy Riders" (Observation 4, Chapter 3). The whole activity is regulated, as shown in Chapters 2–5, by social codes and rules created by the children themselves.

Table 6.1 is a summary of the main stages of make-believe play development as a function of the child's general development.

The Waning of Make-Believe Play

Toward midchildhood most children abandon make-believe play and sociodramatic play for different kinds of play and play-like acitivities, such as computer games, social games, sports, trading picture cards (the current trend favors Pokemon cards) or the like. The age in which this comes about varies. Some children lose interest in make-believe play and qualify it as "childish" as early as in the seventh year of life. Other children continue playing make-believe games until the tenth year of their life or even later. The latter often hide this fact from their friends, fearing to be ridiculed.

Students of make-believe play attribute its disappearance to the process of internalization. As the child grows up, his thoughts and their expression in speech, his feelings and emotions and the products of his imagination tend to go inward and become private, taking the form of daydreaming and merging into the child's stream of consciousness. Their external expression is channeled into socially coded media other than make-believe play, for example, private intimate conversations, organized drama, story writing and other forms of artistic expression.

Table 6.1
Make-Believe Play Development as a Function of the Child's General Development

Dimensions of Development	Complexity	Abstraction	Depth	Objectivity
Areas of Development				
Sense Perception and Attention	from simple signifiers to complex, coherent ad-hoc combinations of signifying raw materials	from concrete signifiers (a cup signifying "a cup") to abstraction of signifying features (a black irrigation hose signifying "a highway")	from random choice of signifiers to choice regulated by deep underlying rules	from choice of signifiers dictated by the child's internal needs to choice by suitability to signified
Memory	from simple, unidimensional signified to long complex, multi-dimensional signified contents, with story lines and coherent dramatic structures; stories continued from session to session, like TV series		from random choice of signified to choice dictated by deep underlying rules	
Creativity	from replication of simple entities and episodes to creation of original story lines forging novel possible		novelty is generated by deep underlying rules	

Table 6.1 *Continued*

	worlds from creating short sequences satisfying immediate emotional needs to inventive creation of complex signifieds and signifiers in the service of solving inter-personal and emotional conflicts	
Insight, Self awareness	from production of ad hoc, random signifiers and signifieds to planned choice based on generalizations concerning main themes purposes, and principles	from lack of out-of play meta-expressions to ample use of meta-expressions commenting on various aspects of the play
Organization and Planning	from ad hoc, incidental choice of signifiers and signified to preplanned play plots and play means / from concrete to organization and planning subject to abstract principles	from subjective to general objective considerations
Knowledge and Understanding	from the child's mundane everyday experience	knowledge and understanding of the world reflected

84

	as the sole source of play contents to books, the mass media etc. as sources	play contents often discuss and debate abstract philosophical issues	in signifieds becomes less subjective and more objective
Socialization	from solitary or parallel play to complex coordination of play means and contents of different children	from solitary play dictated by whims to socio- dramatic play regulated by social codes	from choice of signifiers and signifieds dictated by the child's subjective egocentic needs to taking into account the playmates' viewpoints and needs

SCIENTIFIC RESEARCH

The interface between children's general development and make-believe play development has intrigued many researchers in the fields of child psychology and education. These investigators also have been motivated by the hope that their research might have useful practical applications in early childhood education and psychotherapy. The three main trends in this body of research have been:

1. Correlational studies, concentrating on statistical interrelations between various parameters of make-believe play and of other aspects of the child's development.

2. Intervention studies, in which children are trained in various make-believe play skills. The hoped-for positive effects of this training on specific dimensions of development are then examined.

3. Longitudinal studies, examining the interface between the development of make-believe play and the child's general development through time.

Although the results of some of these studies have been subject to debate, the general trend of this field of investigation has exposed strong positive interrelations between the development of make-believe play and the children's general development. Following is just a sample of relevant findings.

The development of make-believe play has been found to be positively related to the development of language skills, comprehension of texts and pictures and imagery abilities. Children whose make-believe play was found to be higher on a developmental scale also had a better ability to organize their thoughts and actions and express themselves clearly. They also exhibited a more advanced capacity for self-reflection and insight and a keener sense of reality—that is, ability to distinguish between reality and fantasy. They had a clearer, more salient and more positive self-concept. They were more capable of controlling themselves and delaying gratification of urges. They had a stronger tendency toward empathy and a pro-social attitude. They seemed happier. They were found higher in social skills in general and in conflict resolution skills in particular

SUMMARY OF CHAPTER 6

This chapter deals with the interface between children's make-believe play and their general cognitive, emotional and social development. It is argued that there is mutual fertilization between the former and the latter. The evolvement of make-believe play is nourished by the child's cognitive, social and emotional growth.

Practicing make-believe play on the other hand is an opportunity to exercise, rehearse and reinforce all the child's developmental achievements in the following areas: motor skills, memory, creative thinking, reality testing, insight and self-awareness, organization and planning ability, knowledge and understanding of the world, egocentricity versus the ability to understand and consider the feelings, needs and wishes of others, the ability to acquire and act according to common social codes and norms, the ability to achieve social goals through the use of tactics and negotiations and the ability to control one's emotional responses. In each of these areas, make-believe play grows and evolves, with the child's maturation, in complexity, coherence, depth, sophistication abstraction, objectivity and versatility. Although this process is continuous, it can be divided to three main stages:

1. The beginning of make-believe play in the second year of the child's life—at this stage children's make-believe play is solitary, simple and close to the child's immediate everyday experience.
2. The third and fourth years of the child's life—make-believe play at this stage is still solitary or parallel. It is more complex, but structured by the child's egocentric associations.
3. The fifth year and on—make-believe play becomes mainly sociodramatic. It is highly structured and rule-driven. Its contents are drawn from secondary sources such as books, television series and computer games.

The hypothesized mutual fertilization between the child's general development and the development of make-believe play is supported by a considerable body of empirical scientific research.

A CLASSIFIED LIST OF REFERENCES

Make-Believe Play and Social Development

Ariel, 1992; Auwaerter, 1986; Bakeman and Brownlee, 1980; Black, 1992; Boggs, 1978; Bretherton, 1984; Bruner, Jolly and Sylva, 1976; Chang, 1998; Curry and Arnaud, 1974; Eifermann, 1971; Eisenberg et al., 1985; Fineman, 1962; Fisher, 1992; Goencu, 1993; Haight and Miller, 1993; Haight, Wang, Fung, Williams and Mintz, 1999; Howes and Matheson, 1992; Hughes, 1992; E.P. Johnson, 1991; Kessel and Goencu, 1984; Martin and Caro, 1985; Meckley, 1994; Mueller-Schwartz, 1978; Nicolopoulou, 1997; Piaget, 1962; Scales and Almy, 1991; Sutton-Smith, 1966a; Takahama, 1995; Tamaru, 1991; Vespo and Caplan, 1993.

Make-Believe Play and Cognitive Development

Auwaerter, 1986; Boggs, 1978; Bornstein and O'Reilly, 1993; Brainerd, 1982; Bretherton, 1984; Bruner, Jolly and Sylva, 1976; Cohen and MacKeith, 1991; Curry and Arnaud, 1974; Dansky, 1980a, 1980b; Dias and Harris, 1988; Drucker, 1975; Fall, Belvanz, Johnson and Nelson, 1999; Fein, 1978, 1979, 1985; Feitelson, 1972; Fineman, 1962; Fisher, 1992; Flavell, Flavell and Green, 1987; Freyberg, 1973; Goerlitz and Wohlwill, 1987; Golomb, 1979; Golomb and Cornelius, 1977; Gordon, 1993; Goerlitz and Wohlwill, 1987; Gould, 1972; Hughes, 1992; Hutt, Tyler, Hutt and Christophersen, 1989; E.P. Johnson, 1991; Johnson and Christie, 1986; Johnson, Christie and Smilansky, 1990; Yawkley, 1986; Klinger, 1969, 1971; Klugman and Smilansly, 1990; A.K. Levy, 1984; P.H. Lewis, 1973; Lieberman, 1977; McCall, 1974; McCune-Nicolich, 1995, 1997; Pepler, 1982; Pepler and Ross, 1981; Piaget, 1962; Pulaski, 1973; Rosen, 1974; Rubin and Pepler, 1980; Rubin, Watson and Jambour, 1978; Ryan, 1999; Saltz and Brodie, 1982; Saltz, Dixon and Johnson, 1977; Seagoe, 1970; Simon and Smith, 1985; J.L. Singer, 1973, 1998, Singer and Singer, 1985, 1990; Slade and Wolf, 1994; Smilansky, 1968; Smith, 1986; Smith and Dutton, 1978; Sutton-Smith 1966a, 1967, 1971, 1979; Vygotsky, 1966; Wooley, 1995; Yawkley and Pellegrini, 1984.

Research on Play Development

Pepler and Rubin, 1982; Sutton-Smith, 1972, 1982a, 1985.

7   Make-Believe Play in a Cross-Cultural Perspective

ETHNOGRAPHIC RESEARCH OF MAKE-BELIEVE PLAY— THE METHODOLOGICAL LIMITATIONS

Children find the raw materials out of which they create their make-believe play in the physical and cultural environment in which they grow up. One should therefore expect the make-believe play of children who have grown up in different places and social groups to be dissimilar. Describing and analyzing the differences requires a comparative cross-cultural research based on detailed naturalistic observations. A search of the published literature has come up with many ethnographic accounts of children's play in all parts of the world (see "A Classified List of References" at the end of each chapter).

Only pitifully few of these, however, are free of major methodological shortcomings, such as inadequate sampling and data collection methods or impressionistic, sketchy reporting. Consider, for instance, Goldman's (1998) ethnography of the make-believe play of Huli children in Papua, which is one of the best works in this category. His data were obtained by tape-recording the make-believe play speech of the children from a remote microphone. Since, as shown in the previous chapters, the nonverbal ingredients of make-believe play are crucial for understanding its structure and meaning, this technique calls into question his interpretations of the data. Or consider Sever's comparative ethnographic study of conflicts concerning possession of play objects, participation in play groups, play territories and leadership of play activities in children of various Jewish and Arab cultural communities in Israel (The Oranim Project, see Chapter 4). I consider this study a fine piece of work. Still, as Sever (1984) herself admits, this research leaves much to be desired methodologically. The observers did not understand Arabic and had to rely on translations into Hebrew provided by the children's kindergarten teachers. The groups of children observed did not match in their experience in group activities and nursery schooling. The analysis of the data, though brilliant and insightful, was qualitative and somewhat impressionistic.

The danger of ethnocentrism and prejudice lurks behind any ethnographic research. One should therefore be doubly cautious when trying to learn any general lesson from this scanty body of research. One should adopt a particularly guarded attitude toward the following claims, made by various investigators of make-believe play:

• Children of lower social classes or non-Western cultures do not play make-believe games at all.

• Children of these social backgrounds do play make-believe, but their play is dull and underdeveloped in comparison with that of middle-class Western children.

Scientific objectivity would not allow one to reject these claims off hand, but a much larger body of solid ethnographic research is required before anything conclusive can be said about them.

This warning granted, I have tried to review and evaluate some of the tentative relevant findings and insights. The latter, presented below, should be viewed as questions and hypotheses requiring further investigation rather than as valid generalizations.

TYPES OF ANTHROPOLOGICAL EXPLANATION

To assess the above-mentioned ethnographic studies one should take into account the scientific-explanatory frameworks within which they have been conducted. Theories explaining human experience and behavior in social and cultural anthropology may be categorized into the following two general types:

Functionalistic theories. According to these theories, customs, institutions and patterns of behavior in various cultures are there to fulfil specific biological, economic or ecological functions. Functionalistic explanations have been applied also to children's play. A claim expressed over and over again in the literature is that in their play children copy or reproduce patterns of behavior they witness in the adult world. Girls mimic women's behavior: cooking, weaving, putting on makeup. Boys imitate men's behavior: working in the field, hunting, fighting. Boys and girls stage approximations of adults' rituals and ceremonies. This *mimesis* has a function. By imitating the adults, the children practice the skills and aptitudes they will need when they become adults. They prepare themselves for adult life.

Construstivistic theories. Proponents of these theories argue that human experience and behavior take various shapes and forms not just to fulfil varying utilitarian functions. Rather, humans are endowed with an inherent motive to use their intellect, creative thinking and imagination in attempting to explain the world to themselves and exercise influence upon it. In social and cultural anthropology this constructivistic approach is reflected in the structuralistic, symbolic-interpretive and cognitive schools.

Researchers of children's play whose turn of mind is constructivistic emphasize its creative and innovative aspects. They argue that children do not just copy the adults' world in their make-believe play but create a new world of their own, which resembles the reality they have grown into in some respects, but differs from it in other respects. This view is expressed quite eloquently in the following citation from Sutton-Smith (1997, 158): "Children's play fantasies are not meant only to replicate the world, nor to be only its therapy; they are meant to fabricate another world that lives alongside the first one and carries on its own kind of life, a life often much more emotionally vivid than mundane reality."

APPROACHES TO SOCIALIZATION RESEARCH

The two conceptions of play discussed above, play as imitation and play as original invention, are manifested also in research on socialization. In some studies the child is conceived as a passive recipient of the cultural lore and values of his senior socialization agents, who use modeling, training, tutoring, indoctrination and other direct or indirect techniques. In other studies socialization is viewed as an interactive process. The children's minds are not regarded as tabula rasa, but as active, creative producers of ideas and modes of thinking and behavior which influence the adults and contribute to cultural change.

MODERN VERSUS TRADITIONAL CULTURES

Our world is culturally diverse. It consists of numerous societies, each having its own special blend of cultural characteristics. It is an undeniable fact though that some cultures are more akin to each other than other cultures. This has induced anthropologists to classify cultures into types. One such classification is the grading of cultures along the dimension of *modernity versus traditionality*. The most modern cultures are urban, highly literate, technologically advanced, secular and individualistic. The most traditional cultures are rural, illiterate or partly illiterate, untaught in modern technology, adhering to traditional communal religious practices and collectivistic. Social groups all over the world occupy different places along the continuum between these two extremes. Furthermore, with the growing influence of the modern cultures over the world's traditional cultures, the latter are changing gradually and are becoming modernized.

As will be shown below, the dimension *modernity versus traditionality* and the process of modernization are relevant to cross-cultural comparisons of make-believe play. The terms "traditional society" and "modern society" below are shorthand for "a society closer to the traditional pole" and "a society closer to the modern pole," respectively.

ADULTS' ATTITUDES TOWARD CHILDREN'S PLAY IN DIFFERENT CULTURES

The question whether play is imitative or creative as well as the question whether socialization is unidirectional or interactive are empirical ones. It may well be the case that the nature of play is not the same across cultures. These cultural differences can be looked at from various angles, one of which is the question of the extent to which adults endorse and encourage children's play. Different cultural groups show considerable diversity in this respect. In some cultures, notably those which are closer to the modern pole, parents, educators and other caretakers of children encourage play, consider it important, support and promote it and sometimes actively participate in it. In other cultures adults in charge of children regard their play with lack of interest and indifference. And there are cultures in which adults' attitude toward children's play is explicitly negative. They consider it frivolous, disruptive or even immoral. The Victorian saying "Children should be seen, not heard" comes to mind in this juncture. And other things come to mind too.

In the Oranim project (see Chapter 4 and above), Sever sampled the play and social behavior of preschool children in Israel: kibbutz and town Jewish children, urban Christian and Muslim Arab and urbanized Bedouin Arab children. She also conducted home visits and interviewed the children's mothers about their values and socialization practices. I conducted an analogous field study in a seminomadic Bedouin encampment in the Sinai desert. These sociocultural groups may be graded on the modernity versus traditionality dimension as follows: The kibbutz and town Jewish children and their families were the closest to the modernity pole. The Sinai Bedouins were the nearest to the traditionality pole. The urban Israeli Arabs and the urbanized Israeli Bedouins were midway between the latter two extremes. The latter however were more traditional than the former.

This gradation corresponded quite clearly with the adults' attitude to play. The kibbutz equipped the children's communal residence and kindergarten with the best toys, games and play objects. Special places and times were allocated to free play. The parents used to play with their children in the afternoon. Adults held the view that play was good for the children's development and well-being. The same applied to the Jewish town parents and kindergarten teachers. Adults of the urban Muslim and Christian Arab groups considered play as a pastime rather than as an activity that is important for the child's development. Mothers explained that it was natural for children to play, and bought them toys, but did not hold the view that play should be encouraged or promoted by the parents.

In the urbanized Bedouin group, the attitude of adults toward children's play was somewhat negative. Play was seen as a waste of time, or as an activity suitable only for very young children. Toys were conspicuously lacking from both home and kindergarten. In some of the families, the more "modern" ones, a collection of inexpensive, partly broken toys were shown to the interviewer, and their presence seemed to be considered an innovation and a departure from customary ways. The children, having no manufactured toys, played with sticks and other objects they found in a junkyard.

In the Sinai Bedouin group the parents' attitude toward play was definitely hostile. Parents explained that children should be serious, quiet and respectful. They must not make noise, frolic or litter the encampment. On a number of different occasions I witnessed mothers yelling at children who were playing with makeshift toys such as an old car tire they had found somewhere or a "cart" consisting of a can attached to a stick. The mothers confiscated these toys and threw them away. One day I discovered the children hiding behind a hillock, playing fervently, away from the censuring eyes of the mothers.

In some traditional cultures, children's certain kinds of make-believe play are considered foul and corrupt, a manifestation of the bad influence of evil spirits. In an ethnographic study of children's play in the Marquesas Islands, Polynesia, Martini (1994) reports that playing children move away from adults whenever they are near, because adults view their playing as a nuisance, scold them and disrupt their play.

Kim Susan Storey (1976), who conducted a field study of children's play in Bali, reports that the Balinese forbid their children to crawl, expose their teeth or perform other kinds of animal-like behavior in their play. They believe that harmful animal spirits impress themselves upon the children and induce them to behave in these manners.

These examples should not lead one to the conclusion that children's play is discouraged in every traditional society. In some such societies adults enjoy their children's play and even actively participate in it. Rossie (1993b), for instance, describes in his report of Ghrib (Sahara Desert) children's play an episode in which a mother entertained her two and a half year old son by various playful activities. She dug little holes in the sand and covered them with sticks, tied a string to a stone and turned it around and continued amusing her sons by other improvised toys. Likewise, Roopnarine, Hossain, Gill and Brophy (1994) argue that in East India adults take pleasure in playing with their children, although this attitude is not driven by any ideological tenets.

Does the attitude of adults toward children's play affect its quantity and quality? It probably does. The paucity of reliable data and research does not allow one to answer this question in any definitive way. What is absolutely clear, however, is that children in all parts of the world do not refrain from playing just because adults tell them not to.

ARE WORK AND FORMAL SCHOOLING DONE AT THE EXPENSE OF PLAY?

In some social groups children are supposed to do what would be considered in our terms "adult work" at a very early age. Investigators have claimed that children who work do not play, or play very little. This claim has been derived, at least by some of these investigators, from their functionalistic credo. Play, in the functionalistic view, is essentially learning by imitation. In their make-believe games children mimic the adults' work patterns, as a stage in their apprenticeship toward work. Therefore, when they start doing real work, play becomes redundant. This form of reasoning does not appeal, however, to constructivistic play ethnographers. The latter believe that play is motivated by an inner drive to interpret and create. It is therefore perfectly compatible with work.

There are sociocultural communities in which children begin formal schooling at a very early age and spend most of their free time studying. This is the case, for instance, in some Orthodox Jewish communities. Ethnographers of play have asserted also that play is a leisure activity. Children who spend their time working or studying are too busy and tired to play. Bloch and Adler (1994), for instance, report that Senegalese children who had more responsible work duties engaged in less play. By this logic one would not expect Orthodox Jewish Yeshiva children to be engaged in play.

Whether the ethnographers who see a negative correlation between work and schooling on the one hand and play on the other hand are right or wrong is, again, an empirical question. My own experience has not corroborated the claim that hard work and demanding formal schooling preclude play in young children. Girls as young as six in the Sinai Bedouin community with which I conducted the above-mentioned fieldwork spent most of the day helping their mothers do chores such as gathering dry shrubs for making fire, baking bread, cooking, milking the goats, drawing water from the nearby well and serving meals to the whole family. Still, I saw them playing as eagerly as the younger, nonworking boys and girls. I have also conducted many sessions of family play therapy and group play therapy with boys of Ultra Orthodox Jewish families who studied in a Yeshiva from early in the morning till late in the afternoon, and I can bear witness to the fact that these children have never been too tired or preoccupied to play vivid make-believe games.

ARE THERE CULTURES IN WHICH CHILDREN DO NOT PLAY MAKE-BELIEVE GAMES AT ALL?

Some play researchers have alleged that there are such cultures. Feitelson (1959), for instance, observed no instances of make-believe play in Israeli children of the Kurdish Jewish community. Likewise, Ashton (1952) claims that South African Basuto children's play is totally unimaginative. He states that most children's games in this community are "aimless . . . and desultory and consist of roaming about, playing hide and seek, digging on ash heaps and making slides" (cited in Schwartzman and Barbera, 1976).

The possibility that make-believe play is not a culturally universal phenomenon may not be rejected off hand. It can be verified only by empirical observations. One should be wary, however, of methodological pitfalls which can lead one to rash unjustified conclusions. In some cultures children will play make-believe games only in particular places, settings, occasions and times. They will not expose themselves playing such games in the presence of certain categories of people, notably strangers. If I had not found the Sinai Bedouin children's secret play refuge behind that hillock, I could also be liable to conclude that they play no make-believe games at all.

In the above-mentioned Balinese study, Storey relates that during the first two weeks of her stay in the village she witnessed no make-believe play and hardly any play at all. Rather than playing at adult chores, the children actually swept, raked, shoveled, planted and carried rice and water on their heads. Their leisure activities consisted of sitting, staring aimlessly into space, eating and talking quietly. Later it became apparent to Storey that during those two weeks of little play activity, there had been an hiatus in the villages festivals and performances of which Bali is famous world over. With the resumption of these celebrations, children began playing lavish make-believe games.

IS THE MAKE-BELIEVE PLAY OF TRADITIONAL CHILDREN PURELY MIMETIC?

As stated above, many ethnographers of play have maintained that the make-believe play of children of societies that are closer to the traditional pole just mimics adult patterns of behavior. Although modern children also copy adults in their play, they very often incorporate the imitated episodes in unrealistic scenarios which constitute pure figments of their own imagination. Many examples of such scenarios have been described in previous chapters of this book. Such products of imagination are allegedly lacking from the make-believe play of traditional children.

Indeed, many ethnographic reports from various parts of the world describe games which constitute more or less accurate sociodramatic replications of adult work patterns, rituals and ceremonies. Some ethnographers have preferred the term *imitation games* rather than *make-believe games* for such activities.

The make-believe games of Balinese children reported by Storey were classed by her as imitation games, reproductions of adults' ritualized activities, festivals and ceremonies—for example, duplications of cockfights and cremation ceremonies. For instance, a small group of children, feigning a cockfight, flapped their arms like wings and hit each other, running back and forth. Another group of children, staging a cremation ceremony, placed a baby on a bicycle representing the cremation tower, and twirled the bicycle around and around to confuse the adult spirits.

Lancy (1976) observed the play behavior of four- to seven-year-old Kpele children of Liberia. Most of the episodes he describes constitute reproductions of adult work and hunting activities. In one scene he recorded four children playing "blacksmith." One boy was the smith and another a customer. Various sticks signified hammers, a rock represented an anvil and a piece of bamboo stood for the tongs. The smith went through the motions of producing a "machete," signified by a piece of wood. He gave it to "the client" who took it into the jungle to "cut brush."

Rossie (1993b, see above) describes what he calls "games of imitation" performed by Ghrib children. Girls, for instance, feign a wedding ceremony in which they sing and dance just as is done during real marriage festivities. Boys play at being cattle dealers. Children serve as goats, sheep or dromedaries and money is symbolized by pieces of paper, cardboard, white iron and aluminum.

Sever (1980) states that children of the urban Bedouin group (see above) used to reproduce episodes from village festivities in great detail and accuracy. This accords with my own experience. One of the favorite make-believe games of Arab girls in family play therapy and play group therapy has been staging a wedding ceremony.

In his ethnography of Huli (Papua, New Guinea) children's play, Goldman (1998, see above) describes pretend games in which children recreated adults' rituals such as singing dirges for the dead and work activities such as making traps for birds and possums.

Is the make-believe play of traditional children purely imitative then? Unfortunately, the methodological limitations discussed above preclude reaching any definitive answer. The characteristically sketchy, incomplete descriptions of the play episodes observed render it impossible to make out what really happened there. It is quite possible that some children have filled the seemingly mimetic skeleton of the play with original, innovative elements which escaped the notice of the observers or were excluded from the observation protocols. Many of the highly imaginative play scenes described in previous chapters would give the false impression of being purely imitative if they were recounted in a cursory, incomplete manner. Look for instance at the following paraphrase of "The Very Funny Truck" (Observation 10, Chapter 6).

Two six-year-old boys, Ronen and Barak, are playing in Ronen's nursery room. Ronen constructs a large human-like figure with Lego pieces. Barak moves a toy truck across the room. Ronen makes the Lego construction walk.

Ronen: It walked and walked and walked.

Ronen starts to dismantle the Lego construction.

Barak: Let's pretend this was a garbage truck. They threw it into the garbage truck because it broke apart.

Barak makes the truck with the Lego construction bump against a Lego tower the two of them built previously. Barak makes the tower collapse.

Ronen begins to make a different construction out of the Lego pieces of the toppled-down tower. Barak helps him.

With some of the highly inventive elements omitted, this play episode has become a rather dull imitation of everyday activities such as collecting garbage, walking and building.

Not all instances of traditional children's make-believe play reported in the literature are purely mimetic, however. Gougoulis (1999) studied the make-believe play of children of Phocaea, a rural community in Greece. Her observations support her main thesis, that play in this traditional, partly modernized community is a creative activity that reconstructs rather than mimics reality. The children, she argues, comment in their play on their social reality by inverting the hierarchical position they occupy in real life. They also comically exaggerate situations reflecting relationships between authority figures and their subordinates, such as teachers and pupils, parents and their children, policemen and criminals. This is illustrated, for instance, in the following play dialogue between "a teacher" and "a student." The latter was signified by a Playmobil figure. Nine-year-old Stylianos verbalized both roles:

Teacher: Hey you dumb-bird!

Student: Ds ... Ds. ... (nonsensical syllables)

Teacher: Stop it! What was your father's name in the old days?

Student: Saravakos (famous Greek football player)

Teacher: That was his family name. What about his first name?

Student: Dimitris (first name of the above)

Teacher: So, Dimitris Saravakos, You will die!

An interesting question for further research arising in this context is: Are role reversals and comic exaggeration of role relationships in children's make-believe play more prevalent in cultures characterized by a rigid role structure than in cultures in which role relations are flexible?

IS THE MAKE-BELIEVE PLAY OF TRADITIONAL CHILDREN COLLECTIVISTIC?

The handful of published specimens of both mimetic and inventive sociodramatic play of children whose culture is closer to the traditional extreme strikes the reader as having a distinctive, peculiar nature, different in some notable ways from the sociodramatic play of children whose culture is closer to the modern extreme. This impression is produced by a number of different facets of the former and the latter. One facet appears to be the collectivistic nature of traditional sociodramatic play versus the individualistic nature of modern sociodramatic play, at least as reported in these few studies.

In the traditional samples children agree on a conventional theme related to the material, social or spiritual life of their community and stage together a sociodramatic scene elaborating this theme. The sociodramatic play in the modern samples, contrarily, is a product of the conjoint individual improvisational activities of the participants. Each child, drawing on her partly culture-bound and partly private memory store and activating her emotionally colored imagination, contributes her own share of themes and plots. The participants negotiate the right to include their own respective ideas in the mutual production. The final result is a compromise between the individual wills of the participants.

If this difference is real, then the following question arises: Does the make-believe play of traditional children have the same regulative functions with respect to the child's interpersonal proximity and control goals and intrapersonal emotives, discussed in Chapters 3, 4 and 5, as the play of modern children?

Another, related relevant question would be: Are traditional children engaged in solitary make-believe play at all? Apparently they are, as evidenced by the following reports. In three studies done in Senegal by Bloch and O'Rourke (1982), randomized observations of young children in their home setting showed that children were engaged in nonsocial play activities at least a quarter of the day. Bloch and O'Rourke do not specify, however, which of these solitary activities fell under the rubric of make-believe play. Rossie (forthcoming) describes a lengthy episode in which a three-year-old Ghrib boy performs various make-believe activities with a pretend donkey.

IS THE MAKE-BELIEVE PLAY OF TRADITIONAL CHILDREN MOLDED INTO TRADITIONAL FORMATS?

Another facet differentiating between the available make-believe play samples of modern versus traditional children, is, so it seems, the stylistic frames by which they are structured. Children of both modern and traditional societies cast the verbal and nonverbal signifiers of their make-believe play into molds borrowed from customary genres of expression and communication prevailing in their culture. Their repertoire of characters and story lines furthermore includes dominant cultural stereotypes and clichés.

Present-day modern children use figures of speech and behavior patterns borrowed from fairy tales, the movies, television and computer games. Boys introduce into their play cultural stereotypes such as "the hero and the villain" (found in sources such as Power Rangers, Ninja Turtles and Pokemon). Girls adopt ideals of female beauty, erotic appeal and courage such as Barbie and Wonder Woman. Story lines are based on cliches such as "danger-rescue," "child or pet lost and found" and "deprivation-satisfaction" (see Schwartz, 1991).

Children of traditional cultures who have not yet been exposed to the overwhelming influence of the mass media, on the other hand, tend to mold their play into traditional forms of expression and communication found in their culture. They use figures of speech, poetic structures and patterns of verbal and nonverbal behavior borrowed from folk theater, oral traditions of story-telling, singing and prayer, rituals and ceremonies. They appropriate traditional stereotypes such as "the trickster," "the buffoon" or "evil spirits." Like modern children, their play contents are taken not just from primary sources but also from secondary sources such as folk legends and myths.

Gougoulis, in the above-mentioned study of Phocaean children's play, attributes various comic elements found in their sociodramatic play to the influence of traditional Greek shadow theater: The fool-hero stereotype ("Kharagiozis"), caning, beating and insulting the fool, role-reversal, and so forth.

Rossie, in his above-mentioned study of Ghrib children, describes the following sociodramatic game of cattle-stealing: The children who play the roles of the thieves mock the shepherds by sounding the following stylized speech: "The shepherd, oh what a life he is enduring! As a bed, he only has a date tree offshoot bearing a cluster of dates and a knapsack is his pillow!" And then some children, serving as goats, defend their shepherd's honor by reciting the following verses: "The shepherd, he is an apple among the little apple-blossoms! Staying at home never brings along something valuable!"

Goldman, in his above-mentioned Huli study, demonstrates how the Papuan children fashion their sociodramatic play after the conventional format of their community's oral storytelling tradition, termed *bi te*. Stories and myths in the *bi te* frame are performed in a distinctive and melodic recitation style. Poetic conventions include the use of parallel repetition, synonym substitutions and various rhyme devices such as alliteration and assonance. Narrative conventions include repetitions and meta-narrative marks such as "he said." *Bi te* storytelling is not monologic. It has a dialogic structure of discourse exchange. All these features are present in the children's sociodramatic play. Consider for instance the following excerpt, in which the traditional figures of speech are italicized:

Hiyabe (boy, 8), May (boy, 8) and Megelau (boy, 11) create pretend possum traps at the hole of an old tree in the forest:

Hiyabe: Good in mine, the birds used to flock in and out and now the hole is going there.

Mai: In mine then, in mine in mine, the gabiago birds used to flock in through the hole there.

Hiyabe: Oh in mine in mine.

Megelau: Oh in mine in mine.

Mai: With the hole that is there I am building something. *In mine one bird, in mine one bird* went inside.

Hiyabi: We are putting traps.

Megelau: We are putting traps.

The repeated phrase *in mine* and the other repetitions are characteristic of *bi te* formalized style.

Huli children, according to Goldman, often introduce into their play traditional stereotypes such as the haunting spirit, the trickster and the ogre (monstrous giant).

Here is an example:

Ayubi (girl, 8) and Mogai (girl, 9) hide inside a house while Joy (girl, 7) pretends to be "a spirit" about to haunt their home:

Ayubi: I am the dog.

Mogai: We are saying you can be the dog later. Dogs used to be able to see spirits. Come here Ayubi.

Joy: (hooting noises characteristic of spirits)

Mogai: The spirit will be here, so come over here and let's see. Or maybe it's a possum like you can't imagine?

DeMarrais, Nelson and Baker (1994) report about a fascinating traditional, semiritualized genre of play called "storyknifing," practiced by Yup'ik Eskimo girls. The girls tell stories and illustrate them visually by inscribing conventional stick figures in the ground with a knife. Some of these stories are traditional folktales and some their own private, make-believe play, like inventions.

IS THE MAKE-BELIEVE PLAY OF CHILDREN OF LOW-INCOME FAMILIES AND TRADITIONAL SOCIETIES DULLER?

In many ethnographic accounts of the make-believe play of children of low-income families and of sociocultural groups that are closer to the traditional pole, play is portrayed as dull, simple and unsophisticated in comparison with the play of children of modern high-income families.

Granted all the above-mentioned warnings against methodological shortcomings and ethnocentric prejudices, this impression deserves serious consideration. One should beware, however, of sweeping generalizations. Even if there is some grain of truth in this claim in some cases, it is by no means universally true. Admittedly, children who have greater opportunities to enrich their knowledge base and expressive repertoire—through conversations with adults, reading books, travelling, playing computer games and taking continuing education courses in the afternoons—are in general more likely to play richer make-believe games than children who are not exposed to such multifarious stimuli. One should be cautioned against the prejudice that all cultures except that of urban Western middle class fail to inspire and activate their children's intellectual and creative faculties. Consider for instance the following counterexamples.

The high verbal adeptness, creativity and wit manifested in inner city and rural African American children's street games, repartees, stories and make-believe play have been well documented. A beautiful example brought by Sutton-Smith (1981) is the following retort, produced by a 3.9-year-old African American boy of the Piedmont Carolinas in response to his mother's "threat" to tie him up and put him on the railroad track if he continued misbehaving:

"Railroad track
Train all big' n black
On dat track, on dat track, on dat track
Ain't no way I can't get back
Back from dat track
Back from dat train
Big'n black, I'll be back."

In the same article, Sutton-Smith also cites the following statement by Roger Abrahams (1970): "One of the aspects of lower class negro life as an oral culture . . . is the way in which everyday life is suffused with play."

The Balinese negative attitude toward the influence of evil animal spirits on children's play is mentioned above. Balinese culture is, however, one of the richest in the world in traditional theater, music and visual arts. This richness finds ample expression in Balinese children's make-believe games. Here is an excerpt of a play scene, recorded by Storey: "A group of about six boys, seven and eight years in age, gather in the courtyard. Some of the decorations are made into a ring so as to form a headdress. Two boys put the headdress on, face each other, and bow as if two kings greeting one another. They have pretend fights imitating the monkey fights of the Ketjak dance."

CROSS-CULTURAL COMPARISONS OF THE LEVEL OF MAKE-BELIEVE PLAY

To conduct adequate cross-cultural comparisons of make-believe play, one should rely not just on global impressionistic assessments but on explicit, formally defined, operationalized parameters which can serve as yardsticks for systematic comparisons. This is a task for future research. Since the analytic concepts introduced in this book can serve as seminal ideas for such research, these concepts can be enlisted in the service of examining the available evidence. The developmental dimensions presented in Chapter 6 and summarized in Table 6.1 are likely to prove particularly useful for this purpose. These dimensions, appropriately elaborated and refined, can serve not just as scales for measuring the development of make-believe play in the individual child, but also as parameters for rating the level of make-believe play across cultures.

Let me illustrate this application with respect to some of the few ethnographic descriptions of make-believe play cited above. In Chapter 6, the highest developmental level of make-believe play is characterized by the following qualities:

Verbal and nonverbal signifiers are *complex* (e.g., a blanket, crawling out of the blanket, mewing and saying "We are being born now" signify together "the kitten's birth"), *abstract* (e.g., a black irrigation hose signifies "a highway"), *deep* (choice of signifiers is not random, it is dictated by abstract rules) and *objective* (signifiers are selected with view to their suitability, not just to satisfy the player's immediate internal needs). The same applies to the play's signified contents. These add together to long, complex, multidimensional, rule-governed dramatic sequences, having a clearly structured story line. The scenes and plots are often original and highly imaginative.

The play's signifiers and signifieds are harnessed to the purpose of solving emotional and interpersonal problems and difficulties. The latter functions of make-believe play are discussed in Chapters 3, 4 and 5.

The play means and contents exhibit a high degree of self-awareness and introspection. Players plan many ingredients of the play in advance and meta-communicate about them in the course of the play.

The play's signified contents are rich and sophisticated. They reflect not just the children's immediate life experience but also knowledge and ideas drawn from books and the mass media. The children use the play arena to discuss abstract philosophical and moral questions.

Sociodramatic play is highly socialized. The children coordinate their play activities. They negotiate the choice of play means and contents. In this process they exercise empathy, ability to read and take into account each other's ideas, feelings, wishes and needs. In situations of conflict they resort to rules and regulations included in their own self-made "mini-legal systems."

Does the make-believe play of traditional children have these qualities? Let me examine these qualities one by one with respect to the available evidence. Complex ad hoc combinations of signifying features are indeed found in some of the play episodes reported in the literature:

In Rossie's ethnographic research of Ghrib's children's play he describes the girls' use of rags, branches and stones as means for representing daily life in their desert surroundings. His report is accompanied with fascinating photographs. One of the photographs depicts an ad hoc combination of a miniature tent and a miniature weaving loom made out of rags and branches, as well as stones representing goats.

Other complex ad hoc combinations of signifiers are mentioned in the above-cited Kpelle children's "blacksmith" play, recorded by Lancy, as well as in Storey's description of the Balinese children's "cremation" play, also mentioned above. In the adults' cremation ceremony the body is placed in an animal-shaped coffin, and put into a huge colorful tower, which is twirled around to confuse the bad spirits, and then set on fire to burn. The Balinese children reproduced this ceremony as follows: a baby was placed on a bicycle representing the cremation tower, and the bicycle was turned around and around.

The use of the bicycle as a signifier for the rotated cremation tower is a good example of *abstraction* of signifying features. Although the bicycle bears no similarity to the cremation tower, the former was chosen thanks to its *revolvability*.

Another interesting example of abstraction of signifying features is included in Goldman's report of Huli children's play. Hoyali, a five-year-old girl, pretended to breast-feed her baby. The latter was signified by the rubber sole of a running shoe, apparently chosen because of its *elasticity*.

As to signified contents, some of the examples cited above do represent complete dramatic sequences, having a clearly structured story line—such as the Kpelle children's "blacksmith" play (Lancy, 1976), and the Phoacean children's teacher-pupil play (Gougoulis, 1999). The above-mentioned "breast-feeding the shoe-baby" play was part of a rather long and complex dyadic sociodramatic scene, with four-year-old Dagiwa (boy) as the co-player. The scene moved from breast-feeding the shoe-baby to taking him to the hospital because he was sick. The shoe-baby and the foot-baby were given an injection. The boy and the girls pretended to speak like the foreign, white hospital staff members. Then mommy cut pieces of pork and fed the baby.

This scene is characteristic—as far as I can judge by the limited evidence—of the make-believe play of traditional children whose culture has come under modern Western influence. In the eyes of indigenous children of traditional societies, foreigners and their contraptions—cars, airplanes, cameras, and the like—appear to be as exotic and fascinating as extraterrestrial creatures, Spiderman and Pokemons are for modern children. After the children of a traditional society have been exposed to various manifestations of modern life, their make-believe play abounds with contents representing these manifestations.

When I conducted my ethnographic study of Bedouin children in the Sinai desert, Sinai, an Egyptian territory, was occupied by Israel. The Israeli military administration introduced many manifestations of modern life to its seminomadic Bedouin inhabitants: schools, field hospitals, tourism, military vehicles and all the rest. None of these affected the particular encampment in which my fieldwork was conducted, which had been quite isolated, but all these became a part of its inhabitants' surrounding ecology. When I examined my observation protocols, I discovered that over 70% of the make-believe play contents produced by the children had been drawn from these representatives of modern life.

A similar finding is reported in Rossie's ethnography of Ghrib children's play. In the mid-1970s of the 20th century, Ghrib society was going through a quick change, from being nomadic to being sedentary. In the 1980s it had been exposed to television. In the 1990s its oasis settlement had become an important administrative and urbanized center. All these changes were reflected in the children's make-believe games. In the 1970s they began introducing themes of commerce into their play. In the 1980s, after being exposed to a TV series on the crusades, they began play-fighting with bows and arrows, wooden swords and bamboo lances. In the 1990s the boys began playing with pretend motorcars and guns.

It may be concluded from the above examples that traditional children, like modern children, draw their play contents not just from their immediate life experience but also from secondary sources such as stories, myths and, if available, TV drama.

Planning and meta-communication are found in the sociodramatic play of traditional children too. Goldman's observations of the play of Huli children include many examples of this aspect:

Ayubi (girl, 8): I am the dog.

Mogai (girl 9): We are saying you can be the dog later.

Dagiwa (boy 4) mimics a scene he witnessed two days prior when men carrying pigs for a funeral chanted a "pig song."

Nabili (girl 10): Did someone die and that's why you are singing that?

Dagiwa continues singing.

Nabili: What are you going on about? Are you becoming Iba Tiri (a trickster figure)? We only used to say that when someone is dead.

So far no significant qualitative differences between the make-believe play of modern and traditional children have been detected. But what about the parameters of originality and imaginativeness? Is the play of traditional children as fantastic and fanciful as the play of modern children often is? Let us look again at the extract of make-believe play included in the preface to this book:

Gilad and his friend Daliah were busy moving about, chatting vivaciously. Their faces were heavily painted with makeup. They were fancy-dressed with a whole assortment of colorful clothes which they took from my wife's wardrobe. They looked like witch doctors. I overheard parts of their chitchat. Gilad spoke with a funny tone of voice, expressing wonderment and fascination. "We are angels!" he called, "Fire angels! My hair is on fire! My wings are on fire! My belly is on fire! My tushie is on fire! Let's fly to that star over there!" And Daliah echoed him: "We are fire angels! Me too! It's our birthday! We are ten thousand years old! The fire does not burn us. It's a special kind of angels' fire!" Then Daliah began to yell in a panicky voice: "Fire angel! Let's fly away! The electricity monster is coming back!"

I know of no published sample of traditional children's pretend play that includes such flights of fancy. This limitation, if true to fact, may be partly due to the collectivistic nature of traditional children's make-believe play, discussed above. It may be also due to the children's level of literacy. Modern children are exposed to a massive attack of verbal and pictorial fantasy through children's books, the mass media and computer games. This repertoire is not available to most traditional children.

Likewise, I have not encountered any examples of traditional children's make-believe play in which abstract philosophical or moral questions are discussed. The habit of including this level of discourse in the sociodramatic play of modern children is probably a consequence of the individualistic and intellectualizing nature of modern culture. Children are exposed to a variety of different views and opinions on many issues and open discussion and debate are encouraged.

Do traditional children put their play signifiers and signifieds at the service of solving their emotional and interpersonal problems and conflicts? There is hardly any evidence of these functions of make-believe play in the published documentation. I have detected some sequences which may be interpreted as serving self-therapeutic, emotionally regulative functions only in Goldman's observations of Huli children's play. Dagiwa (boy, 4) is reported to have produced the following types of signified contents: chanting a funeral "pig song" (see above); pushing a stick into someone's mouth, causing "the shit to spread everywhere"; a pig is shouting when slaughtered; the shoe-baby is sick, he is taken to the hospital and the nurse gives it an injection.

These contents seem to reflect Dagiwa's age-appropriate fear of being physically hurt (see Chapter 5), which was projected onto the pretend pig and the sick baby. This impression should be backed up by much more data to be of any value.

I have found in the published corpus of observations of traditional children's play no evidence whatsoever to the use of play contents as tools for achieving interpersonal goals. Moreover, in none of the observations recorded did the participants seem to strongly disagree about the play's signifiers or signified contents. The play proceeded smoothly in a spirit of mutual benevolent consent. This may perhaps be attributed to the apparent collectivistic nature of traditional make-believe play, discussed above.

This spirit of cooperation, however, does not strike me as reflective of empathy, reading the other child's individual mind and taking into account his or her feelings, wishes and needs. It looks to me more like a person-to-group relationship than a person-to-person relationship. The sociodramatic play is conceived by the children—so it seems—more as teamwork, a collaborative group endeavor than as an opportunity for individual self-expression.

DO TRADITIONAL CHILDREN HAVE PLAY-RELATED "MINI-LEGAL SYSTEMS"?

As has been demonstrated in Chapter 4, modern children develop systems of social control in order to regulate their conflicts and disagreements concerning formation of playgroups, leadership of the play activities, allocation of play territories and rights of use of play objects.

Does the same apply to traditional children? It seems reasonable to assume that such bodies of rules and regulations are not as necessary for traditional children as they are for modern children. This is so because the former's sociodramatic play is, as suggested above, collectivistic. What renders, perhaps, such social control systems superfluous in these groups is, furthermore, the absence of scarcity in play territories and play means. When children of the same extended family play in an open field, and their toys are stones, leaves and branches, they have no causes for fighting over participation, territories or rights of use.

Sever's comparative ethnographic study of play-related social control systems in groups of children that occupy different places on the modernity versus traditionality scale, as well as my own extension of this study with Sinai Bedouin children, provide an opportunity to scrutinize these speculations more closely.

Sever found considerable between-group differences in the nature of the play-related social control systems. These differences correlated with the *modernity versus traditionality* dimension. The groups closest to the modernity pole had developed mini-legal systems of the kind discussed and illustrated in Chapter 4. The groups closer to the traditionality pole tended to rely on different methods of social control, to be specified below.

The system of play-related social control employed by the modern groups was founded on the following principles:

- The system is geared toward solving interpersonal and intergroup conflicts and disagreements concerning participation in playgroups, rights of use of play territories and play objects and leadership.
- The main mechanism for solving these difficulties is verbal negotiations striving toward a compromise between the parties or acknowledgment of the other party's rights.
- The negotiations bank upon a shared pool of "laws," rules and regulations which have been developed by the children themselves.

The system of play-related social control espoused by the traditional groups was founded on different principles:

- The system is aimed at solving interpersonal (rarely intergroup) conflicts and disagreements about the right of use of play territories and play objects (rarely about participation in playgroup or leadership).
- The main mechanism for solving these difficulties is trying to make one of the parties yield and submit to the will of the other parties. This is achieved mainly by nonverbal means: a threatening posture or tone of voice, grabbing an object and snatching it away, protecting an object or a territory with one's body and so forth.
- These interactions are not based on explicit "laws," except the law of power.

The groups occupying the middle range between the traditional and the modern poles (e.g., the urban Arab group) operate with a mixture of these two systems.

Let me elaborate on some of the above statements. The assertion that a traditional social control system is aimed at solving interpersonal conflicts about the right of use of play objects and play territories is confined to the experimental kindergarten setting in which the observations were taken. There, play territories were limited. Confined toys such as trucks, big dolls and large building blocks were scarce, in high demand and therefore subject to competition and conflict. In an open space such as the Sinai encampment, where no manufactured toys were available and play objects were stones, sticks, junk pieces and dry balls of goats' dung, there were much less occasions on which such conflicts could have developed and therefore less of a need for social control rules.

It has been asserted above that the traditional social control system was rarely called for to solve intergroup conflicts, or disputes about participation in play-groups or leadership. This seems to be due to the following: In the Arab children, stable playgroups have hardly been observed at all. Play alliances among the children were usually random, transitory, momentary, short-lived. They did not all have the nature of fraternities whose membership is restricted. Those few groupings which were more fixed and lasting usually included members of the same extended family. Such associations were accepted as natural and legitimate by the rest of the children and were rarely challenged or intruded on. The same applied to leadership. The social hierarchy among the children was not determined by free contest and bidding for power. It was based on a well-established pecking order, mirroring the community's social structure. Boys had a higher status than girls. Older children had power and authority over younger children. No one lower in the pecking order would dare challenge the prerogatives of the higher. A system of social control regulating group participation and leadership was therefore superfluous for the traditional children.

The claim that play-related social control in traditional children was based on "the law of power," realized by nonverbal forceful means, is liable to give the wrong impression that play interactions in the traditional group were more violent and wild than in the modern groups. This is not so. Since the pecking order among the children was clear and universally accepted by them, truly violent brawls among them were relatively rare. Two children could struggle about a play object for awhile, each of them pulling it, trying to extricate it from the hands of the other one, but very soon one of them would yield and the two would continue to play peacefully together. A boy could direct a threatening nonverbal postural display at another boy, and the latter would get the message and leave. The general atmosphere was therefore not wild at all.

Here is a typical scene, extracted from Sever's observations protocols. My own comments are in square brackets.

Mat'eb and Wa'al are cousins, Mat'eb is almost six years old, Wa'al is five. They both live in Ibtin, the urbanized Bedouin village in the Galilee. Six-year-old Riad is their neighbor. His family's house is situated in the same courtyard as theirs. The three are playing with a toy truck and wooden building blocks [a playgroup based on family ties, residence proximity and age hierarchy].

Mat'eb: Come on. I'll put the boxes in your truck!
Wa'al: Put 'em! Fill it!

Ri'ad: Wa'al ! See what I got! (a green plastic truck)

Wa'al (to Ri'ad): Attention! Don't turn the boxes upside down! Let go through! Move! Give me this one (a long block) and take this one (a shorter one).

Riad complies and exchanges the blocks, without objecting [apparently, Riad, being just a neighbor, is lower on the pecking order than Wa'al, although the latter is younger].

Riad: I want to take my truck to the repairer. Your truck is the repairer's.

A girl passes through by their pile of blocks. She inadvertently bumps against a block (one of the "boxes"), turning it upside down. Wa'al pushes her away [non-verbal]. She looks scared. She extends her hand toward the "box" to put it back in place.

Wa'al: Don't touch it!

The girl goes away [being a girl, lower on the pecking order].

Meanwhile another boy, Suhil, takes advantage of the situation. Sneakingly, swiftly, he gets hold of two "boxes" and then he runs away with them, [a non-verbal way of taking possession]. Wa'al chases Suhil.

Wa'al: Give 'em back!

Suhil stops running. He turns toward Wa'al and hands over the two boxes to him. Wa'al takes them, directing a threatening gesture at him. Then he goes back to his truck [no verbal negotiations; nonverbal means of gaining control].

This scene illustrates some of characteristics of the traditional system quite well: The pecking order among the children (Mat'eb over Wa'al, his younger cousin, Wa'al over Ri'ad, his neighbor, over Mufid and, being a boy, over the girl) and the effective partly verbal and nonverbal power displays: curt imperatives, threatening postures, pushing and chasing.

This analysis can throw perhaps a different light on the above claim that the play-related interactions of traditional children are peaceful, harmonious, cooperative and conflict-free. Although the various cultures represented in the above-mentioned ethnographic studies of play are probably very different in many respects from the Arab and Bedouin groups of the Oranim study, there are perhaps some basic common traits. One of these shared characteristics is, apparently, that serious conflicts are avoided because some children accept without challenge the authority of other children, who are higher in status in their social structure. Consider for instance the following distinct play interactions between a nine-year-old girl, Mogai, an eight-year-old girl, Ayubi, and a seven-year-old girl, Joy in Goldman's study of Huli children:

Excerpt 1

Ayubi: I am the dog.

Mogai: We are saying you can be the dog later. Dogs used to see spirits. Come here, Ayubi.

Joy makes hooting noises characteristic of spirits.

Excerpt 2

Mogai (to Ayubi): You run away now.

Ayubi: I'm the dog, aren't I?

Mogai: You (Ayubi) go shouting like this (dog sounds), after Joy.

Excerpt 3

Mogai: Shall we build a fence? Shall we dig a pretend garden first? Or shall we make a fence before digging?

Ayubi: Yes, fence first.

Excerpt 4

Mogai: Wait, wait. Who's going to be *dama (the spirits)*?

Ayubi: There isn't anyone to be *dama*.

Mogai: Joy, you become *dama*.

In all four excerpts Mogai, the oldest of the three, is the leader. The other two girls, who are younger, accept her suggestions without attempting to suggest their own ideas or challenging hers.

A system of play-related social control which is similar to the traditional and semitraditional systems analyzed by Sever is described in Martini's study of peer interactions in the Marquesas Islands in Polynesia (1994). According to Martini children learn two sets of rules for interacting with others: Compliance with the authority of seniors on the one hand and reciprocity, sharing and status rivalry between age-mates and status equals on the other hand. The means by which status encounters between equals are realized are very similar to the means employed by the Arab and Bedouin groups in Sever's study.

An interesting observation, pertaining to the Oranim study as well as to all the other ethnographic studies of traditional children's play, is that in those sociodramatic scenes in which the traditional children attempted to reproduce adults' rituals and ceremonies, the cooperation among the children was perfect, conflict-free. The same applies to such re-creations in traditional children of the other cultures reported.

RELATIONS BETWEEN SOCIAL STRUCTURE, SOCIALIZATION AND THE NATURE OF SOCIODRAMATIC PLAY

Sever's study and my own extension of it give rise to intriguing questions concerning the interface between the structural properties of a social group, its dominant values and beliefs, its socialization values and practices and the nature of its children's make-believe play.

In the Oranim project the relevant aspects of the culture were elicited by home visits and interviews with the children's parents and grandparents, especially the mothers. The children's sociodramatic play and social behavior were examined by naturalistic observations. In each of the five communities studied (kibbutz, city middle class, city lower class, middle-class urban Arab, urbanized Bedouin and Sinai desert Bedouin) the following areas of culture and socialization were investigated:

1. *Family structure*, as examined by the following parameters:

- Patterns of residence (*patrilocal*—the young couple dwells with the husband's father; *neolocal*—the newly married couple makes a new independent home for themselves, *mixed*—independent but in the vicinity of the family of origin).

- Family extension (*nuclear family* a separate, independent unit versus nuclear family an integral part of the *extended family*).

- Lineality (*patrilineal*—generations traced through fathers; *matrilineal*—generations traced through mothers; *bilineal*—generations traced through both parents).

- Family hierarchy (*authoriatarian*—dominance by gender (males dominate females) and generation (older dominates younger) versus *egalitarian* (equality in rights and duties of genders and generations).

- Subsystems (particularly close relationships between subparts of the family, such as father with teen-age and older sons, mother with daughters, husband with wife).

- Status of children (*high*—the family is child centered; *low*—the family is adult centered, *very low*—children have no rights. Their function is to serve the adults).

- Father's involvement with children (*highly involved* versus *detached*).

2. *Standard of living*, as examined by the following parameters:

- Family income and property ownership (*high income and owning of valuable assets, medium, low*).

- Household technology (*modern* household facilities and electrical appliances versus *traditional* means such as drawing water from a well and cooking on a field oven).

- Parents' occupation (business, academic professional, administrative, blue collar, peasants, shepherds, etc.).

- Family's status in the community (*high*, due to its wealth, education level or political influence; *medium* or *low*).

3. *Family's values*, as examined by the following parameters:

• Individualism versus collectivism.
• Family honor.

4. *Child rearing values and practices*, as examined by the following parameters:

• Attitude to children's intellectual curiosity and creativity (positive, indifferent, negative).
• Parents' attitude toward children's play (positive, indifferent or negative).
• Parents' attitude to the child's independence (positive, indifferent, negative).
• Educational roles of parents (*central and active*—fostering and encouraging the child's intellectual development in all fields and areas. Parents provide their children with educational materials such as books and games. They answer their questions, provide verbal explanations and do things with them versus *peripheral and passive*—parents serve as role models but are not actively involved in their children's development).
• Parent-child communication (*mainly verbal* versus *mainly nonverbal*).
• Discipline and obedience (*high*—children are required to obey their parents, the parents' authority is absolute, the parents owe their children no explanations for their orders, demands and punishments, corporal punishment is sometimes used; *low*—children are expected to cooperate with their parents rather than obey them, requirements and disciplinary measures are accompanied by explanations, punishment is generally avoided, corporal punishment is forbidden.

Table 7.1 sorts the family cultural parameters specified above as well as the level of make-believe play parameters with respect to the cultural groups studied in the Oranim project.

Table 7.1 suggests various interesting correlations—at this stage still hypothetical—between some central cultural characteristics of the children's families on the one hand and the character and level of their play on the other hand. There appears to be a multiple correlation, for instance, between the egalitarian orientation and structure of the Jewish families; their individualism; the high status they accord to their children; the premium they put on their independence, intellectual curiosity and creativity; and their democratic approach to discipline on the one hand, and, on the other hand, the individualistic, creative nature of the children's play and the "legalistic," democratic quality of their play-relevant system of social control. Contrarily, the authoritarian nature of the Bedouin families, their collectivism, their children's low status, their negative attitude to children's independence, intellectual curiosity and creativity and the authoritarian approach to discipline appear to be related to the collectivistic character of their children's sociodramatic play as well as to the arbitrary, nonverbal quality of their play-related system of social control.

Table 7.1

Family Cultural and Level of Play Parameters Applied to the Play of the Jewish and Arab Children Studied in the Oranim Project

	Jewish Groups (Kibbutz, Town)	Urban Arab	Bedouin (Urban, Desert)
Cultural Parameters			
Family structure			
Patterns of residence	neolocal or mixed	patriclocal or mixed	patrilocal
Family extension	nuclear	extended or nuclear	extended
Lineality	bilineal	patrilineal	patrilineal
Family hierarchy	egalitarian	authoritarian or mixed	authoritarian
Subsystems	the married couple, the siblings, parents with all children	the married couple, same-age siblings, fathers with teen-age sons, mothers with daughters	fathers with teen-age and older sons, mothers with daughters, same-age siblings.
Status of children	high	medium	low
Father's involvement with children	high	medium	low
Standards of living			
Family income and property owning	high	mixed	low
Household technology	modern	modern	urban—modern or traditional, desert—traditional
Parents' occupation	business, professional, or administrative; usually both parents work out of home	business, professional or blue collar; usually mothers do not work out of home	desert: fathers— small trade, mothers— household duties, teen-age daughters— shepherds; urban: fathers blue collar

Family's status in the community	kibbutz—by contribution to community life; town—by wealth, education, or professional achievements	by wealth or administrative function	by wealth

Family Values

Individualism vs. collectivism	individualistic	mixed	collectivistic
Family honor	irrelevant	valued	highly valued

Child-rearing Values and Practices

Attitudes to intellectual curiosity and creativity	very positive	moderately positive to indifferent	negative
Attitude toward play	positive and encouraging	moderately positive	indifferent to negative
Attitude to children's independence	positive and encouraging	mildly negative	negative
Educational roles of parents	central, active	mildly active	peripheral, passive
Parent-child communication	mainly verbal	more non-verbal than verbal	mainly non-verbal
Discipline and obedience	low—based on explanation and cooperation	medium	high—based on scolding and arbitrary measures

Table 7.1 *Continued*

Level of Make-Believe Play

Sources of signified
content

	story books, movies and TV shows, computer games as well as everyday life	Adult work and family life, modern technology, traditional rituals and ceremonies

Creativity

	sociodramatic play is created by pooling the individual invention of the participants	sociodramatic play is created collectively by the play group

Stylistic formats

	the play is molded into multifarious stylistic formats	the play is molded into traditional stylistic formats

Nature of
play groups

	relatively stable, based on friendship	unstable, based on social relations in the community

Nature of leadership
of play groups

	based on leader's personal assets	based on power relations

Nature of
play-relevant
social control

	based on mini-legal systems, developed by the children and implemented mainly by verbal negotiations	based on social pecking order dictating dominance-submission and implemented mainly by non-verbal displays

HOW GENERALIZABLE ARE THE RESULTS OF THE ORANIM STUDY?

As asserted above, the Jewish groups observed in the Oranim study were close to the modern pole. The Bedouin groups were close to the traditional pole. The urban Arab group was midway between these two poles. Are the tentative results summarized in Table 7.1 applicable to other modern versus traditional societies? Not necessarily. It should be stressed that the cultural properties of the social groups investigated in the Oranim study are not shared by all modern and traditional societies. Not all modern societies are liberal, democratic and egalitarian and not all traditional societies are authoritarian. There are collectivistic modern societies and individualistic traditional societies. There are traditional societies in which intellectual curiosity and creativity in children is encouraged rather than discouraged. As emphasized over and over in this chapter, the comparative, cross-cultural study of children's make-believe play is still in its infancy.

The purpose of this chapter has not been to present any conclusive summary but to direct the readers' attention to some central questions and map out directions for further research.

SUMMARY OF CHAPTER 7

This chapter is devoted to a comparative cross-cultural view of make-believe play. Due to the paucity of methodologically sound empirical ethnographic research, all the generalizations formulated are of the nature of speculations and questions for further research. In view of the available evidence, I tend toward constructivistic approaches, according to which make-believe play is an original, creative cultural artifact, as opposed to functionalistic views according to which make-believe play is a way of practicing adult roles. The main dimension along which the make-believe play of children of different societies is compared is *modernity versus traditionality*. This basic dimension subsumes the subdimensions specified in Table 7.1. It is hypothesized that these subdimensions correlate with typical features of children's make-believe play, also summarized in Table 7.1.

A CLASSIFIED LIST OF REFERENCES

Theoretical Orientations in Anthropology

Functionalistic: Barnard and Spencer, 1988; Stocking, 1988.

Structuralistic: Barnard and Spencer, 1988; Levi-Strauss, 2000.

Symbolic-interpretive: Geertz, 2000; Turner, 1988.

Cognitive: D'Andrade, 1995; Strauss and Quinn, 1998.

Socialization Research: Gardiner, Mutter and Kosmitzki, 1997; Udwin and Shmukler, 1981; Yawkley and Johnson, 1988.

Modern versus Traditional Societies

Barnard and Spencer, 1998.

Theoretical Studies, Bibliographies and Literature Reviews on the Anthropology of Play

Adams, 1978; Ariel, 1999; Bloch and Pellegrini, 1989; Bower, Ligaz-Carden and Noori, 1982; Centner, 1962; Cheska, 1978, 1981; Child, 1983; Ebbeck, 1973; Feitelson, 1977; Gaskins and Goencu, 1992; Georges, 1969; Haight, Wang, Fung, Williams and Mintz, 1999; Hans, 1981; James, 1998; Lansley, 1968; Lancy and Tindall, 1976; Norbeck, 1974;

Packer, 1995; Pan, 1994; Prosser et al., 1986; Robinson-Finnan, 1982; Roopnarine, Johnson, Hooper and Frank, 1994; Rossie, 1993a, 1993b, 1999a, 2000, forthcoming; Salamone, 1989; Salter, 1977; Schwartzman, 1978, 1980; Schwartzman and Barbera, 1976; Seagoe, 1971; Sever, 1980, 1984; Stevens, 1977; UNESCO, 1978, 1979; Walton, 1990; West, 1988; Whiting and Edwards, 1998; Whiting and Whiting, 1975.

Ethnographic Studies of Make-Believe Play

Adams, 1978; Ariel and Sever, 1980; Bauman, 1975; Beran, 1973a, 1973b; Blanchard, 1981; Bloch and Adler, 1994; Bloch and O'Rourke, 1982; Boggs, 1978; Carlson, Taylor and Levin, 1998; Chang, 1998; de Marrais, Nelson and Baker, 1994; Diamond, 1974; Drewal, 1992; Eifermann, 1970b; Eisen, 1988; Farver, 1993; Farver and Howes, 1993; Farver, Kim and Lee, 1995; Farver and Wimbarti, 1995; Feitelson, 1959; Gougoulis, 1999; Gougoulis and Kouria, 2000; Griffing, 1980; Harkness and Super, 1986; Henry and Henry, 1974; Kloni, 2000; Lancy, 1976; Leacock, 1971; N.T. Martin, 1982; Martini, 1994; Miracle, 1977; Mistry, 1958; Prosser, et al., 1986; Rossie, 1993a; Roopnarine, Hossain, Gill and Brophy, 1994; Rossie, 1999b, 2000, forthcoming; Rubin, Maloni and Hornung, 1976; Salamone and Salamone, 1991; Salter, 1977; Sawada and Minami, 1997; Seagoe, 1971; Storey, 1976; Takahama, 1995; Takeuchi, 1994; Tamaru, 1991.

8 Applications of Make-Believe Play in Education

The value of play in general and make-believe play in particular for early childhood education has been recognized since the mid-19th century. This recognition has been derived from a deep understanding of the crucial role of play in the child's development.

The first kindergarten was established in Germany in 1841 by the great educator Friedrich Froebel. The term kindergarten ("children's garden") was coined by Froebel to convey the idea that like plants in the garden, the child needs fertile soil, care and devotion to grow and fully develop his capacities. In Froebel's kindergartens children were provided with toys and games, which were graded according to their level of development. The rationale behind this choice was that toys and games excite the child's imagination and intellectual curiosity. They encourage the child to explore her environment, experiment with it and express her thoughts and feelings.

Another milestone in the development of early childhood education through play was the institution of The Children's Home in Rome by Maria Montessori in 1907. Montessori also furnished the children with toys and educational games, with the explicit intention of stimulating and enhancing their development. These innovations were paralleled by similar developments in some non-Western countries, such as Japan (see Takeuchi, 1994).

Since these pioneering experiments, the importance of play for early childhood education has become indisputable. Toys and other playthings are now part and parcel of almost every kindergarten and nursery school in the modern world. The necessity to provide the children with ample free play time is considered self-evident. In most educational settings, however, the playing children are more or less left to their own devices. The adult educators supervise the children's behavior but are rarely actively involved in their play. This is partly due to an educational ideology, according to which play should be free from adult interference, and partly to lack of know-how.

Although, as can be gathered from everything written in this book so far, I fully concur with the view that free play contributes considerably to education, I maintain that various kinds of adult involvement are in many cases indispensable for the educational benefits of play to take effect. This is so because very often the children who need educational uplifting most are the least skilled in the use of make-believe play as an accelerator of cognitive, social and emotional development.

The main types of educational activities which can be carried out with respect to children's make-believe play are: diagnosis, training in make-believe play skills, in vivo instruction in such skills and selective active involvement in the children's play with specific educational goals in mind. Let us elaborate on each of these types, with examples.

EDUCATIONAL PLAY DIAGNOSIS

The educator observes and hand-records or videotapes samples of the solitary and sociodramatic play of the children. These samples are analyzed with a view to determining the level of mastery of the language and techniques of make-believe play of each of the participants. The same samples are used to assess the developmental profile of each child, his functioning in interpersonal relations and his emotional concerns.

How is the diagnostic analysis carried out? By all the methods and techniques presented in the previous chapters and in the Appendix. To recapitulate: A textual analysis is performed on samples of observed play behavior of each of the participants in the make-believe play activity. This analysis is carried out by the following steps:

First step: Classifying and tabulating the play signifiers by expressive media across time units, as in Appendix Table 1.

Substep: Analyzing the text, as tabulated in the first stage, into minimal signifier-signified units (see pp. 164–165 in Appendix).

Second step: Identifying and describing structures (see p. 165 in Appendix).

Third step: Deciphering the uses of structures, their creators' presuppositions and purposes (see pp. 166–167 in Appendix).

Fourth step: Identifying out-of-play structures which say something about in-play structures and describing their uses (see pp. 168–169 in Appendix).

Fifth step: Conducting Context-Dependent Componential Analyses of the minimal signifiers-signified units yielded by the second stage (see pp. 170–177 in Appendix).

Sixth step: Revealing and formulating syntactic rules applying to the text of each player as well as to the interactions between the players (see pp. 180–181 in Appendix).

Seventh step: Singling out the proximity and control goals of the play participants with respect to each other; revealing and formulating their strategies for achieving these goals; identifying and describing the types of concrete images of proximity and control and the "diplomatic" means employed in these strategies (see pp. 182–184 in Appendix, and Chapter 3).

Eighth step: Attempting to formulate the children's play-relevant "mini-legal system," the "laws" by which they solve conflicts around issues of leadership, participation in play groups and control of play territories and play means. Trying to determine, for each participant, how well-versed he or she is in these laws, and how skilled he or she is in conducting "legal" arguments and negotiations in the framework of these laws (see Chapter 4).

Ninth step: Trying to interpret the results of the Context-Dependent Componential Analyses conducted in the sixth step in terms of the child's central emotives and his or her cognitive-emotional homeostatic mechanisms (see Chapter 5).

Tenth step: Attempting to determine the level of make-believe play development and the general developmental profile of each child on the basis of the information gathered in the previous stages (see Chapter 6).

All the other educational activities involving make-believe play take into account the results of the diagnostic assessment. Since all these analytic stages have been discussed and illustrated above, they will not be demonstrated here again.

TRAINING IN MAKE-BELIEVE PLAY SKILLS

The play diagnosis of a particular child can give evidence to insufficiently developed make-believe play skills relative to his or her age group. This can be due to cognitive limitations or social inhibitions. One way to help the child improve such skills is systematic training, administered individually or in a group framework. The training course can include any aspect of make-believe play discussed in this book. Its curriculum will include the following topics, among others:

- Distinguishing between make-believe play and non-make-believe play and between in-play and out-of-play verbal and nonverbal expressions.
- Creative choice of signifiers.
- Tapping one's own inner resources and knowledge base, and drawing rich and varied contents to be expressed in make-believe play.
- Using make-believe play for solving technical, social and emotional problems.
- Mastering the group's mini-legal system and learning effective argumentation and negotiation techniques.

Such training courses are offered regularly by the author in The Integrative Psychotherapy Center in Ramat Gan, Israel, for small groups of children who have been referred by kindergarten and nursery school teachers. The children play freely with a variety of toys, props and playthings in a medium-sized room. The educator actively participates in the children's play. The instruction, which includes verbal explanations, leading questioning, modeling and practicing, is done informally, incidentally, often by conveying within-play verbal and non-verbal messages.

IN VIVO INSTRUCTION IN MAKE-BELIEVE PLAY SKILLS

This method serves the same purposes and is carried out by the same didactic techniques as the method of training in make-believe play skills presented above. The only difference is that it is implemented in vivo, in a naturalistic setting, such as free, spontaneous sociodramatic play in a kindergarten or any other educational setting. The educator actively participates in the children's play activity. As a member of a playgroup he or she is in a position to instruct the weaker children in make-believe play skills, using the techniques specified above.

By way of illustration, consider the following vignettes: A kindergaten in Tel Aviv. The teacher, Hava, was specially trained to do in vivo instruction in make-believe play skills. Dor, 5.4, was diagnosed as being weak in this respect. His behavior was often disruptive. This was at least partly due to his being unskilled in make-believe play. The following sequence took place in the Kindergarten's playground during free-play time.

Dor approached a girl, Lilach, who was sitting on the sand in an enormous sand box, making sand cakes. She was using a plastic mold, one among many others scattered on the sand. Dor snatched the mold out of her hand.

Lilach (yelling): Give it back! Give it back!

Dor ignored her. He filled the mold with sand, spilled the sand on the ground, threw the mold on the ground and then stood still, watching Lilach. Two other girls, Hadas and Shosi, joined Lilach. They began pouring water from a mold on the sand to make it wet and then filled other molds with damp sand.

Hadas: It's for a birthday.
Shoshi: It's for Israel's birthday. (This observation was taken a day before the Israeli Independence Day.)

Dor was standing by, watching the girls. He gathered some sand in the palm of his hand and attempted to pour it into Shoshi's container. Shoshi pushed his hand away, calling: "Don't!" He pulled his hand back.

The girls continued playing, ignoring Dor, who was squatting by them, watching them quietly. From time to time the girls directed glances at him, whispering among themselves and giggling. Then Hadas handed a mold full of sand over to him, saying: "Hey, soldier, you should wear this helmet." Dor, helped by Hadas, put the mold on top of his head. The sand spilled all over his face and hair. The girls laughed loudly. Dor stood up and went away.

Dor approached two boys, Erez and Idan, playing in another corner of the sandbox. He started kicking sand at them. Hava, the teacher, saw this. She called: "Dor, what are you doing? You shouldn't do that!" She lay her hand gently on Dor's shoulder and said softly, almost whispering: "Let's watch Erez and Idan and see what they're doing, quietly, because we don't want to disturb them, do we?" She sat down on the sand, inviting Dor to sit by her side. [By encouraging Dor to observe the other children's play, Hava took the first step in teaching Dor play-related social skills.]

Erez and Idan were watching ants crawling in the sand.

Hava (whispering to Dor): What are they doing?

Dor (whispering back): I don't know.

Hava: They're watching ants.

Erez (to Idan): Look, some are big and some are small.

Idan began erecting a sand wall around a group of big and small ants. [Hava, being aware of the children's mini-legal system, understood that Idan wanted to possess a group of ants as play objects, and to mark this he created a territorial boundary.]

Hava (whispering to Dor): You see? Idan has made a sand wall around some ants. He doesn't want anybody to play with them other than himself.

Dor (whispering): Why?

Hava: I don't know.

Erez (to Idan): Give me one big one.

Idan (to Erez): I can't, I need the big ones. [Hava identified *the role suitability law* (see Chapter 4)].

Erez: So give me a medium one.

Idan: No, I need them all.

Erez: That's not fair, *you* didn't find them, *we* found them. [The primacy law of possession.]

Idan: OK.

Idan took a handful of sand with some ants in it and poured it on the sand between Erez' knees.

Hava: Idan gave Erez some ants because both of them found the ants together, so both of them have a right to play with them. [Hava began to explicate, in vivo, the laws of the children's mini-legal system for Dor. Didactic technique—verbal explanation.]

Erez poked his forefinger into the sand, making a hole.

Erez: The big one lives in this cave.

Hava (to Dor): Erez plays as if the hole is the cave in which the ant lives. [Hava's purpose—help Dor distinguish between play and nonplay and between signfier and signified. Didactic technique—verbal explanation.]

Hava: Do you want to find some ants, Dor?

Dor: Yes.

Dor and Hava began looking for ants in the sand. [Didactic method—learning by imitation. Practicing.]

Dor (excited): Here's are two big ones and a little one!

Hava: Let's build a wall of sand around them, so that everybody knows that they are ours and only we are allowed to play with them, because *we* found them.

Dor and Hava began erecting a wall of sand around the ants. [Didactic techniques—verbal explanation, learning by imitation, practicing.]

Idan and Erez watched Hava and Dor curiously.

Hava: Do you want to play with us? [Hava wanted to demonstrate, for Dor, an effective technique of joining a play group: mimicking a group's play near the group until the two groups are coalesced.]

Erez (addressing Hava and Dor): Mine is very big.

Idan: I can see its heart.

Dor picked up a small rubber ball he found in the sand.

Hava: If she is so big maybe she can play with this ball. [Hava's purpose was to suggest, for Dor, a technique of joining a play group: proposing a relevant make-believe play signified content, evoking The Contribution Law (see Chapter 4). Didactic technique—verbal modeling.]

Erez: Her name is Kooky Kadoory (*kadoor* means "ball" in Hebrew).

ACTIVE INVOLVEMENT IN THE CHILDREN'S PLAY FOR SPECIFIC EDUCATIONAL GOALS

The settings and didactic techniques employed in this method are similar to those practiced in the above two methods. Unlike the latter, however, whose purpose is to help the children acquire make-believe play skills, the present method harnesses the children's play to other, play-external, educational goals. The latter can be of various kinds: Helping children evolve their cognitive and social skills and capacities, enhancing their ability to solve problems and difficulties, providing opportunities to develop their imagination and creativity, transmitting knowledge and aptitudes and so forth. The following vignettes exemplify this application.

Enhancing Self-control

Six-year-old Ilan was an impulsive, impatient, jittery boy. Guy, his kindergarten teacher, had been trained to put make-believe play to special educational uses. Guy participated in the children's sociodramatic play regularly, as an equal partner. From time to time, however, he would, from his position as an insider, inconspicuously steer the course of the play toward particular educational goals.

On one occasion a group of children, which included Ilan, played at "monster-hunt." They "hunted monsters" with "paralyzing guns," toy guns emitting "invisible paralyzing waves." When the trigger of such a toy gun was pulled, a click would be heard. Guy observed that Ilan was clicking his gun incessantly. He whispered to Ilan: "You should stop shooting aimlessly. You'll scare the monsters away. Let's hide behind this rock [a chair] and wait quietly for the monsters to come near. I'll tell you when to pull the trigger." Guy attempted to comply, but could not hold himself back and pulled the trigger. "What did you do?!" Guy whispered, all upset, "You shouldn't have done that! You should have waited for my order! Now you scared the monsters away! And what's worse, now they know where we're hiding. They'll soon come and attack us from the other direction!"

Later in the same play Guy suggested: "Let's pretend the monsters took us prisoners and tied us up with invisible ropes." When Ilan moved about Guy said: "No, you can't move, you're tied with an invisible rope." After Ilan lay still for a while, Guy said: "Let's pretend you released yourself by a magic spell and then set all of us free."

Overcoming Negativism

Meera, 5.7, was stubborn, negativistic, insubordinate. When she was asked by Adeena, the kindergarten teacher, to be more cooperative, she would simply run away and hide in one unlikely place or another.

Adeena, who had also been specially trained, would hold group discussions, using partly structured make-believe games. In one of these sessions all the children and Adeena herself held hand puppets and spoke through them. Meera chose a he-goat puppet. Adeena, as "a dog" bark-asked the he-goat why he would always hide behind trees and in caves.

Meera (answering in a goatish voice): Because all the animals here made a kind of washing machine that turns animals into something else and they want to push me into it.

Adeena: Does this washing machine turn animals into something worse or into something better?

Meera: Into something worse.

Adeena (addressing the children): You also think so?

Some animal voices called out "Yes!" and some "No!" One boy, a fox, said: "If you press the red button it turns the animal into a worse animal and if you press the green button it turns the animal into a better animal."

Adeena: Anybody wants to be turned into a better animal?

A number of voices called out: "Me! Me!"

Meera (addressing Adeena): You go into the machine!

Adeena: OK! Do you want to press the button, Meera?

Meera: Yes.

Adeena: But don't press the red button by mistake. Press the green one.

Adeena took a furry handpuppet representing a rabbit out of a box and put it in her pocket. She sat down on the floor, gesturing Meera to approach. She pointed at some point in the air, saying: "Here's the green button, press it." Meera "pressed" the imaginary button. Adeena began to shake, producing machine-like voices with her mouth. Then she replaced the dog's puppet on her hand by the rabbit puppet which she took out of her pocket, stopped shaking and making noises, and spoke in a rabbity voice: "I don't know who I am! Who am I?" A chorus of children answered: "You are a rabbit!"

Adeena: I don't know who I was before, but I feel I am better now.

Other children were now eager to enter the washing machine and change for the better. After some children came out better animals from the machine, Meera wanted to try the machine too. She went in a he-goat and came out a lamb.

As expected, Meera's negativism and her habit of disappearing and hiding were considerably reduced after this session.

Teaching Arithmetic by Make-believe Play

Shimon, a special education teacher, was trained in instructional and educational applications of make-believe play. He was asked by the second-grade arithmetic teacher to work individually with two boys, Eli and Yossi, who could not function as pupils in the class. They were intelligent, but had attention and concentration deficit and were undisciplined.

Shimon saw Eli and Yossi in his room, which was equipped with toys, play objects, games and materials for creative work. Immediately after the two boys entered the room, they began pushing two big toy trucks across the room, very fast, violently, making them collide with each other and crash against the walls and furniture. This went on for a while. After the two boys let out a lot of energy, Shimon began speaking into a toy microphone, announcing: "The big annual truck-race is gonna start in a few minutes! The two greatest racers in the world, Eli Jackson and Yossi Hendrix are going to contend for the world championship!"

He addressed Eli and Yossi, "Mr. Jackson! Mr. Hendrix! Are you ready?"

He directed the two boys with their trucks to a place on the floor bordering on one of the walls of the room and said: "It's a 100-meter race. The winner is gonna be the world's champion! How many meters are there from here to the opposite wall?" The two boys looked confused.

Shimon said: "Count the tiles. Each tile is twenty centimeters. Let's see who can count them faster!" Eli and Yossi began to count the tiles between the two walls. Eli finished first, having counted twenty tiles.

"So how many meters are there between the walls?" asked Shimon. This went on until the two boys learned to calculate the number of rounds they would have to do in order to complete a 100-meter race. And then they began racing with their trucks.

Later the same trucks were used as military vehicles transporting troops of Power Rangers, Spidermen and Supermen to various combat missions. Shimon, assuming the role of the commander-in-chief, commanded his subordinates, General Eli and General Yossi, to perform various calculations related to the number of soldiers allocated to each truck before and after each operation, the number of soldiers posted in each combat position, and so on.

The arithmetic lessons embedded in these games were taught incidentally, as an integral part of the make-believe play. The children were highly motivated to learn and exercise. They were so excited that they refused to leave the room when the bell rang for the break and insisted on continuing playing.

SUMMARY OF CHAPTER 8

This chapter is concerned with applications of make-believe play in early childhood education. The educational and instructional benefits of play have been recognized since the early days of preschool education in the 19th century. Few educational methods have, however, been based on educators' active involvement in the children's play activities. It is argued that such active involvement is required for two main purposes: (1) providing make-believe play training for children who are weak in this respect and (2) facilitating the achievement of particular educational and instructional goals. These are served by active participation in the children's spontaneous or planned play activities, in special settings or in vivo, in the children's natural play environment. To decide on the need for intervention and on its goals and methods, the intervention should be preceded by systematic play diagnosis, which can make use of any of the methods and techniques of analysis introduced in this book.

A CLASSIFIED LIST OF REFERENCES

The Role of Make-Believe Play in Education

Blatchford, 1998; Curtis, 1915; Dasgupta, 1999; Dias and Harris, 1988; Egan, 1988; Eisenberg, et al., 1985; Fein, 1985; File and Kontos, 1993; Froebel, 1887; Gould, 1972; Hanline, 1999; Hellendoorn, van der Kooij and Sutton-Smith, 1994; Howes and Smith, 1996; J.E. Johnson, 1995; King, 1982, 1987; J. Lee, 1922; Makrynioti, 2000; Montessori, 1955; Van der Poel, Bruyn and Rost, 1991; Saracho, Spodeck, et al., 1998; Scales and Almy, 1991; Shmukler, 1984; Smith and Connoly, 1980; Smith and Syddall, 1978; Solomon, 2000; Sutton-Smith, 1979; Sutton-Smith and Sutton-Smith, 1974; Takahashi, 1985; Takeuchi, 1994.

Techniques of Training in Make-Believe Play Skills

Auwaerter, 1986; Dansky, 1980a; Feitelson, 1972; Freyberg, 1973; Hanline, 1999; Packer, 1995; Saltz, Dixon and Johnson, 1977; Singer and Singer, 1985; Smilansky, 1968.

9   Play Therapy

Play in general and make-believe play in particular have been the main treatment vehicles of child psychotherapy since the inception of this specialty in the early years of the Twentieth century. Pioneers such as Anna Freud, Melanie Klein and, later, Virginia Axline have made us aware of the seemingly magical power possessed by play, to ease emotional stress and disentangle disturbances. Since these formative years play therapy has become a fully fledged profession. It has branched into a number of distinct schools, each with their own tenets, techniques and adherents. Here is a brief portrayal of some of the main schools.

MAIN PLAY THERAPY METHODS

Psychoanalytic Play Therapy

This is the oldest play therapy school, an offshoot of Freud's psychoanalysis and its followers' further theoretical elaborations, (e.g., object relations theory, ego psychology and self psychology).

In the Freudian view, child analysis is indicated when the child suffers from *infantile neurosis*. Children who are victims of this condition are not free to direct their energies to the main tasks required for their normal development: study, social relations and creative activities. This is due to crippling, anxiety provoking, unsolved conflicts between the child's basic drives (e.g., the desire to totally possess his mother and get rid of all competitors) on the one hand, and the constraints imposed by society (e.g., the requirement to share his mother with other family members), on the other hand. The child's inability to find a way out of such a conflict can lead him to damaging "solutions": fixation on or regression to earlier stages of development and the onset of various psycholog-ical symptoms.

Later theoreticians of the psychoanalytic school have expanded and elaborated this explanatory framework in various directions. One direction, that of object relations theory, attributes the child's emotional disturbances and their outward manifestations to the child's inadequate internalized self and object (other peo-ple's) representations. According to this theory, the child builds her own self-image and self-concept and internal pictures of other people by gradually internalizing and organizing the numerous impressions she is exposed to in the course of her daily life. Due to various objective and subjective causes, these self and object representations are apt to become distorted, incoherent, infested with conflicts and colored with upsetting emotions. A girl, for instance, is ex-tremely ambivalent about her father, unable to decide whether he is an angel or a devil. She regards herself as ugly and stupid, although she is really good looking and intelligent. Such disturbances in the development of self and object can again lead the child to harmful "solutions" such as fixations and regressions and various psychological symptoms.

Other recent theories have explained emotional and behavioral disturbances in children by making reference to any incongruities and imbalances among the child's internal mental faculties, brought into being in the course of the child's development. Violence, school failure, depression and other psychological symptoms in children are no longer explained just as externalizations of internal conflicts between the child's drives ("id"), perception of reality ("ego") and moral principles ("superego") or of inadequate self and object representations. Such symptoms can be viewed, for instance, as a display of the child's unsatis-fied dependency needs due to her being pushed to early independence by her parents, or as external expressions of a rift between her highly developed ability to analyze her emotions and her still low capacity to contain them.

Current child analysts lay a greater emphasis than earlier ones on environ-mental factors which influence the course of the child's development, such as the presence or absence of adult identification figures, attending appropriately or inappropriately to the child's needs or abuse and exploitation of children. This shift of emphasis has brought about a conceptual change with respect to the therapist's role in child analysis: The therapist is no longer required to be just a passive mirror of the child's psyche, an object onto which transference is projected, and an interpreter of the child's expressions. She is also expected to provide the child with a corrective emotional experience, to give support and encouragement.

The value of play for child analysis has been fully understood and appreciated since the earliest days of psychoanalysis. Sigmund Freud himself gave publicity to his important insights about play and its diagnostic and therapeutic applica-tions in a number of his works. He considered make-believe play a drive-derivative creative activity, in which the child authors an alternative reality, mirroring his unconscious thoughts and feelings. By constructing such a reality and acting upon it, the child gives vent to his internal pressures, fulfils his wishes and desires and gains pleasurable relief.

Freud also attempted to contend with the question why children invoke unpleasant experiences in their play. This seems to contradict *the pleasure principle*, which in his view was the main motivational power in the human psyche. In his article "Beyond the Pleasure Principle" (1959) he attributed this phenomenon to what he called *repetition compulsion*, the tendency to return over and over again to the same traumatic memories, found also in the thoughts and dreams of soldiers who had gone through the First World War. He offered a number of alternative explanations for this phenomenon: the breakdown of defenses, the soothing effect of returning to unpleasant experiences in a safe environment and the habituating influence of repetition. Similar explanations have been offered by many other investigators of play.

Later thinkers and investigators have emphasized the function of play as a workshop for exploring reality issues rather than unconscious wishes and fantasies. They have looked at play as a miniature theater, simulating reality, in which the child can examine at leisure and master developmental demands and cope with stressful events.

All these properties of play have been taken into consideration in the development of psychoanalytic play therapy. A number of theorists have asserted that play has the same role in child analysis as free association and recounting dreams in adult analysis. Children do not yet possess the skills required for exercising the latter major psychoanalytic techniques. Play, however, is a very good substitute, because it shares many structural, thematic and functional properties with free associations and dreams.

An adult analyst is not just a passive listener. He or she interprets the client's free associations and dreams, pointing out core anxieties, underlying conflicts, defenses and manifestations of transference. These interpretations are supposed to have a curative effect.

A child analyst does the same with respect to the child's play. There is a difference, however. A psychoanalytic play therapist, whether he joins the child's play or just accompanies it, interprets within the framework of the child's play. Interpreting directly from fantasy to reality is not recommended. To illustrate, consider the following: A six-year-old girl was overprotective of her newly born brother. Her make-believe play in the session betrayed her wish to get rid of this baby. Her overprotectiveness was understood by the therapist as a defense against this forbidden wish. In her play, the girl created two twin kittens who weren't babies any longer. They found a baby kitten on their way to the circus. They gave the baby kitten to the queen and went to the circus without it. In her interpretation, the therapist did not attempt to connect this scene to the girl's real life. She said instead: "The twin kittens didn't want to take care of the baby kitten. They did not want it in the circus with them. They wanted to enjoy themselves. They refused to be bothered by a crying baby. So they gave it to the queen."

Transference of conflict-laden internalized objects onto the therapist and the latter's interpretation of such transference is of paramount importance in adult analysis. Theorists have emphasized, however, that this is not so in child analysis, since most children still have their love objects present in their daily life. Children in psychoanalytic play therapy do project their conflictual feelings toward these love objects onto the figure of the therapist as well as onto various make-believe play signifiers. The therapist does interpret these projections and assists the child in working through these feelings. These projections, however, are not *transference* properly so-called. They are reflections of the child's living reality and his or her emotional responses to it.

Another key concept in adult analysis is *regression in the service of the ego*. The free-associating client regresses to the developmental stage in which his internal difficulties developed. This regression gives the therapist a direct access to what should be treated by interpretation. This is not necessarily so in child analysis. In most cases the child does not need to regress to an earlier developmental stage. She is still in the stage of problem formation. The expression of this stage in make-believe play provides the therapist with a direct access to it.

As said above, the therapist in psychoanalytic play therapy is not just an object of transference, but a real person: a friend and playmate, a role model, an educator and an aid to development.

Jungian Play Therapy

C.G. Jung (1875–1961) was a Swiss psychiatrist who worked together with Freud, until they went their separate theoretical ways. Unlike Freud, who in his early work saw *libido*, the pleasure principle, as the central human motivating power, Jung, with some other post-Freudian theorists, regarded the individuation process—the drive to separate from parental figures and develop one's own unique identity, as the major driving force in a person's psychic life.

Jung did not accept Freud's conception of a tripartite structure of the psyche: *id, ego* and *superego*. Instead, he proposed his own conception, according to which the psyche consists of *individual unconscious, collective unconscious* and *ego*. The individual unconscious contains both repressed thoughts and feelings and latent, still-underdeveloped potential facets of one's personality. The ego includes one's conscious thoughts and feelings. The collective unconscious, Jung's main innovation and hallmark (although the seminal idea is already found in Freud's theory of dreams) consists of *archetypes*, a concept that bears some similarity to the notion of *emotives* discussed in Chapter 5. Jung's *archetypes* may be viewed as universal unconscious emotives—that is, covert emotional concerns shared by all human beings everywhere. Central archetypes have to do with diverse images of birth, death, love, mother earth, gods and the forces of evil. Their numerous manifestations are found in dreams, fantasies, myths, rituals, folklore and children's make-believe play. Jung believed archetypes to be inherent, genetically transmitted entities in the human brain.

A child's normal development is characterized, according to Jung, by a smooth, undisturbed process of individuation, in which an age-appropriate balance is kept between the child's ego, individual unconscious and collective unconscious. This process is disturbed if the child does not enjoy appropriate parental care, undergoes traumatic experiences or is exposed to manifestations of unfinished individuation in his parental figures. In such cases the child fails to develop his own potentialities to the full. He tends to act out unfinished and underdeveloped sides of his caretakers' personalities.

The purpose of Jungian therapy in general and child therapy in particular is therefore to help one restore his or her full capacity for individuation and personal development and maintain an appropriate balance between his or her ego, personal unconscious and collective unconscious.

Although Jung himself was not a child therapist, his firm belief in the therapeutic power of expressive media such as art, drama and creative writing has induced his followers to develop methods of Jungian play therapy with children. In Jungian play therapy the therapist actively participates in the child's play as a playmate. She lets the child dictate her (the therapist's) roles in the play. From this position of participant-observer the therapist exercises various functions. She encourages the child to express himself in play, reflects his feelings and thoughts, helps him elaborate and explicate his play symbols and points out the relevance of the play contents to his life.

Jungian play therapists divide a session into phases: The phase of entrance from the real world to the play world; the phase of chaos, in which all the forces of the personality are acted out in a disorderly manner; the phase of struggle between the destructive and constructive forces; the phase of reparation and resolution of the conflicts; and the exit phase of returning to reality. The whole process is constructive, change-promoting. Therapeutic change comes, according to Jung's followers, not so much from in-depth interpretations which make the unconscious conscious, but from the creation, evolvement and structuring of play symbols during the above-mentioned phases. The child, assisted by the therapist, grows through playing. The unfolding and elaboration of play symbols stimulate and inspire the child's individuation and revitalize his ability to maintain a suitable balance between the various forces of his personality.

Adlerian Play Therapy

This form of play therapy has been developed within the framework of Alfred Adler's Individual Psychology. This theory is based on the assumption that people are social beings who are motivated primarily by the need to belong, which endows their life with meaning. This need lies behind many other goals toward which people strive. To reach these goals people use judgment and creative thinking. The latter are often based on a person's private logic, which is not necessarily rational or comprehensible to others.

The child's basic need is to belong to her family. She bases her ways of reaching this goal on her own private, not necessarily correct, judgments concerning her family's reality. If the child believes that her attempts to fully belong to her family in positive, constructive ways have failed, she is apt to adopt negative, destructive means to achieve this goal. The main purpose of Adlerian play therapy is helping the child judge her life experience realistically and use her creativity to acquire positive, constructive, effective ways of restoring a full sense of belonging.

In Adlerian play therapy the therapist meets the child alone in a room equipped with a variety of toys and playthings. The therapist sees the child's parents separately for guidance and consultation. The play sessions with the child are divided into four phases:

1. Building a partnership with the child. The therapist observes the child's play, reflects the contents and feelings expressed in it, sets limits and starts interacting with the child in play.

2. Exploring the child's dysfunctional ways of reaching her goals. The therapist attempts, from his position of observer-participant of the child's play, to learn about the child's methods of gaining significance and her self-defeating convictions.

3. Interpreting the child's lifestyle. The therapist helps the child gain insight into her self-defeating strategies. This is done both within the play, by using the child's own play metaphors, and out-of-play, by commenting on the child's play and connecting it to her real life.

4. Reorientation. The therapist, both within the play framework and out of it, guides the child to adopt more positive and effective strategies for reaching her goals.

Child-Centered Play Therapy

The theoretical framework in which this form of play therapy is embedded is Carl Rogers' Client-Centered Therapy. Virginia Axline, Rogers' student and colleague, was the first to apply Rogers' principles to child therapy through play. Axline believed, with Rogers, that every child has an innate capacity for growth, self-fulfilment and self-healing. This innate capacity will be actualized if the child's own subjective construction of her own experience and sense of self is treated with acceptance and respect. Maladjustment occurs when the child's self-concept and her drive toward positive self-realization are denied or perturbed. Play therapy should therefore provide the child with an opportunity, within clearly defined limits, to be her own self and to act out her own wishes and fantasies without being disturbed, directed or criticized. This method of play therapy is child-centered, not problem-centered. The therapist serves mainly as a facilitator. He lets the child exercise her creative faculties and express her emotions freely. The therapeutic process takes place without undue interventions on the side of the therapist.

Some child-centered play therapists have detected the following identifiable stages in the child's emotional development in the course of the play sessions: (1) diffuse feelings, (2) negative feelings directed toward figures representing family members, (3) regression, (4) ambivalent feelings toward figures representing family members, (5) clear, distinct, usually positive attitudes toward figures representing family members.

Cognitive-Behavioral Play Therapy

Cognitive-behavioral therapy is based on the assumption that people's emotional responses and behavior are derived from their internal subjective construction of their experience. The person's conscious or subconscious tenets shape his perceptions and interpretations of events. Psychological difficulties are due to serious errors either in the person's basic tenets or in the perceptions and interpretations derived from them. In cognitive-behavioral therapy the client's ideational system is explored in a supportive, relaxed atmosphere, with view to exposing such dysfunctional errors of judgment and adopting more rational, more efficacious ones instead.

In cognitive-behavioral play therapy, play serves mainly as an audiovisual aid to instruction. Real-life situations in which the child responds inappropriately are simulated through role playing, puppets and other play objects. The child's ideations in these situations are explored through these signifying media. Alternative, more functional ideations are also offered in the framework of the play. Other behavioristic and cognitive techniques such as relaxation, positive reinforcement and behavior shaping are operated within the play arena.

Ecosystemic Play Therapy

This method was developed by Kevin O'Connor and Charles Schaefer. It is derived from a wide-scale integration of biological sciences concepts, various models of child psychotherapy and child development theories.

Although the ecosystemic model is centered on the individual, all the child's internal and external systems are taken into account in all the stages of diagnosis and treatment. Internal systems are the body and its functioning, the cognitive and the emotional profiles. External systems are the family, the school, the various social agencies affecting the child's life, the culture and so on.

Psychopathology is manifested when the child cannot get his needs met and his development is arrested as a result. This can be due to weaknesses and inadequacies in any of the systems listed above and their interrelations. The goal of play therapy is to "facilitate the child's resumption of normal development and to maximize the child's ability to get his or her needs met while interfering as little as possible with the gratification of other's needs" (O'Connor & Schaefer, 1994, p. 71). In order to achieve this the child should gain insight into the dysfunctional elements in his internal or external systems and develop new strategies for rectifying them. This is done inside the make-believe play world. When the therapist identifies the symbolic representation of relevant problematic situations in the child's play, she, speaking in the make-believe play language, looks for alternative explanations and explores creative solutions. Situations are forged, in which the child, free of the impediments characteristic of his real life, can have his needs fully met.

EVALUATION OF PLAY THERAPY METHODS

The multiplicity of play therapy methods bears witness to the universal recognition of the therapeutic power of play. Play therapy methods have been developed within the framework of almost every school of psychotherapy. Theorists of play therapy have drawn on insights and findings made publicly known by investigators of play of various orientations. These insights and findings have been integrated into psychotherapy lore.

Acknowledging these achievements, my conclusion is that the current state of the art leaves much to be desired. Here are the main reasons for this conclusion:

1. None of the methods of play therapy is based on a fully fledged, integrative systematic, rigorous, testable theory of make-believe play and its therapeutic power. Each of them incorporates only a few specific, fragmentary, relevant ideas and findings. This is not the fault of the originators or followers of any of the play therapy methods, because such a fully developed theory still does not exist.

2. In most of these methods there is no organic, inherent connection between the underlying grand clinical theory and the play therapeutic techniques used. With some relatively minor variations, roughly the same play therapeutic techniques are employed in almost all the methods surveyed above. Furthermore, some of the grand theories themselves seem to constitute more or less the same set of ideas in slightly different terminological disguises.

I consider the body of general propositions offered in this book an outline for the kind of comprehensive, systematic theory of make-believe play required for providing an integrative theory of play therapy with a solid foundation. Following is a succinct presentation of the main lines of such an integrative theory.

AN INTEGRATIVE THEORY OF PLAY THERAPY

The Scope of the Theory and the Language in Which It Is Formulated

This play therapy theory is embedded in a general integrative model of psychotherapy I have been developing in the last twenty years or so. This model embraces the family and wider ecological systems, culture, psychodynamics, and the individual's cognitive and socioemotional development. All these have been integrated, systematized and formalized in the language of cognitive science, which borrows its concepts and terms from information-processing theory (see Johnson-Laird, 1989), cybernetics (the science of feedback systems; see Maltz, 1987) and semiotics (the science of signs and symbols; see Cobley, Jansz and Appignanesi, 1997; Deely, 1982).

In this model all the above-mentioned systems are represented as sets of information-processing programs stored in individual minds. A human information-processing program is a rule regulating the kinds and amounts of information received and perceived (input), the ways this information is interpreted, the manner in which it is organized in one's mind and the kinds of outward behavioral responses it leads to (output). To illustrate, consider a *parental discipline* program, stored in the mind of a six-year-old boy. Let us call this boy Timid. This program identifies, classifies and interprets his parents' emotional responses to his own behavior (e.g., anger, disappointment, pride). The same program relates their disciplinary measures to his own previous transgressions. This program also prescribes his own responses—compliance, begging for concessions or the like.

The various rules discussed in the previous chapters can be reformulated as such information-processing programs. Not only intrapersonal systems such as the psychodynamic and the developmental can be represented as sets of information-processing programs, but also interactive systems such as the family and other social bodies (see Ariel 1984, 1987, 1994, 1996, 1997, 1999; Ariel, Carel and Tyano, 1984, 1985; Ariel and Peled, 2000).

Explaining the Etiology of Symptoms—Dysfunctional Attempts to Restore Lost Simplicity

The emergence of psychopathological symptoms and other problems presented to therapy is explained in this model by the concept "dysfunctional attempts to restore the lost simplicity of a set of information-processing programs." To understand this notion one should look into the following rather elaborate account:

The notion of *simplicity* has been borrowed from the philosophy and methodology of science. In this context it comprises the following subnotions:

• *Comrehensiveness*—The simplest set of information-processing programs is capable of processing all the information needed to understand one's relevant experience and respond to it appropriately. For example, Timid's *parental discipline* program is sufficiently simple if it enables Timid to interpret all the relevant responses of his parents correctly and to react accordingly. Suppose for instance that Timid's parents were in the habit of punishing him unjustly, even when he did not do anything to deserve it. If his program did not include clauses referring to this habit, then this program would be incomplete, and therefore not simple enough. Another, different program would be required in order to process the "arbitrary punishing" information. This requirement would complicate Timid's information-processing system.

• *Plausibility*—The simplest set of information-processing programs enables one to assign a plausible, reasonable interpretation to his experience. Using again the *parental discipline* example, if Timid's parents are reasonably loving and benevolent, Timid's program will not interpret their disciplinary measures as expressions of hatred and hostility, designed to harm and destroy him. A subprogram leading to such implausible interpretations would introduce undue complication into his information-processing system.

• *Consistency*—the simplest set of information-processing programs includes no self-contradictory program. For example, if the *parental discipline* program includes a clause which qualifies certain disciplinary measures as just, it would not include another clause which qualifies the same measures as unjust.

The simplicity of a set of information-processing programs can be lost in times of transition and crisis, such as passage from kindergarten to elementary school, death or serious illness in the family, immigration and so on. In such circumstances some people face a new, unfamiliar, complex reality which cannot be fully and easily digested by the set of information-processing programs previously available to them. Their set of information processing programs has therefore lost its *comprehensiveness*. They are exposed to stimuli which cannot be assigned a reasonable explanation by the programs available to them. These programs have therefore lost their *plausibility*. A new experience is assigned contradictory interpretations, which call for incompatible responses by different sets of programs. Their previous set of programs has therefore lost its *consistency*.

Some people adapt themselves to such new circumstances in an adequate, appropriate manner. They vary their previous set of programs to fit it to the new situation. They add new programs or subprograms to it, so that the relevant novel information can be digested. In this way they restore the lost *comprehensiveness* of their information-processing system. They change programs to make them more *plausible* with respect to the new information. They remove contradictory programs or modify them to settle the contradictions, and in this way restore the system's *consistency*.

There are people, however, who are unable, in certain situations of transition or crisis, to introduce such adaptational changes to their information-processing system. They cannot fully restore its simplicity. This is often the case in the following circumstances:

1. The new information is of an extremely painful, stressful nature; for example, in events such as sudden death in the family, war or exposure to extreme violence.

2. The new data are totally incompatible with the information-processing programs available to the person; for example, when a person from a close, isolated, extremely religious community has emigrated to a secular, open, modern urban environment.

3. The person is flooded with a great amount of unfamiliar, extremely confusing and bewildering data, as, again, in the previous example.

Often, when people are unable to restore the lost simplicity of their information-processing system by changing it in the above-mentioned ways, they are reduced to making dysfunctional attempts to regain simplicity. The most common dysfunctional move is a desperate effort to maintain some semblance of simplicity by restoring only one or two of the three subcomponents of simplicity: only *comprehensiveness*, only *plausibility*, only *consistency*, while abandoning any attempt to reestablish the other two components, only *comprehensiveness* and *consistency* but not *plausibility*, and so forth.

To illustrate, let us return to the *parental discipline* program. Imagine the following situation: Until the eighth year of Timid's life his family affairs had been carried on in fairly normal, smooth, congenial ways. But then, when he was eight, crisis befell his family. His mother discovered that his father had an extramarital affair. His parents began going through extremely painful and aggressive divorce procedures. His mother projected her anger at her husband onto Timid, whom she saw as "an exact copy of his father." She would scold Timid and severely punish him for no reason whatsoever. But then she would be tormented with feelings of guilt and would refrain from scolding or punishing him even when he deserved it. His father took the opposite position. He identified with Timid, formed a coalition with him against his wife, and abandoned any attempt to set any appropriate parental limits, even when Timid badly needed such limits.

Obviously, in these circumstances Timid's previous *parental discipline* program would no longer be valid. It would lose its simplicity. This program would not be *comprehensive* anymore, because various kinds of unfamiliar data would not be recognized by its various clauses: his mother's arbitrary penalties, his father's failure to set any limits, and the like. The same program would be no longer *plausible*. It would no longer seem reasonable to interpret his mother's angry accusations and unjustified punishments as benevolent attempts to edify him. Furthermore, the program would not be *consistent* any more, because Timid would have no way of assigning any consistent interpretation to his mother's behavior toward him.

What would Timid do in this imaginary scenario? In all probability, in this critical, traumatic, disoriented time he would be unable to fully restore simplicity by revising his previous program and adapting it to the new family situation. In all likelihood he would attempt one of the following, among other, dysfunctional solutions:

1. Restoring *comprehensiveness* and *consistency*, while forgoing *plausibility*. Timid would convince himself, for instance, that his mother is all bad, a witch, whereas his father is all good, an angel. He would interpret all evidence to the contrary as attempts to deceive and mislead him. Or, Timid would persuade himself that both his parents are all good, angels. He would justify his mother's

unfair treatment by leading himself to believe that he himself is bad, deserving to be punished and mistreated.

2. Restoring *plausibility* and *consistency* while giving up *comprehensiveness*. Timid would ignore, for instance, all evidence indicating that his parents' disciplinary policy has become inconsistent and disconnected from his own behavior. He would process only information bespeaking of a direct, sensible correlation between the nature of his own actions and his parents' reactions.

Such attempts to restore simplicity partially are dysfunctional because they are often costly in terms of the price the child has to pay in making them. Take for instance the former attempt (number 1 above). This could cause serious damage to Timid's own self-esteem or to the representation of his mother in his own mind. Such mental injuries can be manifested by external symptoms of guilt, anxiety or depression. The latter attempt (item 2) can lead Timid to seclusion and isolation, coupled with free-floating anxiety.

It will be noticed that such partial attempts to restore simplicity introduce "bugs" into information-processing programs. In computer jargon "bugs" are snags that have somehow settled themselves in programs. They cause various kinds errors and distortions in the processing of information under the infected programs. This is evident in the above examples. Timid's hypothesized attempts to restore simplicity only partially would cause the intrusion of bugs into his program. I name one of these bugs, which results from the tactic of forgoing comprehensiveness, *horse blinders*, because it restricts the person's vista and leaves a great deal of relevant and important information out. Another bug, caused by forgoing plausibility, I call *the Baron von Munchausen*, because it tells the person false, fantastic tales and distorts her judgment of reality. Another bug I call *topsy-turvy*. It is occasioned by forgoing consistency. It results in an inability to process information in an orderly, consistent manner which makes sense.

To sum up, these are the main stages in the development of dysfunctional solutions to situations of transition and crisis:

1. The normal state of affairs. The set of information-processing programs is sufficiently simple (comprehensive, plausible and consistent).

2. Transitional states and crisis situations—novel, unfamiliar information. The set of information-processing programs loses its simplicity. It is unable to process the unfamiliar information in a comprehensive, plausible and consistent manner.

3. Good adaptation. The set of information-processing programs is changed to accommodate the new unfamiliar information. Simplicity (comprehensiveness, plausibility and consistency) is restored.

4. Inadequate adaptation. Simplicity cannot be fully restored. Either comprehensiveness or plausibility or consistency is sacrificed. Characteristically this is so when the person is flooded with novel, unfamiliar, bewildering stressful information, which is incompatible with previous, familiar experience; changing the previous information-processing system to fully restore simplicity would be too painful. Dysfunctional

attempts to restore simplicity only partially cause the introduction of "bugs" into the person's information-processing system.

5. Psychopathological symptoms or other manifestations of stress are developed as outward signs of the failure to restore simplicity fully.

The Goals of Play Therapy—"Debugging" the Information-Processing System and Restoring its Simplicity

Integrative play therapy is great fun. The therapist plays together with the clients—an individual child, a group of children or a family. Both therapist and client can give free rein to their imagination, inventiveness and creativity. The means of expression and communication at their disposal are endless. They can talk, sing, make music, draw, paint, use or create all kinds of objects and materials, move, dance, jump, roll on the floor, whatever. Play therapy is extremely flexible and rich. Still, the therapist, in the midst of all this excitement, should never lose sight of his goals and purposes. He has to carefully monitor the happenings in the room, interpret them and respond self-consciously. He should at all times know what he is doing and why, because integrative play therapy is a precision instrument. The play therapeutic moves should be pinpointed, like laser beams in an eye operation. Play in this form of therapy is used in two different but interrelated ways: (1) as a debugging instrument by which the bugs settled in the client's information-processing system are removed or at least weakened; (2) as a vehicle of therapeutic communication.

These uses of play are realized in the following three kinds of therapeutic moves:

1. *Main (debugging) moves*—designed to free the system from particular bugs.

2. *Preparatory moves*—preparing the ground for the main moves by securing the co-operation of the clients and helping them get ready for change. Since the therapist is a senior co-player, she is entitled and able, like a dominant child in a sociodramatic playgroup, to influence the course of the play and divert it to her own chosen directions by performing a series of preparatory play moves. (See elaboration below.)

3. *Auxiliary moves*—geared toward neutralizing undesirable side effects of main moves. Such moves are required mainly in family play therapy or group play therapy, where main moves affect the other participants in ways that are not always predictable or advantageous.

All these moves together are expected, in the course of time, to empower the client to introduce the necessary changes into his or her information-processing system, so that its simplicity with respect to changed reality is fully restored.

Make-Believe Play as a Debugging Instrument—Bug-Busters

The use of make-believe play as a precision debugging instrument in main moves requires understanding of the therapeutic power of make-believe play.

This power is embodied in various properties that make-believe play has. I call these properties *bug-busters*. The bug-busters are derived from the following three sources:

1. The formal definition of make-believe play, presented in Chapter 1.
2. The function of make-believe play as an homeostatic mechanism for balancing emotional concerns. This function is discussed in Chapter 5.
3. The function of make-believe play in regulating interpersonal conflicts of proximity and control. These functions are discussed in Chapters 3 and 4.

Bug-busters, with their main therapeutic applications, are discribed in the following sections.

Bug-Busters Derived from the Definition of Make-Believe Play

Owning-Alienation. Since the player performs the mental operations of *animation* and *identifying*, he or she *owns* the content of his or her play (i.e., is committed to its being real). Since, however, the player also performs the mental operation of *disclaiming seriousness*, he or she is also alienated from this content, not committed to its being real.

Therapeutic applications: This property can be used to shake one's deep convictions about oneself or others (from owning to disowning), or to make one accept previously rejected truth about oneself or others (from disowning to owning).

Examples: This property can be used to help Timid disown his view of his mother as a witch. Imagine for instance the following make-believe play: The therapist, Timid and his mother play at "a masks parade." Each participant tries on a series of masks, some representing good characters, such as a guardian angel or a faithful watchdog, and some bad characters, such as a devil, a witch or a vulture. Each participant pretends that his or her masked face is in fact his or her own real face. The play-property *owning-alienation* is supposed to induce in Timid's mind a cognitive-affective mental state of doubt in the validity of his image of his mother as bad.

The same therapeutic play property can be used to have Timid's mother own her denied projection of her anger at her husband onto Timid. Consider for instance the following make-believe play scene: The therapist, assuming a distorted version of Timid's father's name, is engaged in "a boxing match" with Timid's mother. Timid is the referee. The therapist keeps evading Timid's mother and playing it foul. Timid's mother is demanding of Timid, the referee, to take a stand against the therapist. If he finds it difficult to comply, she is accusing him of being on the therapist's side and starts fighting with him instead of with the therapist.

Basic Duality. Owing to the mental claim of *disclaiming seriousness*, the player is both inside the play and outside it, a self-observer.

Therapeutic applications: Increasing self-awareness regarding bugs; making contradictions between different levels of communication explicit.

Examples: The above "boxing match" example illustrates this application. Both Timid and his mother are perfectly aware that the contents of their play apply not just to the imaginary characters in the staged boxing match but also to their real selves. This forces them to reflect about their own real-life behavior and psychological maneuvers. Another example: Timid's mother "plays as if she is punishing her son for his misbehavior." In this make-believe play the property of *basic duality* is activated with view to explicating the contradiction between two levels of communication, one overt and one covert. On the overt level her penalties are educative. On the covert level they are manifestations of aggression.

Arbitrariness of Signifier. Thanks to the claims of *animation* and *identification*, there should not necessarily be any similarity between the signifier and its signified content.

Therapeutic applications: Softening the emotional impact of emotive-related information. Exaggerating contradictions.

Examples: Shoshana, a divorcee, wanted to send her ten-year-old daughter, Yudit, to a boarding school. Both of them claimed they could not get along with one another. They were getting on each other's nerves. In one session Shoshana and Yudit staged the following play scene: Shoshana as "queen" sent Yudit as "princess" to the forest. The therapist, imitating the howling of wolves, assumed the role of a fairy. He promised to lead the princess to a hut in the forest, where she would be safe. Then he asked Shoshana to "be" the hut. Yudit sat in her lap and Shoshana hugged her. In this example, Shoshana's body, especially her lap, served as an arbitrary singifier for the signified "a hut in the forest," alluding to the boarding school. The contrast between the physical closeness of mother and daughter, the warmth and softness of Shoshana's lap, on the one hand and the cold, distant hut (boarding school) was designed to make Shoshana and Yudit aware of their covert dependency needs, hiding behind conflict and teasing.

Possible Worlds. Thanks to the claims of *animation* and *identification* any potential or imaginary situation can come alive in make-believe play.

Therapeutic applications: Information left out by bugs can be reintroduced in make-believe play.

The above example of "the hut in the forest" illustrates this property too. The scene in which Shoshana hugged and protected Yudit was taken from a possible world in which their overt relations would be characterized by love, warmth and support.

Bug-Busters Derived from the Emotional-Homeostatic Functions of Make-Believe Play

Distancing. The mechanism by which the child distances his play signified contents and signifiers from the hard core of his emotives to their periphery (see Chapter 5) can be operated under the therapist's direction.

Therapeutic applications: Facilitating the expression of emotionally difficult contents; softening the impact of such messages and working them through.

Example: Bella, an eight-year-old girl, was sexually harassed by a neighbor. Whenever this event was mentioned she had a fit of unbearable stomach ache and then she would start crying and yelling. She refused to talk about that traumatic experience.

A play therapist helped Bella work through this experience by playing with her. She encouraged Bella to choose signifiers and signified contents remotely associated in Bella's mind with the emotive "fear of being attacked," such as a cat lying in wait for a mouse, a pickpocket and a bothersome friend.

Repetition. Emotionally loaded contents are repeated over and over again through make-believe play symbols.

Therapeutic applications: Softening the emotional impact of loaded themes and working through, by habituation and rehearsing in a benign environment.

Example: The therapist encouraged Bella (see the above example) to reintroduce the above-mentioned signifiers and signified into her play over and over again.

Bug-Busters Derived from the Social-Communicational Functions of Make-Believe Play

Covert Communication. Communication concerning interpersonal conflicts are transferred to the realm of make-believe play (see Chapter 3).

Therapeutic applications: Facilitating the expression of complex and stressful interpersonal messages; detouring resistance.

Example: Oz, Bella's seven-year-old brother (see example above) felt neglected by his parents. They considered him strong and independent and turned all their attention to Bella who was viewed as "weak" and needy. Overtly, Oz shared this family myth and behaved accordingly. In a family session he was encouraged by the therapist to express his covert feelings and wishes. He staged a make-believe play scene in which he was a baby monkey whose surrogate parents and protectors, a couple of hunters, had been devoured by a lion. He was left alone and was looking for foster parents.

Make-Believe Play as a Vehicle of Therapeutic Communication

The property of *covert communication*, discussed above, is used not just in main, debugging, moves, but also in preparatory and auxiliary moves. Most of the interpersonal messages exchanged between the therapist and the clients and among the latter are in-play rather than out-of-play expressions. The latter are the main tools of therapeutic communication in this form of therapy.

As already realized by the readers, the therapist's moves in integrative play therapy are often directive. Even though the clients initiate their own spontaneous play, the therapist subtly diverts the course of the play to directions which serve the goals of therapy—debugging and fully restoring simplicity. It should be realized however that the directive role of the therapist is not radically different from the roles dominant children have in sociodramatic play.

In Chapter 4 it was shown that playgroup leaders have a final say not only about play-external decisions, such as rights of participation, play territories and right of use of play objects, but also about in-play roles, choice of signifiers and signified contents and storylines. It will be recalled furthermore that in socio-dramatic play the participants continuously negotiate every aspect of the play, using all kinds of direct and indirect strategies and tactics of persuasion. The therapist's attempts to influence the course of the play does not deviate therefore from the children's own rules and norms. Moreover, some of the kinds of pre-paratory, auxiliary or main tactical moves used in integrative play therapy have been borrowed from children.

Having observed children's sociodramatic play for many years, I have learned their own stratagems for arguing their playmates into playing as they, the former, wish. Another source of stratagems has been the strategic therapeutic techniques developed by master therapists such as Milton Erickson, Cloe Madanes and other like-minded contributors (see references at the end of the chapter). Here is a partial list of such types of strategic moves, with their main therapeutic func-tions.

1. *Mimicking*—imitating clients' play behavior.

Therapeutic functions: Joining: When children want to join a play activity they simply imitate the play of the children they want to play with. The therapist can do the same. Reflecting, commenting: By imitating aspects of the clients' play behavior, such as an accusing finger pointed by a mother at her daughter. The therapist reflects these aspects and comments on them.

2. *Pacing*—channeling behavior to specific routes.

Therapeutic functions: After the therapist mimics the play of a client, she gradually modifies her own play, until the client begins to imitate her play.

Example: A child is playing as if he is a very noisy elephant. The therapist is mimicking his play, pretending to be another noisy elephant. But then the therapist is gradually lowering his voice, until the child has become a quiet elephant.

3. *Focusing*—stressing aspects of play behavior, by sound and lighting ef-fects or verbal and nonverbal comments.

Therapeutic functions: Turning attention to important features; interpreting.

Examples: A mother, Batya, worked hard to set limits to her children. Her husband Gad, as usual, remained passive, uninvolved. To emphasize his avoid-ing, uncommitted attitude the therapist sat astride on a chair by Gad and began whistling the tune of a popular Israeli song whose opening line is "I am sitting on the fence, neither here nor there."

4. *Explicating*—making hidden entities explicit, by verbalizing them or act-ing them out nonverbally.

Therapeutic functions: Emphasizing important features; interpreting.

Example: A family staged a "bank robbery" make-believe game. Sari, the therapist, thought the choice of this story, as well as the roles preferred by the family members and their actions, were not coincidental. They reflected the out-of-play family dynamics. To explicate the family members' hidden messages, Sari assumed the role of a TV reporter at the end of the scene. She interviewed "the bank manager"(the father), "the witness" (the mother), "the police officer" (the older sister) and "the robber" (the brother) about their feelings and their motives for acting as they did.

5. *The double*—the therapist, directly or through a doll, represents a client.

Therapeutic functions: Speaking for a client who refuses to participate in the play activity or is unable to express his hidden feeling and thoughts.

Example: A mother, speaking through a doll, poured a torrent of accusations on her son. Her son's doll, frightened and intimidated, remained silent. His mother's doll began accusing him of treating her with disrespect. "You don't respect me enough to apologize," she shouted. The therapist took hold of a doll which was identical to the son's and said: "I am afraid of you."

6. *Providing stimuli*—the therapist provides behavioral or material stimuli which are to provoke the kind of play he is interested in.

Therapeutic functions: Encouraging certain kinds of activities or changing the course of an activity.

Example: To encourage a girl to express her jealousy of her newly born brother in play, the therapist placed a baby doll, a toy baby cradle and other toys representing baby things on the carpet in front of the girl.

7. *Illusion of alternatives*—the therapist suggests two alternative play ideas. The more attractive alternative is the one he wants the family member to choose.

Therapeutic functions: Enabling the therapist to join the clients' play or influence its course.

Example: A therapist who wanted to encourage a timid little boy to express his strong side in play asked him: "Do you want to be Mickey Mouse or Mighty Mouse?"

8. *Obedient actor*—the therapist asks clients for permission to join their play and lets them choose his role in it. Once inside, he is free to make his own choices.

Therapeutic functions: Enabling the therapist to become an equal play partner.

9. *Willynilly*—the therapist performs a play act which engages a client in a complementary play act.

Therapeutic functions: Engage clients in play or influence their play in accordance with the therapist's aims.

Example: The therapist who wanted to cast a boy in the role of a hunter said to him: "I am the rabbit. Hunter, please don't shoot me!"

MAKE-BELIEVE PLAY DIAGNOSIS

The spontaneous make-believe play of an individual child, a group of children or a family can be a singularly rich source of diagnostic information. The method of using play observations for clinical diagnosis is a somewhat modified version of the educational play diagnosis method specified in Chapter 8. The therapist observes and records or videotapes samples of the clients' spontaneous make-believe play. These samples are analyzed by the same ten steps that were described in Chapter 8.

The therapist's subsequent play therapy interventions will be based on a diagnosis from these stages. Please notice that the seventh analytic step includes the requirement to pinpoint and describe bugs in the participants' strategies for achieving their proximity and control goals. This requirement is needed for what was called "debugging" to take effect. Such bugs are the targets of some of the "bug-busters" described above. Notice also that the ninth step of the analysis instructs the therapist to identify and describe inadequacies in the functioning of this homeostatic mechanism for regulating the child's emotions. This is required, because such inadequacies are the targets of bug-busters such as *distancing* and *repetition*.

INDICATIONS FOR REFERRAL

Integrative play diagnosis and play therapy can be carried out properly only by specially trained professional therapists. However, laypersons—parents, educators and other caretakers of children—who are worried about a child under their care, can include careful observations of the child's spontaneous play in their sources of information about the child's emotional condition. It should be stressed that not every aspect of children's play, or, for that matter, nonplay behavior, that might look worrying to an adult is really a cause for concern. Perfectly normal young children are often irrational, irresponsible and absurd. The make-believe play of well-adjusted children often includes themes of patricide, matricide, suicide, sadism and a whole assortment of ideas that might look way out, bizarre and crazy from an adult standpoint.

What in children's play should be a cause for concern then? In some cases the very lack of such frightening elements. Suppose for instance that a child has been going through extremely stressful experiences, such as death of a parent, abuse, traumatic divorce or the like. If his or her make-believe play exhibits at that period no trace whatsoever of these experiences but depicts an ideal, beautiful world without any trouble or difficulties, it would be reasonable to surmise that this child is not coping with the bad experience well and has perhaps no way of working through his or her emotional reactions. In this case it would perhaps be advisable to refer the child to professional counseling.

Another feature of children's play that can be viewed as an indication for referral to counseling is obsessive, persistent repetition of certain negative signified contents. If, for instance, a child has brought up the theme of matricide in his make-believe play once or twice, among a variety of other contents, this is not necessarily a cause for concern. But if a child plays only about matricide, over and over again, for weeks, then this should perhaps be taken as an alarm.

Another sign of possible serious difficulties is what looks like a persistent loss of the distinction between play and reality. This can take various forms, such as fear of toys, as if they can really do harm, slipping from play aggression to real aggression toward people, animals or objects and insisting stubbornly that the imaginary make-believe characters and events are real.

Parents and other caretakers are also advised to be watchful of signs of regression in play. If for instance a six-year-old child whose make-believe play used to be highly developed appears to have gone back to the earliest stage of make-believe play development (see Chapter 6) and remains only there for a considerable period of time, this is perhaps a sign of regression due to emotional distress.

It should be stressed, however, that identifying emotional distress which requires counseling should never be based only on the child's make-believe play. The functioning of the child in all areas of life should be taken into account. Make-believe play is only one of a variety of sources of information that should be considered.

SUMMARY OF CHAPTER 9

This chapter is devoted to make-believe play as a source of clinical diagnostic information and as a therapeutic instrument. These applications of play in general and make-believe play in particular have been exercised since the early days of professional psychotherapy and counseling. Almost every school of professional therapy has developed its own version of play therapy. Some of the major play therapy methods are briefly surveyed: psychoanalytic, Jungian, Adlerian, child-centered, cognitive-behavioral and ecosystemic. None of these methods, however, was based on a general integrative model of psychotherapy which incorporated a theory of make-believe play and its therapeutic power.

To rectify this, a method of integrative play therapy, embedded in a general integrative model of psychotherapy has been develop by the writer. This model embraces the family and wider ecological systems, culture, psychodynamics, and the individual's cognitive and socioemotional development. All these systems are represented as sets of information-processing programs stored in individual minds.

The integrative play therapy method, which is subsumed under this model, incorporates everything said about make-believe play in this book. Psychopathological phenomena and other difficulties brought to therapy are explained in this model as manifestations of one's inability to fully restore the simplicity (comprehensiveness, consistency and plausibility) of one's information-processing system in situations of transition and crisis. In such situations one's information-processing system cannot process the new, unfamiliar information one is exposed to in the simplest way. The system has lost its simplicity. If the individual is flooded with bewildering, stressful information which is incompatible with the information-processing system available to her, she can restore simplicity only partially, achieving only comprehensiveness, only consistency, only plausibility and so forth.

This partiality causes the introduction of "bugs" into one's information-processing system. The goal of therapy is to remove these bugs and help the clients reach adequate adaptation by fully restoring simplicity. In play therapy these can be achieved by the self-conscious, creative activation of "bug-busters," curative properties of make-believe play. The bug-busters are derived from the very definition of make-believe play (*owning-alienation, basic duality, arbitrariness of signifier* and *possible worlds*), from the emotional-homeostatic function of play (*distancing, repetition*) and from its social-regulative function (*covert communication*). The activation of these properties is intertwined in the fabric of spontaneous, creative and imaginative sociodramatic play initiated and conducted conjointly by the therapist and the clients. The therapist diverts the play to the desired, therapeutically useful directions by making *preparatory, auxiliary* and *main* play moves.

Observations of make-believe play can serve as a rich source of data for clinical diagnosis. The observations are analyzed by all the tools introduced in this book, with special attention to bugged strategies for achieving proximity and control goals as well as to flaws in the functioning in the emotional homeostatic play mechanism.

Lay caretakers of children can learn to detect signs of emotional distress in children by keeping a watch on some features of the make-believe play, mainly total avoidance of unpleasant themes in times of crisis; obsessive, persistent repetition of distressing themes, loss of ability to distinguish between play and reality and regression to early stages of play development.

A CLASSIFIED LIST OF REFERENCES

Play Diagnosis

Harper, 1991; J. M. Lewis, 1993; Solnit, Cohen and Neubauer, 1993; Tyndall-Lynd, 1999.

Methods of Play Therapy

Psychoanalytic: Cohen and Solnit, 1993; Esman, 1983; A. Freud, 1965; S. Freud, 1959; Hartmann, 1950; Kernberg, Chazan and Normandin, 1998; Klein, 1932; Kohut, 1971; A. C. Lee, 1997; Loewald, 1987; Mahler, 1979; Parsons, 1999; Sandler, Kennedy and Tyson, 1980; Schaefer and O'Connor, 1983; M. E. Scott, 1998; Waelder, 1933; Winnicott, 1971; Zhang, 1998.

Jungian: Allan, 1997.

Adlerian: Kottman, 1997; White, Flynt and Jones, 1999.

Child-centered: Axline, 1947, 1964; Kot, Landreth and Giordano, 1998; Landreth, Baggerly and Tyndall-Lynd, 1999; Landreth and Sweeney, 1997; Moustakas, 1955; Parsons, 1999; Zhang, 1998.

Cognitive-behavioral: Conning, 1999; Fall, Balvanz, Johnson and Nelson, 1999; Knell, 1997.

Ecosystemic: O'Connor, 1997; O'Connor and Schaefer, 1994; Sweeney and Homeyer, 1999; Sweeney and Rocha, 2000; Schaefer and O'Connor 1983.

Integrative Play Therapy

The notion of simplicity: Cohen and Stewart, 1995; Hempel, 1966; Slobodkin, 1993.

Cybernetics: Abramovitz, 1995; Bateson, 1977; Maltz, 1987; Moray, 1963;

Human information-processing: Izard, 1991; Johnson-Laird, 1989.

Semiotics and linguistics: Akmajian, Demers, Farmer and Harnish, 1995; Beaugrande, 1980; Cobley, Janscz and Appignanesi, 1997; Deely, 1982.

Models Guiding Practice

Ariel, 1984, 1987, 1994, 1996, 1997, 1999; Ariel, Carel and Tyano, 1984, 1985; Ariel and Peled, 2000; Erickson, 1982; Fall, 1997; Hellendoorn, 1988; Keith and Whitaker, 1981; Van der Kooj and Hellendoorn, 1986; Madanes, 1981; O'Connor and Braverman, 1977; O'Connor and Schaefer, 1994; Phillips and Landreth, 1995; Schaefer, 1974; E. Scott, 1999; Singer and Singer, 1990; Vanfleet, Lilly and Kaduson, 1999.

Summary and Apologia

This book may be viewed as a general, comprehensive introduction to the whole field of children's imaginative, make-believe play. It includes a formal definition of the concept "make-believe play," an anatomical analysis of make-believe play as a semiotic system—a language in the wide sense of this term, a scrutiny of the cognitive and socioemotional functions of make-believe play, a survey of the development of make-believe play against the background of the child's general development, a review of make-believe play from a cross-cultural view-point and a discussion of applications of make-believe play in education and psychotherapy. All these divergent perspectives have been studied in different disciplines, within the framework of heterogeneous theoretical and methodological orientations.

The goal of the work presented in this book has been more ambitious than just surveying all of these elements. It constitutes an attempt to systematize, synthesize and integrate all these studies of make-believe play within a single theoretical and methodological framework. This required trying to translate the most important insights concerning make-believe play into a single theoretical meta-language. As evidenced by many examples in the history of science, such an endeavor can lead to considerable improvement over the current state of the art in a number of important respects, such as exposing systematic interrelations among entities previously considered unrelated; uncovering inaccessible, deep layers of the phenomena investigated; facilitating the construction of exact, rigorous, explicit, testable hypotheses; and founding practical applications on a solid, systematic theoretical and methodological basis. As is shown below, the work reported in this book does indeed boast such achievements.

The theoretical meta-langauge chosen for this work is one that borrows its concepts, terms and principles from what has in recent years been termed *cognitive science*, an overall discipline embracing general systems theory, cybernetics (the science of homeostatic feedback systems), cognitive, human information-processing psychology and semiotics (the science of signs and symbols).

The reasons why I opted for this theoretical and methodological integrative framework are multifold. Here are some:

- Cognitive science has been a "winning" meta-theory in the human and social sciences in recent years. It has led to systematization, deepening and rapid scientific development in many subareas of psychology, anthropology and other fields.

- Cognitive science has provided rigorous and precise methods for analyzing various aspects of human behavior.

- The genre of human behavior investigated in this work, children's make-believe play, yields itself quite naturally to analysis by the theoretical and methodological tools of cognitive science.

As has been claimed above, the attempt to translate heterogeneous aspects of make-believe play into this homogeneous theoretical language has yielded various useful outcomes, such as:

Exposing systematic interrelations among entities previously considered unrelated. The insights gained by the analysis of make-believe play in this theoretical and methodological framework throw light on covert interrelations among seemingly isolated aspects of make-believe play as well as on hidden connections between make-believe play and other phenomena. Thus, the cognitive complexity of make-believe play, explicated by its formal definition in Chapter 1, has been shown to be systematically related to various aspects of the child's cognitive development (see Chapter 6) as well as to the effectiveness of some play educational and play therapeutic techniques (see Chapters 8 and 9).

Likewise, it has been demonstrated that the social functions of make-believe play are interconnected with the child's social development and with its social success or failure in educational settings (see Chapter 4 and Chapter 8). It has also been exhibited that the emotional functions of make-believe play are derivatives of the child's general congitive-emotive mechanisms, which are manifested in other forms of experience and behavior such as free associations and dreams. The therapeutic value of make-believe play is closely related to these mechanisms (see Chapter 9).

Uncovering inaccessible, deep layers of the phenomena investigated. The semiotic analysis of "The Shrunken People," using heuristic techniques such as CDCA and goals and plans analysis, exposed covert classificatory dimensions of signifiers and signified contents and deep structural, syntactic inter-relations among these dimensions. (See Appendix Tables 1 and 3 and pp. 178–184 in the

Appendix). The same applies to the semiotic analysis of "Easy Riders" in Chapter 3 and "The Soldier and the Submarine" in Chapter 5.

Facilitating the exact, explicit rigorous construction of interesting testable hypotheses. The results of the systematic microanalysis and macroanalysis of make-believe play texts in the Appendix and Chapters 3 and 4 constitute such hypotheses, which can be validated or refuted by examining further samples of play by the same methods. (See discussion in Chapter 5.)

The theoretical concepts and terms and the analytic methods proposed in this work can serve as yardsticks for a systematic study of the development of make-believe play as well as for systematic cross-cultural comparisons of make-believe play. One of the developmental parameters of make-believe play discussed in Chapter 6 is the gradual evolvement of deep, covert dimensions and rules governing the choice of both signifiers and signified, (see Table 7.1). The theoretical and methodological framework proposed in this work offers the concepts, terms and techniques for studying this developmental process in detail. In Chapter 7 it has been proposed to apply the same developmental parameters in a cross-culture comparative analysis of the level of make-believe play. Again, the theoretical and methodological meta-language offered in this work includes the apparatus necessary for doing such in-depth cross cultural comparisons.

Founding practical applications on a solid, systematic theoretical and methodological basis. The guidelines for a systematic educational and clinical play diagnosis proposed in Chapters 8 and 9 are identical to the steps in a semiotic analysis of make-believe play and its socioemotional functions proposed in the Appendix and in Chapters 2, 3 and 5.

The "bug-busters," that is, the play therapeutic principles and techniques for remedying information-processing errors due to the clients' inability to restore the simplicity of their information-processing system, are logically derived from the formal definition of make-believe play in Chapter 1 and from the in-depth analysis of its socioemotional functions in Chapters 3, 4 and 5.

I would like to conclude with the following confession: I am not just a play therapist and a play researcher. I am a musician too. When I studied music I was upset by the contradiction between my being enchanted and fascinated by the beauty and mystery of music and the tiring mental and physical efforts required in the process of acquiring the dry, formal concepts of music theory and the technical performance skills. I am perfectly aware of a similar contradiction between the playfulness of play and the complicated, dry, pedantical quality of some parts of the model presented in this book, defying all my genuine efforts to make it reader-friendly. Nevertheless, I truly hope you have found the effort of reading through this book worthwhile.

Appendix: Analyzing a Make-Believe Play Text—Procedures and Heuristic Techniques

INTRODUCTION

These analytic procedures and techniques will be discussed and illustrated with respect to the following observation:

Observation 13: The Shrunken People

The participants in this play scene are Avshalom (boy) and Sharon (girl), both six years old. Another dyadic play episode produced by these two children, entitled "Peace Forever," is presented and analyzed in Chapter 2. "The Shrunken People" took place in the living room of Avshalom's home, a week after "Peace Forever."

Many plastic dolls representing human and semihuman figures of television adventure series such as Power Rangers, Ninja Turtles, Batman, and the like were scattered on the floor.

Avshalom sat on the floor, holding a green doll, representing a human figure whose hands resembled a crab's pincers. Avshalom called this doll Tzvaty, a Hebrew name whose English equivalent would be something like Pincey. Avshalom held Tzvaty on the floor, in a standing position. Sharon stood near him. Avshalom spoke in a childish voice:

Avshalom: Can't you see that I am little?

Sharon looked confused.

Sharon: Are you little? How come you are little?

Avshalom raised Tzvaty toward Sharon and replied in a funny, high-pitched screeching voice:

Avshalom: Can't you see me?!

Apparently "me" was Tzvaty, not Avshalom himself. He played little Tzvaty so convincingly that I, through the video lenses, could hardly see him.

Sharon: Yes, I can see you.

And then Sharon picked up another doll off the floor, representing a strong man, which she and Avshalom had named Jack. She changed her voice to make it "manly." She became Jack.

Sharon: Do you want me to become little too?

She didn't wait for Avshalom's answer. She squatted by Avsahlom, holding Jack very close to Tzvaty. And then she changed her voice again. It became babyish.

Sharon: Yes, I have become little.

Avshalom didn't like the idea. He spoke angrily:

Avshalom: But I didn't *know* I'd become little! So why are you becoming little? . . . It's not that I want you to become little! I want us . . . (pausing) to get over this situation!

I tried to figure out what Avshalom was trying to tell Sharon. It was not an easy task, because the scene kept rolling on. Apparently what he meant was that his own volition had nothing to do with what happened to him, or to Tzvaty. He contracted, became little, not because he wanted to. It just happened to him, took him by surprise. He wanted it to happen neither to himself nor to Jack. He expected Sharon to understand this and was angry when she didn't, although she tried.

Sharon (quietly): So what do you want?
Avshalom (emphatically): I want to be big again!

Avshalom now picked up a Ninja Turtle off the pile of dolls. He got it close to Tzvaty. Sharon tried to say something, but Avshalom cut her short.

Avshalom (speaking from the Ninja Turtle's mouth, in a "grown up" voice): Is anybody speaking here?

Sharon (as Jack, still in a babyish voice): Yes, it's us. Tommy and Tommy. Me and him.

Tommy and Tommy were familiar figures. Sharon and Avshalom invented them when they were five years old. They were twin brothers. One represented Avshalom and the other Sharon. I saw Sharon rotating Jack, upside down and upside again, as if doing acrobatic feats.

Avshalom began speaking from the Ninja Turtle's mouth. His tone of voice was cynical, derisive:

Avshalom: Really. From my class at school!? I am not a member of your class!

By saying this, I thought, Avshalom rejected Sharon's contention that he and she were Tommy and Tommy, the twins. He was big, a Ninja Turtle, whereas she was tiny, a baby Jack. How could they be twins?

Sharon (still in a childish voice): But we've become little.

And then, all of a sudden, Avshalom, as the Ninja Turtle, began speaking in a babyish voice too.

Avshalom (as baby Ninja Turtle): But me too, I was a Ninja fighter, but I've become teeny weeny.

Sharon (in a babyish voice): Teeny weeny, teeny weeny. Everybody here is teeny weeny. Me too. I'm tiny.

At that, Avshalom got up abruptly. He stood in front of Sharon and began speaking in a "grown up" voice again.

Avshalom: Tommy and Tommy! Tommy and Tommy! I'm Merdy! I've come here to visit you!

I figured it out: Since both Jack and the Ninja Turtle were tiny now, they could be considered twin brothers by Avshalom, unlike before, while he himself assumed another role, that of Merdy, a grown up, signified by his own standing body.

Avshalom (as Merdy): Where are you?

Sharon: Down here.

Avshalom: Where?

Sharon: Here. Look.

Avshalom: What happened to you?

Sharon: We've become little.

Avshalom: mmm . . .

Sharon didn't respond. Avshalom began making funny convulsive movements, accompanied by strange, hoarse voices. Then he stopped and sat down quietly.

Avshalom (in a choking voice): Someone has pounced upon me.

He began rotating the Ninja Turtle, upside down and then upside again, in much the same way as Sharon did with Jack before.

The two kids sat quietly for a while. Then Sharon drew Jack near Avshalom, making the doll stand on the floor. Avshalom began to speak in a babyish voice:

Avshalom (as the Ninja Turtle): Hey, Tommy and Tommy, I've shrunk too!
Sharon: Yes, but I should return myself to . . .

She got up and hurried to another pile of dolls in the corner of the room. She returned with a silvery doll representing a strong man. She spoke in a determined intonation:

Sharon: Yes, and I've become bad, and I would like to stay this way.
Avshalom (as baby Ninja Turtle): But how can we become big again?

Sharon placed the silvery doll in front of his Ninja Turtle and spoke.

Sharon: I don't know. Maybe my brother knows.

Then Avshalom changed his voice again, apparently speaking as "Tommy," her twin brother:

Avshalom: I don't know anything about such a thing!

He crawled toward the pile of dolls and picked up a big doll representing a strikingly strong man. He spoke in a loud, self-assured voice:

Avshalom: Maybe I know!
Sharon: O, that's not bad.

There was a moment of silence. I noticed that Avshalom, as the strong man, didn't try to suggest any way of becoming big again.

Avshalom: Excuse me . . . I am your classmate.
Sharon (as the silvery doll): Our classmate? But you are not on our football team.
Avhshalom: I am not on the football team because I don't participate in football games.
Sharon (drawing the silvery doll back, mumbling): I can see something . . . everything is alright . . . everything is alright.

Avshalom: Alright (pause). Not really. We have shrunk. Is this alright?

Sharon: No, everything is alright in the town, but with us nothing is alright . . . I'm going to call Bob . . . Bob's brother . . . not the little one . . . his twin brother. He is the most giant of them all.

The twin brother thing again, I said to myself.

Sharon went to the pile of dolls in the corner of the room. She came back with a very big silvery, winged doll, Bob's brother. She picked up the silvery doll and held it in the same hand in which she was holding Bob's brother.

Avshalom: He is not his brother. Bob is the son of this Robot. I know all the names here. So how have we got shrunk?

Sharon (rubbing the silvery doll and Bob's brother against each other): How have we got shrunk? . . . By the power of . . .

Avshalom (cutting her short): You know . . . what our names are?

Sharon: Yes, Tommy and Tommy.

Avshalom picked up Tzvaty. He raised it high in the air, rotating it.

Avshalom (shouting very loudly): We want to come back to being grown!

Sharon, holding Bob's brother in her right hand and the silvery doll in her left hand, spoke quietly:

Sharon: You two come with me and I'll show you where it comes from.

Avshalom: Where do you know us from?

Sharon: I used to be in your class.

Avshalom (cynically): Yes, of course. What's your name?

Sharon (aggressively): What do you mean?

Sharon, angry, began to push Tzvaty, which was held in Avshalom's hand, with Bob's brother, quite hard. I wondered what made her so angry. Both Sharon and Avshalom seemed to have forgotten Sharon's intriguing promise to show Bob's brother and the silvery doll "where it comes from."

Sharon (poking Tzvaty again): Don't you know that I'm Batman? Don't you know that I used to be in your class?

Avshalom: What did you say your name was?

Sharon (drawing Bob's brother back): Maybe Jack. Haven't you thought about me?

The reason for Sharon's anger seemed to be clear now. She was hurt because Avshalom "forgot her."

Avshalom (emphatically): From our class? No. Jack is *not* from our class.

Sharon took hold of the silvery doll.

Sharon: Jack, you are not from our class, so why are you talking like that? . . . Last year . . .

Avshalom, angry, began to hit Bob's brother with Tzvaty.

Avshalom: You are in second grade. Your are not in . . . sixth grade!
Sharon: Jack?
Avshalom: Yes. There's a Jack in sixth grade.
Sharon: Jack is in second grade. There's another Jack in eighth grade. He [Tzavaty?] didn't know.
Avhsalom: Are you Jack in eighth grade?
Sharon (as Bob's brother): Yes.
Avhaslom: We're Jack in the army . . . eh . . . Tommy, Tommy in the army.
Sharon (insistently): In eighth grade, eighth! Eighth! You are in eighth!

Avshalom, worked up, hit Bob's brother very hard with Tzvaty, tossing Bob's brother two yards away.

Avshalom (shouting): We're in the army!

Sharon, preserving her equanimity, went to retrieve Bob's brother.

Sharon (returning with Bob's brother): Army? First of all we are sixth grade. One should always choose the first decision.
Avshalom: That's something I know.

Avshalom, feeling defeated, hit Bob's brother, held in Sharon's hand, again, quite hard.

Avshalom (shouting): Shut up then! We made a mistake!
Sharon: Watch it!
Avshalom (yelling, shaking Tzvaty violently): I'm not gonna watch it until you agree!
Sharon: OK. Alright. I agree. If you are insisting so.

Sharon made Bob's brother stand on the floor. Avshalom did the same with Tzvaty and got up.

Avshalom (quietly): I can see I've been dreaming. I'm not a soldier.

Sharon (looking up toward Avshalom): He turned into . . .

Avshalom: Tommy and Tommy! Tommy and Tommy! What happened to you?

Sharon: Who's speaking?

Avshalom: A friend of his.

Sharon: We've shrunk.

Avshalom: I'm Ofree. I don't know why you've shrunk. Did you drink a potion your mother prepared?

Sharon (squatting, holding the silvery doll): No, but I believe . . . he knows why.

Avshalom: I know why?!! Yeah, I do know why!

Avshalom gets hold of the strong doll, assuming his harsh voice:

Avshalom: I did it!

Sharon: Why?

Avshalom: I wanted to show that there are cuter types, more than you think. Cuter than me. I'll show you. Come after me.

Avshalom started walking away. Sharon got up, following him.

AN INFORMAL ANALYSIS OF "THE SHRUNKEN PEOPLE"

As this observation came to a close, I felt as if I had been a spectator in the theater of the absurd. What I had seen seemed like a display of a bewildering assortment of characters talking nonsense. I transcribed the videotaped scene and read the transcript over and over again, and then it started to make sense. It became obvious that it had in it, underneath the surface, more than met the eye. Some general patterns began to take shape, such as the following: The whole scene revolves around one central theme—"littleness" versus "bigness." This theme manifests itself in several variations: shrinking and growing again, the appearance and departure of little figures and big figures, discussions about whether the characters are in second grade, sixth grade, eighth grade or in the army service, trying to understand what makes people shrink and grow, and so on.

The signifiers and signified contents fall into fairly clear categories:

Size of characters: Little people (represented by little dolls); big, strong people (represented by big, strong dolls) and big people who are not particularly strong (represented by the upright bodies of the players). The little people are people who have shrunk. The big, strong people don't want to shrink. They attempt to explain to the little people why they have shrunk and help them return to their previous size. The big nonstrong people are visitors who are surprised to find out that their friends have shrunk.

Age of characters: 2nd grade, 6th grade, 8th grade, army service age. These categories are organized in the following sequence: little people, followed by big, strong people, followed by big nonstrong people, followed by discussions about age, back to little people, and the sequence repeats itself. The two players keep going back and forth between preferring to be of the same size or age and wanting to be differentiated from each other in this respect. This is evidenced in the following excerpts.

Excerpt 1

(Sharon as Jack wants to become little like Avshalom, as Tzvaty, but he wants her to remain bigger than he is.)
Sharon changed her voice to make it "manly." She became Jack.

Sharon: Do you want me to become little too?

She didn't wait for Avshalom's answer. She squatted by Avsahlom, holding Jack very close to Tzvaty. And then she changed her voice again. It became babyish.

Sharon: Yes, I have become little.

Avshalom didn't like the idea. He spoke angrily:

Avshalom: But I didn't *know* I'd become little! So why are you becoming little? . . . It's not that I want you to become little!

Excerpt 2

(At first Avshalom denies that he is of the same age ["class"] as Sharon. Then he admits that both of them are of the same size ["little"].)
Avshalom began speaking from the Ninja Turtle's mouth. His tone of voice was cynical, derisive:

Avshalom: Really. From my class at school!? I am not a member of your class!
Sharon (still in a childish voice): But we've become little.
Avshalom (as baby Ninja Turtle): But me too, I was a Ninja fighter, but I've become teeny weeny.

Excerpt 3

(Sharon does not want to remain little, as Avshalom. She wants to be big, strong and "bad.")

Avshalom (as the Ninja Turtle): Hey, Tommy and Tommy, I've shrunk too!

Sharon: Yes, but I should return myself to . . .

She returned with silvery doll representing a strong man. She spoke in a determined intonation.

Sharon: Yes, and I've become bad, and I would like to stay this way.

Excerpt 4

(Avshalom tells Sharon that he is of the same age as she is [her classmate]. This time it is Sharon who is casting doubt upon this contention.)

Avshalom: Excuse me . . . I am your classmate.

Sharon (as the silvery doll): Our classmate? But you are not on our football team.

Excerpt 5

(Sharon says that Bob's brother is of the same age as Bob [being his twin brother]. Avshalom denies this and tells her that Bob is the son of the robot.)

Sharon: . . . I'm going to call Bob . . . Bob's brother . . . not the little one . . . his twin brother. He is the most giant of them all.

Avshalom: He is not his brother. Bob is the son of this Robot. I know all the names here. So how have we got shrunk?

Excerpt 6

(Sharon tells Avshalom that Jack is of the same age as him [his classmate]. Avshalom insists that Jack is younger. Then the children go on inventing other "Jacks," some of the same age, some younger and some older.)

Avshalom: Where do you know us from?

Sharon: I used to be in your class.

Avshalom (cynically): Yes, of course. What's your name?

Sharon (aggressively): What do you mean? . . .

Sharon (poking Tzvaty again): Don't you know that I'm Batman? Don't you know that I used to be in your class?
[And so forth . . .]

A FORMAL ANALYSIS OF "THE SHRUNKEN PEOPLE"

The formal analysis has the following purposes: corroborating the informal analysis; revealing other, less overt and manifest, patterns. The formal analysis proceeds according to the following steps:

1. Identifying and describing signifier-signified units, and their combinations into structures.

2. Sorting out the context-dependent uses of structures—their creators' presuppositions and purposes.

3. Distinguishing structures which say something about other structures and defining their uses.

4. Classifying signifier-signified units into categories, and formulating rules constraining both their combinations into structures and the context-dependent uses of these structures.

First Step: Identifying and Describing Signifier-Signified Units

This step can be broken down into substeps:

Substep 1 (analyzing signifiers into types of expressive media across time)

To facilitate the detection of signifier-signified units, observed play which has been videotaped or otherwise recorded can be analyzed and tabulated by the following simple technique.

The axis of time is divided into equal consecutive intervals. The length of each interval is determined by the analyzer in accordance with the question how fine one wants the analysis to be. It can be five seconds, twenty seconds, thirty seconds, one minute, and so on. The verbal and nonverbal in-play and out-of-play behavior of each of the participants in the activity in each time interval is analyzed into its linguistic and vocal, spatial, motional and tactile components. The results can be displayed in a tabular form (see Appendix Table 1).

Let me illustrate this technique by applying it to the following short excerpt of "The Shrunken People":

Avshalom sat on the floor, holding a green doll, representing a human figure whose hands resembled a crab's pincers. Avshalom called this doll Tzvaty, a Hebrew name whose English equivalent would be something like Pincey. Avshalom held Tzvaty on the floor, in a standing position. Sharon stood near him. Avshalom spoke in a childish voice:

Avshalom: Can't you see that I am little?

Sharon looked confused.

Appendix Table 1
Analysis of Observed Play Behavior by Expressive Media Across Time Units

Expressive Media	verbal-vocal	spatial	motional	tactile
Time units (length of unit, 1 minute)				
Time unit 1				
Avshalom	"Can't you see that I'm little?"; childish voice	having Tzvaty stand on the floor		holding Tzvaty
Sharon			standing by Avshalom looks confused	
	"Are you little? How come you are little?"			
Time unit 2				
Avshalom			raising Tzvaty toward Sharon	
	"Can't you see me?"; a funny, high-pitched, screeching voice			
Sharon	"Yes, I can see you."			
Time unit 3				
Sharon			picking up Jack off the floor	
	"Do you want me to become little too?"; manly voice			
			squatting by Avsahlom, very close to Tzvaty	holding Jack
	"Yes, I have become little"; babyish voice			

Sharon: Are you little? How come you are little?

Avshalom, raising Tzvaty toward Sharon, replied in a funny, high-pitched, screeching voice:

Avshalom: Can't you see me?!
Sharon: Yes, I can see you.

And then Sharon picked up another doll off the floor, representing a strong man, which she and Avshalom had named Jack. She changed her voice to make it "manly." She became Jack.

Sharon: Do you want me to become little too?

She didn't wait for Avshalom's answer. She squatted by Avshalom, holding Jack very close to Tzvaty. And then she changed her voice again. It became babyish.

Sharon: Yes, I have become little.

The results of the analysis are displayed in Appendix Table 1.

Substep 2 (analyzing the tabulated observation into minimal signifier-signified units)

The second step in analyzing a make-believe play text is identifying and listing the building blocks of which the text is constructed, the basic, minimal signifier-signified units of which it is composed. Easier said than done. As will be seen below, this is not at all a simple task and conclusive results are difficult to come by.

A minimal unit is a unit that cannot be separated into constituent parts which still keep their original identity. A vase with water and flowers, for instance, is a complex structure, not a minimal unit. It can be separated into three constituent parts: the vase, the flowers and the water. Each of these parts, having been separated from the other parts, preserves its original identity. The vase itself, however, is a minimal unit. If it is broken to pieces, none of the pieces will be a vase any more.

Let us look at Appendix Table 1 again. Which of the behavioral features classified by this table constitute together minimal units? What about the following features, for instance?

1. Avshalom: I'm little (verbal-vocal marker of "littleness").
2. childish voice (vocal marker of "littleness").
3. Tzvaty (a "little" doll).
4. Tzvaty stands on the floor (*the lowest plane*, apparently a spatial marker of "littleness" or perhaps of Tzvaty's humble position).

Is the aggregate consisting of these features a minimal unit or a complex structure? On the face of it, it should definitely be taken to be a complex structure, because in this aggregate each of the features, considered separately, seems to preserve its original identity. There is a flaw in this argument, however. The relevant question is not whether the distinct identity of each feature is preserved in the English language or in our general knowledge base, but whether each feature has an independent singularity in Avshalom and Sharon's language of make-believe play. It may well be that in this language various features which appear to us to be independent have become, taken together, an inseparable unit. Comparing this to idioms such as "kick the bucket" or "cream of the crop" or frozen compounds such as "horseback" and "backbone" the constituent words in such expressions have lost their independent status as separate units. Children create ad hoc combinations of signifying features in their make-believe play (see below). In some cases such ad hoc combinations get stabilized. They become the idioms of the make-believe play of particular children or specific groups of children.

One way to find out whether what looks like an ad hoc combination of features constitutes a single signifier-signified unit or not is the following. All the occurrences of the features in question in a sufficiently large make-believe play text are inspected. The purpose of the inspection is to learn whether the incidences of these features are independent or interdependent. This can be determined by the question whether the occurrence of any of the features in the aggregate is regularly accompanied by the occurrence of all the other features, or not. If the features are interdependent in this sense, one must conclude that they constitute together a single minimal unit.

Admittedly, Observation 13 is not sufficiently detailed or accurate for such an inspection to yield conclusive results. A quick look at Appendix Table 1 indicates, however, that the feature *occupying the lowest plane* (standing on the floor) is not interdependent with the other features mentioned above. Soon enough, Avshalom raised Tzvaty to a higher plane, toward Sharon. This shows that *occupying the lowest plane* is not an inseparable part of the signifier-signified unit "littleness."

Since the accurate dissection of a text to valid minimal signifier-signified units is, as shown above, a complicated task, one can rely, for most practical purposes, mainly on one's intuition in accomplishing this task.

Second Step: Identifying and Describing Structures

A structure is a combination of minimal signifier-signified units. Not every such combination is a structure, however. For a combination of units to be considered a structure, the signified contents of the units must be interrelated, adding up together to a significant whole.

Consider the following combination of units, produced by Sharon (see the table): [*holding Jack* + *squatting by Avshalom, very close to Tzvaty* + *saying* "Do you want me to become little too?" + *manly voice*]. This combination is a structure in the above sense, because the units are thematically interrelated and convey a complete idea, which can be paraphrases as "A big, strong man called Jack is asking little Tzvaty, who became little, if he wants him to become little too."

Structures can be simple or complex. Complex structures consist of simple structures embedded within other simple structures or chained to other simple structures:

Avshalom: I'm Ofree. I don't know why you've shrunk. Did you drink a potion your mother prepared?

Third Step: Identifying and Describing the Uses of Structures, Their Creators' Presuppositions and Purposes

Most structures have well-defined *uses*. Children use the structures they create in their make-believe games as tools for achieving their interpersonal goals. This use is discussed in detail in Chapter 3.

There are structures whose uses are derived from their very nature. This is the case for instance with salutations such as "good morning" and gestures such as a military salute. This is not always the case, however. On many occasions the maker of a structure is free to decide about its particular context-dependent uses.

In order to describe a use of the latter, elective, kind, one has, as it were, to read the mind of the creator of the structure, to guess his *presuppositions* and *purposes* with respect to his mate.

In the example above Sharon, as Jack, asked Avshalom, assuming a "manly" voice: "Do you want me to become little too?" She didn't wait for Avshalom's answer. She squatted by Avsahlom, and then said in a babyish voice: "Yes, I have become little." Obviously, her presupposition (spelled out explicitly by her question "Do you want me to become little too?") was that Avshalom expected her to shrink to his size. Her purpose was to please Avshalom by fulfilling his expectation.

People's presuppositions and purposes are not always so obvious or explicit, however. In most cases, since people's minds cannot be read directly, the elective uses of structures, their creators' presuppositions and purposes, can only be inferred from the verbal and situational contexts in which the structures in question are embedded. Such deductions necessarily involve a considerable component of guesswork and conjecture. To demonstrate how such inferences are carried out, please look at the following structure extract of "The Shrunken People":

. . . *Avshalom*: I don't know anything about such a thing!

He crawled toward the pile of dolls and picked up a big doll representing a strikingly strong man. He spoke in a loud, self-assured voice.

Avshalom: Maybe I know!

What were Avshalom's presuppositions and purpose in saying "Maybe I know!"? Let us inspect the context for clues. We must be good detectives to find relevant clues because they are often concealed in the most unlikely places:

Avshalom (as The Ninja Turtle): Hey, Tommy and Tommy, I've shrunk too!
Sharon: Yes, but I should return myself to . . .

She got up and hurried to another pile of dolls in the corner of the room. She returned with a silvery doll representing a strong man. She spoke in a determined intonation.

Sharon: Yes, and I've become bad, and I would like to stay this way.

Avshalom (as baby Ninja Turtle): But how can we become big again?

Sharon placed the silvery doll in front of his Ninja Turtle and spoke.

Sharon: I don't know. Maybe my brother knows.

Then Avshalom changed his voice again, apparently speaking as "Tommy," her twin brother.

Avshalom: I don't know anything about such a thing!

He crawled toward the pile of dolls and picked up a big doll representing a strikingly strong man. He spoke in a loud, self-assured voice.

Avhshlom: Maybe I know!

Sharon: O, that's not bad.

With some effort, I have managed to find what looks to me like significant clues in the above extract. Prior to the production of this structure by Avshalom, he attempted to persuade Sharon to "be" the knowledgeable adult who can help him grow ("I've shrunk. . . . How can we become big again?"). Sharon consistently repelled these attempts of his. Although she did "become" big and strong (through the silvery doll), she refused to be helpful and supportive. She insisted on being "bad" ("Yes, and I've become bad, and I would like to stay this way"). Afterward she threw the ball back to Avshalom. It was he who was supposed to be resourceful and knowledgeable ("I don't know. Maybe my brother knows"). Avshalom, as Tommy, Sharon's "twin brother," refused to play this role ("I don't know anything about such a thing"), but subsequently he changed his identity and did "become" the big, strong, self-confident man who might be able to solve the problem.

It may be concluded that Avshalom produced the structure "strong man saying 'Maybe I know' in a loud, self-assured voice" on the *presupposition* that Sharon did not want to assume the role of the knowledgeable, helpful adult and expected him to be in this role instead. His *purpose* therefore was to live up to this expectation of hers, to show her that he was willing to comply with her wish.

Fourth Step: Spelling Out the Uses of Out-of-Play Structures that Say Something about In-Play Structures

The task of describing structures and their context-dependent uses is complicated by the fact that texts are often multilayered. Some structures are used to say something about other structures. Consider for instance the following conversation:

Mary: How much did this dress cost you?
Jane: What kind of question is that?

Jane's response belongs to a higher textual level than Mary's question. The former is a comment about the former.

One manifestation of this phenomenon is the distinction between in-play and out-of-play verbal and nonverbal structures in the language of make-believe play. Out-of-play structures are often used to say something *about* the play.

The uses of out-of play structures with respect to in-play structures can also be characterized by the concepts *presupposition* and *purpose*. Look for instance at Sharon's utterance "One should always choose the first decision." It seems to be an out-of-play structure referring to in-play structures. You are invited again to scrutinize the context of this utterance for clues to Sharon's presuppostions and purpose:

Sharon (poking Tzvaty again): Don't you know that I'm Batman? Don't you know that I used to be in your class?
Avshalom: What did you say your name was?
Sharon (drawing Bob's brother back): Maybe Jack. Haven't you thought about me?

The reason for Sharon's anger seemed to be clear now. She was hurt because Avshalom "forgot her."

Avshalom (emphatically): From our class? No. Jack is not from our class.

Sharon took hold of the silvery doll.

Sharon: Jack, you are not from our class, so why are you talking like that? . . . Last year. . . .

Avshalom, angry, began to hit Bob's brother with Tzvaty.

Avshalom: You are in second grade. Your are not in . . . sixth grade!
Sharon: Jack?
Avshalom: Yes. There's a Jack in sixth grade.

Sharon: Jack is in second grade. There's another Jack in eighth grade. He (Tzvaty?) didn't know.

Avhsalom: Are you Jack in eighth grade?

Sharon (as Bob's brother): Yes.

Avhaslom: We're Jack in the army . . . eh . . . Tommy, Tommy in the army.

Sharon (insistently): In eighth grade, eighth! Eighth! You are in eighth!

Avshalom, worked up, hit Bob's brother very hard with Tzvaty, tossing Bob's brother two yards away.

Avshalom (shouting): We're in the army!

Sharon, preserving her equanimity, went to retrieve Bob's brother.

Sharon (returning with Bob's brother): Army? First of all we are sixth grade. One should always choose the first decision.

The relevant in-play structure in this context seem to be Sharon's preceding expression "First of all we are in sixth grade," which, in turn, can be traced back to Avshalom's previous words "Jack is not from our class . . . You're not in sixth grade . . . Yes, there's Jack in sixth grade." Sharon's out-of-play structure "One should always choose the first decision" is an arbitrary rule she made up in order to beat Avshalom in the rather impassioned negotiations between them about Jack's age and school class affiliation. In this argument, Sharon, who had identified herself as Jack, wanted to convince Avshalom (as Tzvaty) that Jack used to be in the same class and of the same age as him, whereas Avshalom insisted that Jack was younger. It may be concluded that Sharon produced the structure "One should always choose the first decision" on the following *presuppositions*: (1) Avshalom wants me to "be" younger than he is. (2) His resistance to "being" of the same age as I am is not insurmountable, as evidenced by his previous willingness to admit that "There's a Jack in sixth grade." Sharon's *purpose* in having produced this structure was then to persuade Avshalom to agree to "be" close to her in age and past school class.

Clearly, the analysis of the presuppositions and purposes of in-play and out-of-play structures and the formulation of rules applying to these presuppositions and purposes can throw light on central aspect of the interpersonal relations among playmates. This subject is taken up again below and was discussed in detail in Chapters 3 and 4.

MACROSCOPIC ANALYSIS AND RULE FORMULATION

Fifth step: Formulating Rules

The next step in a rigorous analysis of play texts is formulating rules. Rules are generalizations. They are formulas describing general constraints on combinations of categories of units into structures. The word "categories" should be stressed. Rules say something about categories of units, not about single units. The rules of English do not apply to specific words but to word categories such as nouns, verbs and prepositions. The rules of musicology apply to such categories as major scales, minor scales and rhythmic patterns, not to particular notes. Likewise, formulating the rules of make-believe play requires the classification of signifiers-signified units into categories. A major heuristic technique involving such classification is *Context-Dependent Componential Analysis*. It helps categorize signifiers and signified by meaningful dimensions and reveal important hierarchical interrelations among these dimensions. It therefore considerably facilitates the subsequent formulation of rules.

Context-Dependent Componential Analysis

Componential Analysis is a technique developed by anthropological linguists as a method for revealing and describing semantic systems, that is, covert interrelations among meanings of words in various "exotic" languages (see Hammel, 1965). *Context-Dependent Componential Analysis* (CDCA) is my own elaboration of this technique. To illustrate this technique, let me apply it to samples of signifiers and signified units of "The Shrunken People."

CDCA of a Sample of Minimal Signifiers Produced by Avshalom

First Step (listing units with the contexts in which they occur).

Signifying unit: small-size doll called Tzvaty

Contexts: held in hand while player is sitting on the floor; held close to Ninja Turtle doll; facing the latter; raised toward doll held by standing player; hitting doll called Bob's brother, shouting loudly; hitting doll called Jack; shaking violently; rotating high in the air; speaking in a babyish voice.

Signifying unit: doll called Ninja Turtle

Contexts: facing Tzvaty, close to it; speaking in a choking voice; speaking in a cynical intonation.

Signifying unit: strong doll

Contexts: speaking loudly; speaking in a self-assured voice; speaking in a harsh voice.

Signifying unit: body of player as signifier

Contexts: standing erect; speaking in soft, quiet voice or in an ordinary speaking voice.

Signifying unit: hitting
Contexts: Jack with Tzvaty; Bob's Brother with Tzvaty; angry voice.

Signifying unit: raising Tzvaty
Context: after having hit Jack.

Signifying unit: speaking in a high-pitched, screeching voice
Context: while raising Tzvaty.

Signifying unit: loud shouting
Contexts: Tzvaty, while hitting Bob's Brother; Tzvaty, shaking violently.

Signifying unit: speaking in an angry voice
Context: Tzvaty, while hitting Jack.

Signifying unit: speaking in a harsh voice
Context: strong doll

It will be observed that all the units and all the contexts, being signifiers rather than signified contents, consist of perceptible entities, which can be seen, heard or otherwise directly sensed.

Second Step (pairwise comparisons of units with their contexts, extracting common components)

Each unit with its contexts is compared with each other unit-contexts. For each pair, the following questions are asked: (a) What are the common dimensions (components) shared by the units-contexts compared? (b) What contrasts or differentiates these units-contexts along these common components?

To get the hang of these questions, let us apply them to the pair "the tall man versus the short woman." The components common to the members of this pair are *height* and *gender*. The contrasts along these common components are the values *greater* and *lesser* for *height*, and the values *male* and *female* for *gender*.

Since presenting this step in detail requires a great deal of space, let me illustrate the comparisons just with two pairs of units-contexts:

First pair:

Small-size doll called Tzvaty—held in hand while player is sitting on the floor; held close to Ninja Turtle doll; facing the latter; raised toward doll held by standing player; hitting doll called Bob's brother, shouting loudly; hitting doll called Jack; shaking violently; rotating high in the air; speaking in a babyish voice.

Body of player as signifier—standing erect; speaking in soft, quiet voice or in an ordinary speaking voice. Common components and differentiating values: size (big, small); loudness (loud, normal, soft).

Second pair:

Body of player as signifier—standing erect; speaking in soft, quiet voice or in an ordinary
    speaking voice.
Strong doll—speaking loudly; speaking in a self-assured voice; speaking in a harsh voice.

Common components and differentiating values: loudness (loud, soft), intonation (straight, self-assured).

The complete analysis has yielded the following components, with their differentiating values:

line of movement (straight, rotational, twisted)

height of movement (high, low)

direction of movement (horizontal, upward, downward)

proximity (distant, close, touching lightly, touching pressingly)

power of contact (powerful, light)

posture (erect, lax)

strength (strong, weak)

size (big, small)

pitch (high, low)

loudness (loud, normal, soft)

intonation (straight, cynical, surprised, self-assured)

Third Step (drawing supercomponents)
Supercomponents are common to components extracted in the third step.

Supercomponent 1: power (common to the components *strength, power of contact, size,
    loudness* and *proximity*).
Supercomponent 2: plane (common to the component *line of movement, height of move-
    ment, direction of movement, posture* and *pitch*).
Supercomponent 3: linearity (common to the components *line of movement* and *intona-
    tion*).

Fourth Step (drawing supersupercomponents)
The fourth step is drawing at least one supersupercomponent, common to all
the supercomponents drawn in the third step. If no single supersupercomponent
has been found, supersupercomponents common to subgroups of supercomponents will be searched for. The supersupercomponent common to all the above
supercomponents is *energy*.

Fifth Step (organizing the results in a single configuration)
The fifth and last step is organizing all the results of the previous steps in a
single configuration (a table, a diagram or the like) displaying their interrelations. A word of caution: This step is far from being easy, straightforward or

Appendix Table 2
Results of CDCA for Avshalom's Signifiers in The Shrunken People

Energy	very energetic	less energetic	least energetic
Power			
force	strong	not too strong	weak
power of contact	powerful	not too powerful	light
magnitude	large	average	small
loudness	loud	normal	soft
voice maturity	mature		childish
proximity	touching pressingly	touching lightly; close	distant
Plane			
height of movement	high	intermediate	low
direction of movement	upward (all the way)	same level; upward (part of the way)	downward
posture	erect		lax
pitch	high	intermediate	low
Linearity			
line of movement	rotational	twisted	straight
intonation	cynical, surprised		straight

self-evident. It takes power of abstraction and creative thinking. Such a configuration is a theory about the data. If it is not insightful and revealing then it should not be considered a good theory.

Appendix Table 2 is one such configuration. It tells us that the signified contents produced by Avshalom in "The Shrunken People" are conveyed by varying the level of energy invested in moving the player's body and dolls in space and in the players' speech. In order to express his concerns, Avshalom alternates between putting out more powerful and less powerful gestures and speech sounds. He goes from movements on the horizontal plane to the more energy-consuming movements on the vertical plane and back. He takes turns between linear and nonlinear motions and intonations.

For comparison, CDCA was conducted with respect to Sharon's signifiers in "The Shrunken People" too. The results, which, due to shortage of space, are not presented here, justify the postulation of *energy* as the single super-supercomponent common to all the signifiers in Sharon's play. The main difference between Sharon's and Avshalom's resulting configurations is the absence of the components subsumed under the supercomponent *plane* in Sharon's configuration. This means that Sharon, in distinction to Avshalom, did not express signified contents by moving alternately on the horizontal and vertical planes. Another difference between Sharon's and Avshalom's system of signifiers has to do with the use of voice. Sharon did not use varied intonations, but did employ variations in maturity of voice.

Appendix Table 3
Results of CDCA of Avshalom's Signified in The Shrunken People

Potency	potent	somewhat potent	not potent
Growth			
size	big	intermediate	little
change of size	growing		shrinking
size-difference	different		same
age	adulthood	older childhood	young childhood
age-difference	different		same
strength	great	intermediate	little
generation	parental		sibling
cuteness		non-cute	cute
visibility	visible		invisible
shrinking-			
causing agents	potion, magic		
Relationships			
Closeness	close	intermediate	distant
group relationships	stranger coming	visiting	in-group
level of relationship	vertical		horizontal
physical aggression	aggressor		victim
States of mind			
knowledge	knowing		ignorance
volition	wanting		not wanting

The same technique was applied to the signified contents of Avshalom's and Sharon's play. Appendix Table 3 shows the results for Avshalom.

CDCA of a Sample of Minimal Signified Produced by Avshalom in "The Shrunken People"

First Step (List of minimal signified units in contexts)

Signified unit: The person Tzvaty

Contexts: has become little (shrunken); surprised that Tommy cannot see that he has become little; rose toward Tommy for him to see that he has become little; wanted to know if Tommy could see him; Tzvaty did not know that he had become little; Tzvaty hit Jack; Tzvaty wanted to get over the situation (of having become little), to be big again; the Ninja turtle came close to Tzvaty.

Singnified unit: the person Jack

Contexts: Tzvaty hit Jack; Tzvaty did not want Jack to become little; Jack was in second grade; Jack was not in sixth grade.

Signified unit: the person Ninja Turtle

Contexts: the Ninja Turtle came close to Tzvaty; the Ninja Turtle wanted to know if anybody was speaking; the Ninja Turtle derided the idea that Jack was of the same class in school as he; the Ninja Turtle used to be a fighter but had become little (teeny weeny); the Ninja Turtle was choking; somebody pounced upon the Ninja Turtle.

Signified unit: strong man

Contexts: the strong man knew perhaps how to make the shrunken people big again; the strong man claimed that he was the silvery doll's classmate; the strong man shrank Tommy and Tommy.

Signified units: Tommy and Tommy

Contexts: Merdy came to visit Tommy and Tommy; Merdy did not know where Tommy and Tommy were; Jack was not Tommy and Tommy's classmate; Ofree asked Tommy and Tommy what happened to them; Tommy and Tommy's mother perhaps prepared a shrinking potion; the strong man shrank Tommy and Tommy

Signified unit: Merdy

Contexts: Merdy came to visit Tommy and Tommy; Merdy did not know where Tommy and Tommy were.

Signified unit: Ofree

Contexts: Ofree asked Tommy and Tommy what happened to them.

Signified unit: little (shrunken)

Contexts: Tzvaty became little (shrunken); Tzvaty didn't know that he had become little; Tzvaty did not want Jack to become little; the Ninja Turtle had become little (teeny weeny); Tommy and Tommy became little, perhaps because they had drunk a potion their mother prepared.

Signified unit: big (grown)

Contexts: Tzvaty wanted to become big (grown) again; Tommy and Tommy were big; Merdy was big; Tzvaty wanted to know how to become big again.

Signified unit: want

Contexts: Tzvaty wanted to become big (grown) again; Tzvaty wanted to know how to become big again.

Signified unit: see

Context: Tzvaty wanted to know if Tommy could see him.

Signified unit: know

Contexts: Merdy did not know where Tommy and Tommy were; Tzvaty did not know that he had become little; Tzvaty wanted to know how he had become shrunken; Tzvaty wanted to know how to become big again; Tommy did not know how to make the shrunken people become big again; the strong doll knew perhaps how to make shrunken people big again.

Signified unit: visit

Context: Merdy (with others) came to visit Tommy and Tommy.

Signified unit: classmate

Contexts: the Ninja Turtle derided the idea that he was Tommy and Tommy's classmate; the strong man claimed that he was the silvery doll's classmate; Jack was not Tommy and Tommy's classmate.

Signified unit: second grade

Contexts: Jack was in second grade.

Signified unit: sixth grade

Context: Jack was not in sixth grade.

Signified unit: army

Contexts: there's a Jack in the army; we are in the army; I am not a soldier (not in the army).

Signified unit: brother

Context: the silvery, winged doll was not Bob's brother.

Signified unit: son

Context: the winged doll was the son of the Robot.

Signfied unit: mother

Context: Tommy and Tommy's mother perhaps prepared a shrinking potion.

Signified unit: potion

Context: Tommy and Tommy shrank perhaps because they drank a potion their mother prepared.

Signified unit: cuter types

Contexts: the strong man shrank Tommy and Tommy because he wanted to show that there were cuter types than himself.

Second Step (pairwise comparisons, extracting common components)

Again, the analysis itself will not be presented here. Here are the resulting components:

size (big, little)

change of size (shrinking, growing)

size-difference (same, different)

age (baby-age, 2nd grade, 6th grade, 8th grade, army)

age-difference (same, different)

strength (strong, weak)

level of relationship (horizontal, vertical)

generation (parental, sibling)

cuteness (noncute, cute)

visibility (visible, invisible)

shrinking causing agents (potion, magic)

proximity (distant, close)

group relationship cohesion (in-group, visiting, stranger coming)

knowledge (knowing, ignorance)

volition (wanting, not wanting)

physical aggression (aggressor, victim)

Third Step (drawing supercomponents)

Supercomponent 1: growth (common to the components *size, change of size, size-difference, age, age-difference, strength, generation, cuteness, visibility, shrinking causing agents*).

Supercomponent 2: relationships (common to the components *proximity* and *group relationship, level of relationship* and *physical aggression*).

Supercomponent 3: states of mind (common to the components *knowledge and volition*).

Fourth Step (drawing super-supercomponents)

The super-supercomponent common to all the above supercomponents is *potency*.

Fifth Step (organizing the results in a single configuration)

One possible configuration is presented in Appendix Table 3.

What the configuration in Appendix Table 3 tells us is that Avshalom's signified contents in "The Shrunken People" center around the single super-superdimension of *potency*. These contents alternate between potent and less potent ones. Potency is manifested in the areas of *growth, relationships* and *states of mind*. Growing or grown characters such as "Jack" before he shrank and "the strong doll" are more potent than shrinking or undergrown ones such as "Tzvaty." Asymmetric relationships between grown-up outsiders approaching in-group undergrown characters with good or bad intentions (e.g., "Merdy" versus shrunken "Tommy and Tommy") are more potent than symmetric in-group relationships among undergrown characters (e.g., shrunken "Tommy and Tommy" versus shrunken "Ninja fighter"). States of mind of knowing and wanting are more potent than ignorance and indifference.

For comparison, the same analysis was conducted with respect to Sharon's signified contents. The results were very similar to Avshalom's but there were some noticeable differences. Sharon's configuration lacked a component of physical aggression, but did include three components representing states of mind that were absent from Avshalom's play: *badness, well-being* and *empathy*. The component of closeness in Sharon's play included, furthermore, a greater variety of manifestations of physical touching than in Avshalom's.

It should be noted also, that although this is not reflected in the results of the CDCA, Sharon, in her play, attributed ignorance to characters representing herself and knowledge to other characters, contrary to Avshalom.

Notwithstanding these differences, the results of the CDCAs for Avshalom's and Sharon's play are strikingly similar. This resemblance reflects the like-mindedness of these close friends, whose play partnership had been long-standing.

How Do the Results of the CDCAs Facilitate the Formulation of Rules?

CDCA has been introduced here, it will be recalled, as a heuristic technique, facilitating the process of inferring rules (constraints on combinations of categories of units into structures) from observed data. How can the results presented above assist one in this process? First, by displaying a nonarbitrary, well-grounded, meaningful classification of minimal units found in the play text into categories and subcategories such as *moving upward as a sign of heightened energy* or *growth from invisibility to visibility*. Second, the results of the analysis imply possible constraints on interrelations among these categories and subcategories. Signifiers of the same energy level and signified of the same potency level, for instance, are more likely to co-occur in the same structures than signifiers and signified of different levels of energy and potency. For example, *standing erect* is more likely to co-occur, within the same structure, with *speaking loudly* than with *speaking softly*. Likewise, *shrinking* may be expected to go together with *being a victim* rather than with *being an aggressor*.

Following are characterizations of some general structural interrelations among categories of signifiers and signified implied by the above CDCAs. These characterizations represent a further step toward the formulation of rules.

Correspondence Between Signifiers and Signified

Since the function of signifiers is to convey contents, the components of signifiers must somehow correspond to the components of signified for each player. In general, for both Avshalom and Sharon, greater exertion of *energy* signifies greater *potency*. In terms of the supercomponents and the components subsumed under them, stronger, bigger and louder puppets and humans (e.g., "Jack," "the Ninja Turtle"), movements in or toward the higher plane (e.g., "Avshalom got up abruptly . . . and began speaking in a 'grown up' voice"), erect postures, rotational line of movement and higher pitch—all these signify bigger, more grown characters and also greater dominance or aggression in relationships, as well as a knowing, highly motivated state of mind, and vice versa.

An examination of the correspondences between signifier and signified components in "The Shrunken People" revealed one-to-many relations. With few exceptions, each component of signifiers was found to correspond to several components of signifies. The expressive means (signifiers) of make-believe play are economical. Each type of signifiers marks more than one and usually many types of signifieds.

Fluctuations of Energy and Potency in the Play Text

"The Shrunken People" is characterized by continuous fluctuations between higher and lower levels of energy and potency. These fluctuations assume the form of a wave, whose curves alternate between peaks and valleys of energy and potency. This wave form represents the core conflict expressed in "The Shrunken People": The conflict between wishing to grow up and wanting to remain very young or even become babies again.

Consider, for instance, Avshalom's curve of growing and then diminishing energy and potency in the following excerpt. The values of components in square brackets are taken from Appendix Tables 2 and 3.

Avshalom (as baby Ninja Turtle): But how can we become big again? [small magnitude, childish voice maturity=low energy; little size, young childhood, ignorance=low potency]

Sharon placed the silvery doll in front of his Ninja Turtle and spoke.

Sharon: I don't know. Maybe my brother knows.

Then Avshalom changed his voice again, apparently speaking as "Tommy," her twin brother.

Avshalom: I don't know anything about such a thing! [ignorance = low potency; normal loudness = growing energy]

He crawled toward the pile of dolls and picked up a big doll representing a strikingly strong man. He spoke in a loud, self-assured voice.

Avhshlom: Maybe I know! [strong force, large magnitude, loud voice, mature voice = high energy; big size, adulthood, great strengh, knowing state of mind = high potency]

Sharon (raising the silvery doll, directing it toward the strong man): O, that's not bad. (silence). . . . Everything is alright . . .

Avshalom: Not really. We have shrunk. Is this alright? [shrinking, ignorance = low potency]

The following lists display the sequences of low, medium and high levels of energy and potency reflected in the succession of signifiers and signified in "The Shrunken People".

Avshalom's Sequence List

Energy: low, medium, high, low, high, medium, high, medium, high, high, medium, high, low, high, high, high, high, high, high, low, high.

Potency: medium, low, medium, high, medium, high, medium, low, medium, high, medium, low, low, low, low, low, high, low, high, low, medium, high, low, high, high, high, high, low, medium, low, high, high, high, high, low.

Sharon's Sequence List

Energy: high, medium, low, low, high, low, low, low, medium, high, high, low, medium, high, high, medium, high, high.

Potency: low, medium, high, low, low, low, medium, low, high, low, low, low, low, low, medium, high, low, medium, medium, medium, low, high, high, high, high, high, low, medium, medium, high.

These lists reflect the continuous fluctuations discussed above quite well.

It will be observed that there is a very high correlation between the levels of energy and potency for each player. That is, in the great majority of cases when the level of energy is low, medium or high, the level of potency is also low, medium or high, correspondingly.

A Syntactic Rule Governing the Play Interactions Between Avshalom and Sharon

The following informal analysis was proposed above: "The two players (Avshalom and Sharon) keep going back and forth between preferring to be of the same size or age and wanting to be differentiated from each other in this respect." This analysis can be extended to incorporate the results of the CDCAs, presented above. The following syntactic rule is the end product of this extended analysis:

- IF a player (Avshalom or Sharon) has produced a structure containing signifiers and signified of the same level of energy-potency as the other player's,
- THEN the other player will respond by generating a structure of a different (higher or lower) energy-potency level.

And, vice versa:

- IF a player has produced a signifier-signified structure of a different (higher or lower) energy-potency level,
- THEN the other player will respond by generating a unit (structure) of the same energy-potency level as the other player's.

This rule accords with the picture of continuous fluctuations between higher and lower levels of energy and potency discussed above.

The following analysis of the beginning part of "The Shrunken People" illustrates the validity of this rule. At the onset of the observed activity, Avshalom was sitting on the floor (the low plane) holding Tzvaty (a small doll). According to Appendix Table 2, *low height of movement* and *small magnitude* are least energetic signifying features. Sharon was standing near him, occupying a high plane of movement, a *very energetic* signifying feature. Then Avshalom began speaking in a childish voice, a *least energetic* feature. He said "Can't you see that I am little?" These words, implying that he took Sharon to be *big* (high energy and potency), include the signified features of *littleness* and *invisibility*, least potent according to Appendix Table 3.

So far the energy-potency polarity between Avshalom and Sharon's play were complete. At this point Sharon said: "Are you little? How come you are little?" This utterance already includes some rapprochement, approaching Avshalom's lower energy-potency level, because it implies the signified feature of *ignorance*, a least potent feature according to Appendix Table 3.

Avshalom responded by raising Tzvaty toward Sharon (*moving upward part of the way*, a component of medium level of energy according to Appendix Table 2). He said in a high-pitched, screeching voice (a very energetic signifying feature): "Can't you see me?" Sharon answered: "Yes, I can see you." This reply included the signified feature *visible*, highly potent according to Appendix Table 3.

The partners, whose play had exhibited opposed levels of energy and potency at first, were moving gradually to equivalent, high energy-potency levels, in accordance with the syntactic rule spelled out above.

Sharon remained on this high level for a while, but then began going down, differentiating herself from Avshalom. She picked up Jack, a doll representing a strong man. She changed her voice to make it "manly" (*strong force* and *adult voice*, very energetic signifying features and very potent signified ones). But immediately afterward she asked Avshalom: "Do you want me to become little too?" By saying these words she yielded her own will to Avshalom (*low volition*—a least potent feature). She squatted by Avshalom (low plane = low energy), holding Jack very close to Tzvaty (close proximity, a feature of a medium energy level). She began speaking in a babyish voice (low energy-potency). She said: "Yes, I have become little" (low energy-potency).

Avshalom responded by saying: "But I didn't know I'd become little! So why are you becoming little?" In this question he professed his *ignorance*, a low-potency signified feature.

Both partners were now again on roughly the same energy-potency level. This equality would not last for long though. Soon enough, Avshalom began heightening the energy-potency level of his play. He began hitting Jack with Tzvaty (*aggressor*-high potency) and said: "I want us to get over this situation! . . . I want to be big again!" (*wanting* and *big*-high potency).

Such energy-potency fluctuations, summarized by the above syntactic rule, are manifested in all other parts of "The Shrunken People."

Tracing Purposes and Presuppositions to Arrive at the Players' Goals and Plans

As stated above, the analysis of the presuppositions and purposes of in-play and out-of-play structures and the formulation of rules applying to these presuppositions and purposes can throw light on a central aspect of the interpersonal relations among playmates. More specifically, it is hypothesized that all the play structures produced by each player are aimed at reaching specific interpersonal *goals* with respect to other players. Each player, furthermore, has a *plan* or a strategy for reaching his or her goals.

The task of uncovering and formulating the goals and plans of the playmates can be facilitated by examining the sequences of the players' purposes and presuppositions. Let me illustrate this from the beginning part of "The Shrunken People." Sharon's and Avshalom's hypothesized purposes and presuppositions of the participants are enclosed in square brackets:

Avshalom held Tzvaty on the floor, in a standing position. Sharon stood near him. Avshalom spoke in a childish voice.

Avshalom: Can't you see that I am little?

[*Avhsalom's presupposition*: "Sharon does not understand my play move." *Avshalom's purpose*: making Sharon understand my play move.]
    Sharon looked confused.

Sharon: Are you little? How come you are little?

[*Sharon's presupposition* "Avshalom is trying to make me understand his play move." *Sharon's purpose*: to convey to Avshalom my surprise at his play move and my difficulty to understand why he chose this move and how the change happened.]
    Avshalom raised Tzvaty toward Sharon and replied in a funny, high-pitched, screeching voice:

Avshalom: Can't you see me?!

[*Avshalom's presupposition*: Sharon still cannot refuses to understand my play move. *Avhsalom's purpose*: to make Sharon understand my play move.]

Sharon: Yes, I can see you.

[*Sharon's presupposition*: Avshalom wants me to accept his play move even if I don't fully understand it. He has no patience to explain. *Sharon's purpose*: to let Avshalom know that I accept his move and his unwillingness to explain.]
    And then Sharon picked up another doll off the floor, representing a strong

man, which she and Avshalom had named Jack. She changed her voice to make it "manly." She became Jack.

Sharon: Do you want me to become little too?

She didn't wait for Avshalom's answer. She squatted by Avsahlom, holding Jack very close to Tzvaty. And then she changed her voice again. It became babyish.

Sharon: Yes, I have become little.

[*Sharon's presuppostion*: Avshalom wants me to join him and make the same play move as his. *Sharon's purpose*: to comply with Avshalom's supposed wish.]
Avshalom didn't like the idea. He spoke angrily:

Avshalom: But I didn't *know* I'd become little! So why are you becoming little? . . . It's not that I want you to become little!

[*Avshalom's presuppositions*: Sharon has not understood what I have been trying to express by my play move and how I have been expecting her to respond. *Avshalom's purpose*: to express my disapproval of Sharon's having made a play move without understanding my own play move and without taking into account what I have been expecting of her.]
To expose the participants' *goals* one should examine their *purposes*, with view to tracing a common direction. The common thread linking Avshalom's purposes seems to be his wish that Sharon read his mind and follow his lead. His goal was therefore to control her mind and her behavior. Sharon's purposes on the other hand were characterized by efforts to understand Avshalom's whims and comply. Her goal appears to be submission.
The players' *plans* or *strategies* for reaching their goals can be exposed by inspecting both their presuppositions and their purposes. When a player presupposes that he or she cannot achieve his or her purpose, this player can, as a tactical move, adopt a different purpose, which however is aimed at the same goal. A player's *plan* for reaching his or her goal consists of such tactical moves. For example, Sharon at first presupposed that Avshalom was trying to make her understand his play moves. Accordingly, her purpose was to convey to Avshalom her surprise at his play move and her difficulty to understand why he chose this move and how the change happened. Afterward, however, having encountered Avshalom's responses, she discarded the previous presupposition and adopted a new one: "Avshalom wants me to accept his play move even if I don't fully understand it. He has no patience to explain." And then, maintaining her goal of submitting to Avshalom's whims, she switched to a different purpose: "to let Avshalom know that I accept his move and his unwillingness to

explain." Such analysis facilitates the formulation of the players' plans for reaching their goals:

Sharon's plan for reaching her goal of submitting to Avshalom's will: IF I don't understand Avshalom's thoughts and expectations of me, I ask him to explain himself so that I can comply. IF he refuses to explain, I try to read his mind, and do what I have guessed he wanted me to do.

Avshalom's plan for reaching his goal of controlling Sharon's mind and behavior: IF Sharon is unable to read my mind and understand my expectations of her, I provide minimal explanations. IF she misunderstands me and acts not in accordance with my expectations, I scold her.

Let me stress that the sole purpose of the above analysis has been to illustrate a heuristic technique. The extract analyzed is too short to draw any valid generalizations about Avshalom's and Sharon's goals and plans.

The technique of tracing the players' purposes and presuppositions as a way of arriving at their goals and plans was discussed and illustrated, in more detail, in Chapter 3.

Other kinds of rules of the language of make-believe play were discussed in Chapters 3–5.

References

Abramovitz, R. (1995). *Cybernetics of cybernetics*. Minneapolis: Future Systems.

Adams, C.R. (1978). Distinctive features of play and games: A folk model from Southern Africa. In Schwartzman, H.B. (Ed.), *Play and culture*. West Point, NY: Leisure Press. pp. 150–162.

Akmajian, A., Demers, A., Farmer, A.K. and Harnish, R.M. (1995). *Linguistics: An introduction to language and communication*. Boston: MIT Press.

Aldis, O. (1975). *Play fighting*. New York: Academic Press.

Allan, J. (1997). Jungian play psychotherapy. In O'Connor, K.J. and Braverman, L.M. (Eds.), *Play therapy, theory and practice: a comparative presentation*. New York: Wiley, pp. 100–130.

Amen, E.W. and Renison, N. (1954). A study of the relationship between play patterns and anxiety in young children. *Genetic Psychology Monographs* 50, 3–41.

Ardrey, R. (1966). *The territorial imperative: A personal inquiry into the animal origins of property and nations*. New York: Atheneum.

Ariel, S. (1984). Locutions and illocutions in make-believe play. *Journal of Pragmatics* 8, 221–240.

Ariel, S. (1987). An information processing theory of family dysfunction. *Psychotherapy* 24, 477–494.

Ariel, S. (1992). Semiotic analysis of children's play: A method for investigating social development. *Merrill-Palmer Quarterly* 38, 119–138.

Ariel, S. (1994). *Strategic family play therapy*. 2nd paperback edition. Chichester: Wiley.

Ariel, S. (1996). Re-storying family therapy. *Contemporary Family Therapy* 18, 3–17.

Ariel, S. (1997). Strategic family play therapy. In O'Connor, K.J. and Braverman, L.M. (Eds.), *Play therapy, theory and practice*. New York: Wiley, pp. 368–395.

Ariel, S. (1999). *Culturally competent family therapy: A general model*. Westport, CT: Praeger.

Ariel, S., Carel, C. and Tyano, S. (1984) A formal explication of the concept of family homeostasis. *Journal of Marital and Family Therapy* 10, 337–349.

Ariel, S. Carel, C. and Tyano, S. (1985). Make-believe play techniques in family therapy. *Journal of Marital and Family Therapy* 11, 47–60.

Ariel, S. and Peled, O. (2000). Group work with children and adolescents in an integrative therapeutic framework [Hebrew text]. *Mikbatz, The Journal of the Israeli Association of Group Therapy* 5, 42–60.

Ariel, S. and Sever, I. (1980). Play in the desert and play in the town: On play activities of Bedouin Arab children. In Schwartzman, H.B. (Ed.), *Play and culture*. West Point, NY: Leisure Press, pp. 164–175.

Aronson, K. and Thorell, M. (1998). Family politics in children's play directives. *Journal of Pragmatics* 31, 25–47.

Asher, S.R. and Coie, J.D. (1990). *Peer rejection in childhood*. New York: Cambridge University Press.

Auwaerter, M. (1986). Development of communicative skills: The construction of fictional reality in children's play. In Cook-Gumpertz, C., Corsaro, W. and Strecks, J. (Eds.), *Children's worlds and children's language*. Amesterdam: Mouton de Gruyter, pp. 205–230.

Axline, V. (1947). *Play therapy: The inner dynamics of childhood*. Boston: Houghton Mifflin.

Axline, V. (1964). Non-directive therapy. In Haworth, M. (Ed.), *Child psychotherapy: Practice and theory*. New York: Basic Books, pp. 34–39.

Bach, G.R. (1945) Young children's play fantasies. *Psychological Monographs* 59, 3–69.

Bakeman, R. and Brownlee, J.R. (1980). The strategic use of parallel play: A sequential analysis. *Child Development* 51, 873–878.

Barnard, A. and Spencer, J. (Eds.) (1998). *Encyclopedia of social and cultural anthropology*. London: Routledge.

Bateson, G. (1955). A theory of play and fantasy. *Psychiatric Research Reports* 2, 39–51.

Bateson, G. (1956). The message "This is play." In Schaffner, B. (Ed.), *Group processes*. New York: Josiah Macy.

Bateson, G. (1977). *Steps to an ecology of mind*. New York: Ballantine.

Bauman, R. (Ed.) (1975). *Black girls at play: Folkloristic perspective on child development*. Washington DC: National Institute of Education.

Beaugrande, R.A. (1980). The pragmatics of discourse planning. *Journal of Pragmatics* 44, 15–42.

Beran, J.A. (1973a). Characteristics of children's play and games in the Southern Philippines. *Silliman Journal* 20, 100–113.

Beran, J.A. (1973b). Some elements of power in Filipino children's play. *Silliman Journal* 20, 194–207.

Black, B. (1992). Negotiating social pretend play: Communication differences related to social status and sex. *Merrill-Palmer Quarterly* 38, 212–232.

Blanchard, K. (1981). *The Mississippi Choctaws at play*. Urbana: University of Illinois Press.

Blaney, P.H. (1986). Affect and memory: A review. *Psychological Bulletin* 99, 229–246.

Blatchford, P. (1998). The state of play in schools. *Child Psychology and Psychiatry Review* 3, 58–67.

Bloch, M.N. and Adler, S.M. (1994). African children's play and the emergence of sexual division of labor. In Roopnarine, J.L, Johnson, J.E. and Hooper, F.H. (Eds.), *Children's play in diverse cultures*. Albany: State University of New York Press, pp. 148–178.

Bloch, M.N. and O'Rourke, Sh. (1982). The non-social play behavior of young Senegalese children: Sex differences and the effect of maternal employment. In Loy, J. (Ed.), *Paradoxes of play*. West Point, NY: Leisure Press.

Bloch, M.N. and Pellegrini, A.D. (1989). *The ecological context of children's play*. New York: Academic Press.

Boggs, S. (1978). The development of verbal disputing in part-Hawaiian children. *Language in Society* 7, 325–344.

Bornstein, M.H. and O'Reilly, A.W. (Eds.) (1993). *The role of play in the development of thought: New direction for child development*. San Francisco: Jossey-Bass.

Bower, E., Ligaz-Carden, A. and Noori, K. (1982). Measurement of play structures: Cross-cultural considerations. *Journal of Cross-Cultural Psychology* 13, 315–329.

Brainerd, C.J. (1982). Effects of group and individualized dramatic play training on cognitive development. In Pepler, D.J. and Rubin, K.H. (Eds.), *The play of children: Current theory and research*. Contributions to Human Development 6. New York: S. Krager, pp. 114–129.

Bretherton, I. (Ed.) (1984). *Symbolic play: The development of social understanding*. New York: Academic Press.

Bretherton, I. (1989). Pretense: The form and functions of make-believe play. *Developmental Review* 9, 383–401.

Bruner, J.S., Jolly, A. and Sylva, K. (1976). *Play: Its role in development and evolution*. Middlesex: Penguin.

Carlson, S.M., Taylor, M. and Levin, G.R. (1998). The influence of culture on pretend play: The case of Mennonite children. *Merrill-Palmer Quarterly* 44, 538–565

Cattanagh, A. (1998). The role of play in the life of the child. *Child Psychology and Psychiatry Review* 3, 113–114.

Centner, T. (1962). *L'enfant africain et ses jeux*. Elisabetville, Congo: CEPSI.

Chang, Ch. J. (1998). The development of autonomy in pre-school Mandarin Chinese-speaking children's play narratives. *Narrative Inquiry* 8, 77–111.

Cheska, A.T. (Ed) (1978). The study of play from five anthropological perspectives. In Slater, M.A. (Ed.), *Play: Anthropological perspectives*. West Point, NY: Leisure Press, pp. 17–35.

Cheska, A.T. (Ed) (1981). *Play as context*. West Point, N.Y.: Leisure Press.

Child, E. (1983). Play and culture. A study of English and Asian children. *Leisure Studies* 2, 169–196.

Cobley, P., Jansz, L. and Appignanesi, R. (1997). *Introducing semiotics*. New York: Totem Books.

Cohen, D. and MacKeith, S.A. (1991). *The development of imagination: The private worlds of childhood*. London: Routledge.

Cohen, J. and Stewart, I. (1995). *The collapse of chaos: Discovering simplicity in a complex world*. London: Penguin.

Cohen, P.M. and Solnit, A.J. (1993). Play and therapeutic action. *Psychoanalytic Study of the Child* 48, 49–63.

Conning, E. (1999). Integration of play therapy and transactional analysis. *Transactional Analysis Journal* 29, 139–140.

Corsaro, W. (1983). Script recognition, articulation and expansion in children's role play. *Discourse Processes* 6, 1–19.

Corsaro, W. A. (1985). *Friendship and peer culture in the early years.* Norwood, NJ: Ablex.

Corsaro, W.A. (1992). Interpretive reproduction in children's peer cultures. *Social Psychology Quarterly* 55, 160–177.

Curry, N. and Arnaud, S. (1974). Cognitive implications in children's spontaneous role play. *Theory into Practice* 13, 173–277.

Curtis, H. (1915). *Education through play.* New York: Macmillan.

D'Andrade, R. (1995). *The development of cognitive anthropology.* Cambridge: Cambridge University Press.

Dansky, J. L. (1980a). Cognitive consequences of sociodramatic play and exploratory training for economically disadvantaged preschoolers. *Journal of Child Psychology and Psychiatry* 20, 47–58.

Dansky, J.L. (1980b) Make-believe: A mediator between free play and associative fluency. *Child Development* 51, 576–579.

Dasgupta, C. (1999). Listening to children through play. In Milner, P. and Carolin, B. (Eds.), *Time to listen to children: Personal and professional communication.* New York: Routledge, pp. 175–187.

Deely, J.N. (1982). *Introducing semiotics: Its history and doctrine.* Bloomington: Indiana University Press.

DeMarrais, K.B., Nelson, P.A. and Baker, J.H. (1994). Meaning in mud: Yup'ik Eskimo girls at play. In Roopnarine, J.L., Johnson, J.E. and Hooper, F.H. (Eds.), *Children's play in diverse cultures.* Albany: State University of New York Press, pp. 179–209.

Diamond, S. (1974). Introduction. *Doll play of Pilaga Indian children.* New York: Vintage.

Dias, M.G. and Harris, P.L. (1988). The effect of make-believe play on deductive reasoning. *British Journal of Developmental Psychology* 6, 207–221.

Dinsmore, J. (1981) Toward a unified theory of presupposition. *Journal of Pragmatics* 5, 335–363.

Dixon, W. and Shore, C. (1993). Language style dimensions and symbolic play. *Play Theory and Research* 1, 259–289.

Doyle, A.B. and Connolly, J. (1989). Negotiation and enactment in social pretend play: Relations to social acceptance and social cognition: *Early Childhood Research Quarterly* 4, 289–302.

Doyle, A., Doering, P., Tessler, O. and de Lorimier, S. (1992). Transitions in children's play: A sequential analysis of states preceding and following social pretense. *Developmental Psychology* 28, 137–144.

Drewal, M.T. (1992). *Yoruba rituals: Performers, play, agency.* Bloomington: Indiana University Press.

Drucker, J. (1975). Toddler play: Some comments on its functions in the developmental process. *Psychoanalysis and Contemporary Science* 3, 13–28.

Duncan, M. (1988). Play discourse and the rhetorical turn: A semiological analysis of "Homo Ludens." *Play and Culture* 1, 28–42.

Ebbeck, F. (1973). Learning from play in other cultures. In Frost, J. (Ed.), *Revisiting early childhood education.* New York: Wiley, pp. 321–326.

Eckler, J.A. and Weininger, O. (1989). Structural parallels between pretend play and narratives. *Developmental Psychology* 25, 736–743.

Egan, K. (1988). *Imagination and education.* New York: Teachers College Press.

Eifermann, R.R. (1970a). Level of children's play as expressed in group size. *The British Journal of Educational Psychology* 40, 161–170.

Eifermann, R.R. (1970b). Co-operativeness and egalitarianism in Kibbutz children's games. *Human Relations* 23, 579–587.

Eifermann, R.R. (1971). Social play in childhood. In Herron, R. and Sutton-Smith, B. (Eds.), *Child's play.* New York: Wiley.

Eisen, G. (1988). *Children's play in the holocaust.* Amherst: University of Massachusetts Press.

Eisenberg, N., Wolnick, Sh.A., Hernandez, R. and Pasternak, J.A. (1985). Parental socialization of young children's play: A short-term longitudinal study. *Child Development* 56, 1506–1513.

Ellis, M.J. and Scholtz, G. (1978). *Activity and play in children.* Englewood Cliffs, NJ: Prentice-Hall.

Erickson, M. (1982). *My voice will go with you.* New York: Norton.

Erikson, E. (1940). Studies in the interpretation of play. *Genetic Psychology Monographs* 22, 557–671.

Erikson, E. (1972). Play and actuality. In Piers, M.W. (Ed.), *Play and development.* New York: Norton, pp. 127–168.

Erikson, E. (1977). *Toys and reasons.* New York: Norton.

Esman, A. (1983). Psychoanalytic play therapy. In Schaefer, C. and O'Connor, K. (Eds.), *Handbook of play therapy.* New York: Norton.

Evaldsson, A.C. and Corsaro, W.A. (1998). Play and games in the peer cultures of preschool and preadolescent children: An interpretive approach. *Childhood: A Global Journal of Child Research* 5, 377–402.

Evans, J. (1986). In search of the meaning of play. *New Zealand Journal of Health, Physical Education and Recreation* 19, 16–19.

Fall, M. (1997). From stages to categories: A study of children's play in play therapy sessions. *International Journal of Play Therapy* 6, 1–21.

Fall, M., Balvanz, J., Johnson, L. and Nelson, L. (1999). A play therapy intervention and its relationship to self efficacy and learning behaviors. *Professional School Counseling* 2, 194–204.

Fantuzo, J.W. (1995). Assessment of preschool play interaction in young low-income children: Penn Interactive Peer Playscale. *Early Childhood Research Quarterly* 10, 105–120.

Farver, J.A.M. (1993). Cultural differences in scaffolding pretend play: A comparison of American and Mexican mother-child and sibling-child pairs. In Macdonald, K. (Ed.), *Parent-child play: Descriptions and implications.* Albany: State University of New York Press, pp. 349–366.

Farver, J.A.M. and Howes, C. (1993). Cultural differences in American and Mexican mother-child pretend play. *Merrill-Palmer Quarterly* 39, 344–358.

Farver, J.A.M, Kim, Y.K. and Lee, Y. (1995). Cultural differences in Korean and Anglo-American preschoolers' social interaction and play behavior. *Child Development* 66, 1088–1099.

Farver, J.A.M. and Wimbarti, S. (1995). Indonesian children's play with their mothers and older siblings. *Child Development* 66, 1088–1099.

Fein, G. (1975). A transformational analysis of pretending. *Developmental Psychology* 11, 291–296.

Fein, G. (1978). Pretend play: Creativity and consciousness. In Goerlitz, D. and Wohlwill, J.F. (Eds.), *Curiosity, imagination and play*. Hillsdale, NJ: Lawrence Erlbaum, pp. 281–304.

Fein, G. (1979). Play in the acquisition of symbols. In Katz, L. (Ed.), *Current topics in early childhood education*. Norwood, NJ: Ablex., pp. 195–225.

Fein, G. (1980). Pretend play in childhood: An integrative review. *Child Development* 52, 1095–1118.

Fein, G. (1984). The self-building potential of pretend play as "I got a fish, all by myself." In Yawkley, T.D. and Pellegrini, A.D. (Eds.), *Child's play: Developmental and applied*. Hillsdale, NJ: Lawrence Erlbaum.

Fein, G. (1985). Learning in play: Surfaces of thinking and feeling. In Frost, J.L. and Sunderlin, S. (Eds.), *When children play*. Wheaton, MD.: Association for Childhood Education International.

Fein, G. (1986). The affective psychology of play. In Gottfried, A.W. and Caldwell, C. (Eds.) *Play interactions*. Lexington, MA: Lexington Books, pp. 31–49.

Fein, G. (1989). Mind, meaning and affect: Proposals for a theory of pretense. *Developmental Review* 9, 345–363.

Fein, G. (1995). Toys and stories. In Pellegrini, A. (Ed.), *The future of play theory*. Albany: State University of New York Press, pp. 151–164.

Fein, G. and Kinney, P. (1994). He's a nice alligator: Observations on the affective organization of pretense. In Slade, A. and Wolf, D. (Eds.), *Children at play: Clinical and developmental studies of play*. New York: Oxford University Press, pp. 188–204.

Fein, G. and Rivkin, M. (Eds.) (1986). *The young child at play*. Washington, DC: National Association for the Education of Young Children.

Feitelson, D. (1959). Some aspects of the social life of Kurdish Jews. *Jewish Journal of Sociology* 1, 201–216.

Feitelson, D. (1972) Developing imaginative play in preschool children as a possible approach to fostering creativity. *Early Child Development and Care* 1, 181–195.

Feitelson, D. (1977). Cross cultural studies of representational play. In Tizard, B. and Harvey, D. (Eds.), *Biology of play*. Philadelphia: J.B. Lippincott.

File, N. and Kontos, S. (1993). The relationship of program quality to children's play in integrated early integration settings. *Topics in Early Childhood Special Education* 13, 1–18.

Fine, G. A. (1980). Children and their culture: Exploring Newall's paradox. *Western Folklore* 39, 170–183.

Fine, G. A. (1983). *Shared fantasy: Role-playing games as social worlds*. Chicago: University of Chicago Press.

Fineman, J. (1962). Observations on the development of imaginative play in early childhood. *Journal of Child Psychiatry* 1, 167–181.

Fisher, E.P. (1992). The impact of play on development: A meta-analysis. *Play and Culture* 5, 159–181.

Flavell, J.H., Flavell, E.R and Green, F.L. (1987). Young children's knowledge about the apparent-real and pretend-real distinction. *Developmental Psychology* 23, 816–822.

Forbes, D., Katz, M. and Paul, B. (1986). Frame talk: A dramatic analysis of children's fantasy play. In Mueller, E. and Cooper, C. (Eds.), *Process and outcome in peer relationships*. New York: Academic Press, pp. 249–265.

Forbes, D. and Yablick, G. (1984). The organization of dramatic content in children's fantasy play. In Kessel, F. and Goencu, A. (Eds.), *Analyzing children's play dialogues*. San Francisco: Jossey-Bass, pp. 23–36.

Freud, A. (1965). *Normality and pathology in childhood: Assessment of development.* New York: International Universities Press.

Freud, S. (1959). Beyond the pleasure principle. In Starchey, J. (Ed.), *The standard edition of the complete psychological works of Sigmund Freud*. London: The Institute of Psychoanalysis.

Freyberg, J.T. (1973). Increasing the imaginative play of urban disadvantaged children through systematic training. In J.L. Singer (Ed.), *The child's world of make-believe*. New York: Academic Press, pp. 129–154.

Froebel, F. (1887). *The education of man*. Translated by Hailmann, W.N. New York: Appleton.

Fromkin, V. and Rodman, R. (1998). *An introduction to language*, 6th edition. Forthwork, TX: Harcourt Brace College Publishers.

Frost, J. and Sunderlin, S. (Eds.) (1985). *When children play*. Washington D.C.: Association for Childhood Education International.

Furth, H.G. and Kane, S. (1992). Children constructing society: A new perspective on children at play. In McGurk, H. (Ed.), *Childhood social development: Contemporary perspectives*. Hillsdale, NJ: Lawrence Erlbaum, pp. 149–173.

Galda, L. and Pellegrini, A. (1985). *Play, language and stories*. Norwood, NJ: Ablex.

Gardiner, H.W., Mutter, J.D. and Kosmitzki, C. (1997). *Live across cultures: Cross cultural human development*. Boston: Allyn and Bacon.

Garvey, C. (1974). Some properties of social play. *Merrill-Palmer Quarterly* 20, 163–180.

Garvey, C. (1977). *Play*. Cambridge, MA: Harvard University Press.

Garvey, C. (1979). Communication controls in social play: Peer play dyads, verbal rituals. In Sutton-Smith, B. (Ed.), *Play and learning*. New York: Gardner Press, pp. 109–125.

Garvey, C. (1993). Diversity in the conversational repertoire: The case of conflicts and social pretending. *Cognition and Instruction* 11, 251–264.

Garvey, C. and Berndt, R. (1977). *The organization of pretend play*. JSAS Catalog of Selected Documents in Psychology, vol. 7

Garvey, C. and Kramer, T. (1989). The language of social pretend. *Developmental Review* 9, 364–382.

Gaskins, S. and Goencu, A. (1992). Cultural variations in play: A challenge to Piaget and Vygotsky. *The Quarterly Newsletter of the Laboratory for Comparative Cognition* 14, 31–35.

Geertz, C. (2000). *The interpretation of cultures*. New York: Basic Books.

Georges, R. A. (1969).The relevance of models for analyses of traditional play activities. *Southern Folklore Quarterly* 33, 1–23.

Gerstmyer, J.S. (1991). *Toward a theory of play as performance: An analysis of video-taped episodes of a toddler's play performance*. Ph.D. Dissertation., Univerity of Pennsylvania.

Giffin, H. (1984). The coordination of meaning in the creation of a shared make-believe reality. In Bretherton, J. (Ed.), *Symbolic Behavior*. New York: Academic Press.

Goencu, A. (1993). Development of intersubjectivity in social pretend play. *Human Development* 36, 185–198.

Goldman, L.R. (1998). *Child's play: Myth, mimesis and make-believe*. Oxford: Berg.

Golomb, C. (1979). Pretense play: A cognitive perspective. In Smith, N. and Franklin, M. (Eds)., *Symbolic functioning in childhood*. New York: Wiley.

Golomb, C. and Cornelius, C. (1977). Symbolic play and its cognitive significance. *Developmental Psychology* 13, 246–252.

Golomb, C. and Goodwin, C. (1987). Children's arguing. In Philips, S., Steele, S. and Tanz, C. (Eds.), *Language, gender and sex in comparative perspective*. Cambridge: Cambridge University Press, pp. 200–246.

Goerlitz, D. and Wohlwill, J.F. (Eds.) (1987). *Curiosity, imagination and play*. Hillsdale, NJ: Lawrence Erlbaum.

Gordon, M.H. (1993). The inhibition of pretend play and its implications for development. *Human Development* 36, 215–234.

Gottfried, A.W. and Caldwell, C. (Eds.) (1986). *Play interactions*. Lexington, MA: Lexington Books.

Gougoulis, C. (1999). The "rules" of mockery: Folk humor and symbolic inversion in Greek children's pretend play. *Acta Ethnographica Hungarica* 44, 199–208.

Gougoulis, C. and Kouria, A. (Eds.) (2000). *Children's play in modern Greek society; 19th and 20th centuries* [Greek text]. Athens: Kastaniotis Publishers and Foundation for Research in Childhood "Spyros Doxiadis."

Gould, R. (1972). *Child studies through fantasy*. New York: Quadrangle.

Griffing, P. (1980). The relationship between socioeconomic status and sociodramatic play among black kindergarten children. *Genetic Psychological Monographs* 101, 3–34.

Griffiths, R. (1935). *The study of imagination in early childhood*. London: Kegan Paul.

Groos, K. (1901) *The play of man*. New York: Appleton.

Haight, W.L. and Miller, P.J. (1993). *Pretending at home: Early development in sociocultural context*. Albany: State University of New York Press.

Haight, W.L, Wang, X., Fung, H., Williams, K. and Mintz, J. (1999). Universal, developmental and variable aspects of young children's play: A cross-cultural comparison of pretending at home. *Child Development* 70, 1477–1488.

Hammel, E.A. (Ed.) (1965). Formal semantic analysis. *American Anthropologist*, Special Issue.

Hanline, M.F. (1999). Developing a pre-school play-based curriculum. *International Journal of Disability, Development and Education* 46, 289–305.

Hans, J.S. (1981). *The play of the world*. Amherst: University of Massachusetts Press.

Harkness, S. and Super, C.M. (1986). The cultural structuring of children's play in a rural African community. In Blanchard, K. (Ed.), *The many faces of play*. Champaign, IL: Human Kinetics, pp. 96–103.

Harper, J. (1991). Children's play: The differential effects of intrafamilial physical and sexual abuse. *Child Abuse and Neglect* 15, 89–98.

Harris, P.L. and Kavanaugh, R.D. (1993) *Young children's understanding of pretense*. Monograph of the Society for Child Development. Chicago: University of Chicago Press.

Hartmann, H. (1950). Comments on the psychoanalytic theory of the ego. *Psychoanalytic Study of the Child* 5, 74–96

Hellendoorn, J. (1988). Imaginative play techniques in psychotherapy with children. In

Schaefer, C. E. (Ed.), *Innovative interventions in child and adolescent therapy*. New York: Wiley, pp. 43–67.

Hellendoorn, J., Van der Kooij, R. and Sutton-Smith, B. (Eds.) (1994). *Play and intervention*. Albany: State University of New York Press.

Hempel, G.G. (1966). *Philosophy of natural science*. Englewood Cliffs, NJ: Prentice-Hall.

Henry, J. and Henry, Z. (1974). *Doll play of Pilaga Indian children*. New York: Vintage-Random House.

Herron, R.E. and Sutton-Smith, B. (1971). *Child's play*. New York: Wiley.

Howes, C. (1985). Sharing fantasy: Social pretend play in toddlers. *Child Development* 56, 1253–1258.

Howes, C. and Matheson, C.C. (1992). Sequences in the development of competent play with peers: Social pretend play. *Developmental Psychology* 28, 961–974.

Howes, C. and Smith, E.W. (1996). Relations among child care quality, teacher behavior, children's play activities, emotional security and cognitive activity in child care. *Early Childhood Research Quarterly* 10, 381–404.

Howes, C., Unger, O.A. and Matheson, C.C. (1992). *The collaborative construction of pretend*. Albany: State University of New York Press.

Hudson, J. and Nelson, K. (1984). Play with language: Over-extensions as analogues. *Journal of Child Language* 11, 337–346.

Hughes, F.P. (1992). *Children, play and development*. Boston: Allyn and Bacon.

Huizinga, J. (1955). *Homo ludens: A study of the play element in culture*. Boston: Beacon Press.

Hutt, S. J., Tyler, S., Hutt, C. and Christophersen, H. (1989). *Play, exploration and learning*. London: Routledge.

Izard, C. (1991) *The psychology of emotions*. New York: Plenum.

James, A. (1998). Play in childhood: An anthropological perspective. *Child Psychology and Psychiatry Review* 3, 104–109.

Johnson, E.P. (1991). Searching for the social and cognitive outcomes of children's play: A selective second look. *Play and Culture* 4, 201–213.

Johnson, J.E. (1995). The challenge of incorporating research on play into the practice of preschool education. *Journal of Applied Developmental Psychology* 15, 603–618.

Johnson, J.E. and Christie, J.F. (1986). Pretend play and logical operations. In Blanchard, K. (Ed.), *The many faces of play*. Champaign, IL: Human Kinetics, pp. 50–58.

Johnson, J.E., Christie, J.F. and Yawkley, T.D. (1986). *Play and early childhood development*. Glenview, IL: Scott, Foresman.

Johnson-Laird, Ph.N. (1989). *The computer and the mind: An introduction to cognitive science*. Cambridge, MA: Harvard University Press.

Kaarby, G. (1986). Children's conceptions of their own play. Department of Education and Research, Goteborg, Sweden: Goteborg University.

Kane, S.R. and Furth, H.G. (1993). Children's constucting social reality: A frame analysis of social pretend play. *Human Development* 36, 199–214.

Katz, M.M., Forbes, D., Yablick G. and Kelly, V.C. (1983). Disagreements during play: Clues to children's constructs of reality. In Blanchard, K. (Ed.), *The many faces of play*. Champaign, IL: Human Kinetics, pp. 104–114.

Keith, D.V. and Whitaker, C.A. (1981). Play therapy: A paradigm for work with families. *Journal of Marital and Family Therapy* 3, 243–251.

Kernberg, P.F., Chazan, S.E. and Normandin, L. (1998). The children's play therapy instrument (CPTI): Description, development and reliability studies. *Journal of Psychotherapy Practice and Research* 7, 196–207.

Kessel, F. and Goencu, A. (Eds.) (1984). *Analyzing children's play dialogues*. San Francisco: Jossey-Bass.

King, N.R. (1982). Work and play in the classroom. *Social Education* 446, 110–113.

King, N.R. (1987). Elementary school play: Theory and research. In Block, J.H. and King, N.R. (Eds.), *School play*. New York: Garland, pp. 143–165.

Klein, M. (1932). *The psychoanalysis of children*. London: Hogarth Press.

Klinger, E. (1969). Development of imaginative behavior: Implications of play for a theory of fantasy. *Psychological Bulletin* 74, 277–298.

Klinger, E. (1971). *Structure and functions of fantasy*. New York: Wiley.

Kloni, A. (2000). Children, work and play in rural Greece: The case of Lygaria, Epirus [Greek text]. In Gougoulis, C. and Kouria, A. (Eds.), *Children's play in modern Greek society: 19th and 20th centuries*. Athens: Kastaniotis Publishers and Foundation for Research in Childhood "Spyros Doxiadis," pp. 417–473.

Klugman, E. and Smilansky, S. (Eds.). (1990) *Children's play and learning*. New York: Teachers College Press.

Knell, S.M. (1997). Cognitive-behavioral play therapy. In O'Connor, K.J. and Braverman, L.M. (Eds.), *Play therapy, theory and practice: A comparative presentation*. New York: Wiley, pp. 79–99.

Kohut, H. (1971). *The analysis of the self*. New York: International Universities Press

Van der Kooj, R. and Hellendoorn, J. (Eds.) (1986). *Play, play therapy, play research*. Lisse, The Netherlands: Swets and Zeitlinger.

Kot, S., Landreth, G.L. and Giordano, M. (1998) Intensive child-centered play therapy with child witnesses of domestic violence. *International Journal of Play Therapy* 7, 17–36.

Kottman, T. (1997). Adlerian play therapy. In O'Connor, K. and Braverman, L.M. (Eds.), Play therapy theory and practice: A comparative presentation. New York: Wiley, pp. 310–340.

Kyratzis, A. (1992). Gender differences in the use of persuasive justification in children's pretend play. In Hall, K., Buchholtz, M. and Moonwomon, B. (Eds.), *Locating power*. Berkeley: University of California Press, pp. 80–92.

Lancy, D.F. (1976). The play behavior of Kpele children during rapid cultural change. In Lancy, D. and Tindall, A. (Eds.), *The anthropological study of play: Problems and prospects*. West Point, NY: Leisure Press, pp. 72–79.

Lancy, D.F. and Tindall, B.A. (1976). *The anthropological study of play: Problems and prospects*. West Point, NY: Leisure Press.

Landreth, G., Baggerly, J. and Tyndall-Lynd, A. (1999). Beyond adapting adult counseling to use with children: The paradigm shift to child-centered play therapy. *Journal of Individual Psychology* 55, 272–287.

Landreth, G.L. and Sweeney, D.S. (1997). Child-centered play therapy. In O'Connor, K.J. and Braverman, L.M. (Eds.), *Play therapy, theory and practice: A comparative presentation*. New York: Wiley, pp. 17–45.

Lansley, K. (1968). *A collection and classification of the traditional Melanesian play activities with a supplementary bibliography*. MA Thesis. Edmonton: University of Alberta.

Leacock, E. (1971). At play in African villages. Special Supplement of Play, *Natural History* 80, 60–65.

Lee, A.C. (1997). Psychoanalytic play therapy. In O'Connor, K.J. and Braverman, L.M. (Eds.), *Play therapy, theory and practice: A comparative presentation*. New York: Wiley, pp. 46–78.

Lee, J. (1922) *Play in education*. New York: Macmillan.

Lein, L. and Brenneis, D. (1978). Children's disputes in three speech communities. *Language in Society* 7, 299–323.

Leslie, A.M. (1987). Pretense and representation: The origins of a theory of mind. *Psychological Review* 94, 412–426.

Levi-Strauss (2000). *Structural anthropology*. New York: Basic Books.

Levy, A.K. (1984). The language of play: The role of play in language development. *Early Child Development and Care* 17, 49–62.

Lewis, J.M. (1993). Childhood play in normality, pathology and therapy. *American Journal of Orthopsychiatry* 63, 6–15.

Lewis, P.H. (1973). *The relationship of sociodramatic play to various cognitive abilities in kindergarten*. Ph.D. Dissertation. Ohio State University.

Lieberman, J.N. (1977*)*. *Playfulness: Its relationship to imagination and creativity*. New York: Academic Press.

Lillard, A.S. (1993a) Pretend play skills and the child's theory of mind. *Child Development* 64, 348–371.

Lillard, A.S. (1993b). Young children's conceptualization of pretense: Action or mental representation state? *Child Development* 64, 372–386.

Lloyd, B. and Goodwin, R. (1995). Let's pretend: Casting the characters and setting the scene. *British Journal of Developmental Psychology* 13, 61–70.

Lodge, K.R. (1979). The use of the past tense in games of pretend. *Journal of Child Language* 6, 365–369.

Loewald, E.L. (1987). Therapeutic play in space and time. *Psychoanalytic Study of the Child* 42, 173–192.

Loy, J.W. (1982). *The paradoxes of play*. West Point, NY: Leisure Press.

Madanes, C. (1981). *Strategic family therapy*. San Francisco: Jossey-Bass.

Mahler, M.S. (1979). Separation-individuation. In *The selected papers of Margaret S. Mahler*. Northvale, NJ: Jason Aronson.

Makrinioti, D. (2000). Play in the curriculum of Greek preschool education. A critical reading of child-centered educational discourse [Greek text]. In Gougoulis, C. and Kouria, A. (Eds.), *Children's play in modern Greek society: 19th and 20th centuries*. Athens: Kastaniotis Publishers and Foundation for Research in Childhood "Spyros Doxiadis," pp. 85–172.

Maltz, M.D. (1987). *Psycho-cybernetics*. Pocket Books.

Martin, N.T. (1982). Socialization through traditional play and games in the Hanahan society of Buka. In Parrington, J.T., Orlicj, T. and Salmela, J.H. (Eds.), *Sport in perspective*. Ottawa: Sport in Perspective, Inc.

Martin, P. and Caro, T.M. (1985). On the functions of play and its role in behavioral development. *Advances in the Study of Behavior* 15, 59–103.

Martini, M. (1994). Peer interactions in Polynesia. In Roopnarine, J.L., Johnson, J.E. and Hooper, F.H. (Eds.), *Children's play in diverse cultures*. Albany: State University of New York Press, pp. 73–103.

Mathews, W. (1977). Modes of transformation in the initiation of fantasy play. *Developmental Psychology* 13, 212–216.

Maynard, D. (1985). How children start arguments. *Language in Society* 144, 1–30.

McCall, R.B. (1974). Exploratory manipulation and play in the human infant. *Mono-graphs of the Society of Research in Child Development*, serial number 155, 15, 2.

McCune-Nicolich, L. (1995). A normative study of representational play at the transition to language. *Developmental Psychology* 31, 198–206.

McCune-Nicolich, L. (1997). Beyond sensorimotor intelligence: Assessment of symbolic maturity through analysis of pretend play. *Merill-Palmer Quarterly* 23, 89–99.

McCune-Nicolich, L. (1981). Toward symbolic functioning: Structure of early pretend games and potential parallels with language. *Child Development* 52, 785–797.

Meckley, A.M. (1994). *The social construction of young children's play*. Ph.D. disser-tation, University of Pennsylvania.

Miller, S. (1974). The playful, the crazy and the nature of pretense. In Norbeck, E. (Ed.), *The anthropological study of human play*. Houston, TX: Rice University Studies 60, 31–51.

Minuchin, S. (1974). *Families and family therapy*. Cambridge, MA: Harvard University Press.

Miracle, A. (1977). Some functions of Aymara games and play. In Stevens, P. (Ed.), *Studies in the anthropology of play*. West Point, NY: Leisure Press.

Mistry, D.K. (1958). The Indian child and his play. *Sociological Bulletin* [Bombay], 9, 48–55.

Montessori, M. (1955). *Childhood education*. New York: New American Library.

Moray, N. (1963). *Cybernetics*. New York: Hawthorn Books.

Moustakas, C. (1955). Emotional adjustment and the play therapy process. *Journal of Genetic Psychology* 86, 79–99.

Muller-Schwartz, D. (1978). *Evolution of play behavior*. Stroudsburg, PA: Dowden, Hutchinson and Ross.

Neubauer, P.B. (1987). The many meanings of play. *Psychoanalytic Study of the Child* 42, 3–9.

Nicolopoulou, A. (1997). Children and narratives: Toward an interpretive and sociocul-tural process. In Bamberg, M. (Ed.), *Narrative development: Six approaches*. Hillsdale, NJ: Lawrence Erlbaum, pp. 179–215.

Norbeck, E. (1974). The anthropological study of human play. In Norbeck, E. (Ed.), *The anthropological study of human play*. Houston, TX: Rice University Studies 60, 1–8.

O'Connor, K. (1997). Ecosystemic play therapy. In O'Connor, K. and Braverman, L.M. (Eds.), *Play therapy theory and practice: A comparative presentation*. New York: Wiley, pp. 234–284.

O'Connor, K. and Braverman, L.M. (Eds.) (1977). *Play therapy theory and practice: A comparative presentation*. New York: Wiley.

O'Connor, K. and Schaefer, C. (1994). *The handbook of play therapy*. New York: Wiley.

Packer, M. (1995). Cultural work on the kindergarten playground: Articulating the ground of play. *Human Development* 37, 5, 259–276.

Pan, H. (1994). Children's play in Taiwan. In Roopnarine, J., Johnson, J. and Hooper, F. (Eds.), *Children's play in diverse perspectives*. Albany: State University of New York Press, pp. 31–50.

Parsons, M. (1999). The logic of play in psychoanalysis. *International Journal of Psy-choanalysis* 80, 5, 871–884.

Parten, M. (1932). Social participation among preschool children. *Journal of Abnormal and Social Psychology* 27, 243–369.

Pellegrini, A.D. (Ed.) (1995). *The future of play theory*. Albany: State University of New York Press.

Pepler, D.J. (1982). Play and divergent thinking. In Pepler, D.J. and Rubin, K. (Eds.), *The play of children: Current theory and research*. New York: S. Karger.

Pepler, D.J. and Ross, H.S. (1981). The effects of play on convergent and divergent problem solving. *Child Development* 52, 1202–1210.

Pepler, D.J. and Rubin, K. (Eds.) (1982). *The play of children: current theory and research*. New York: S. Karger.

Phillips, R. and Landreth, G. (1995). Play therapists on play therapy I: A report of methods, demographics and professional practices. *International Journal of Play Therapy* 4, 1, 1–26.

Piaget, Jean (1962). *Play, dreams and imitation in childhood*. New York: Norton.

Van der Poel, L., de Bruyn, E.E. and Rost H. (1991). Parental attitude and behavior and children's play. *Play and Culture* 4, 1–10.

Prosser, G.V. et al. (1986). Children's play in Sri Lanka: A cross-cultural study. *British Journal of Developmental Psychology* 4, 170–186.

Pulaski, M.A. (1973). Toys and imaginative play. In Singer, J.L. (Ed.), *The child's world of make-believe*. New York: Academic Press, pp. 74–103.

Riga, A.V. (2000). Descriptive representation of children's daily routines in a Greek summer camp. Observing intra-group behavior in self-organized group games of middle childhood [Greek text]. In Gougoulis, C. and Kouria, A. (Eds.), *Children's play in modern Greek society: 19th and 20th centuries*. Athens: Kastaniotis Publishers and Foundation for Research in Childhood "Spyros Doxiadis," pp. 475–531.

Robinson-Finnan, C.L. (1982). The ethnography of children's spontaneous play. In Spindler, G. (Ed.), *Doing the ethnography of schooling*. New York: Holt, Rinehart and Winston.

Roopnarine, J.L., Johnson, J.E. and Hooper, Frank H. (Eds). 1994. *Children's play in diverse cultures*. Albany: State University of New York Press.

Roopnarine, J.L. Hossain, Z., Gill. P. and Brophy, H. (1994). Play in the East Indian Context. In Roopnarine, J.L., Johnson, J.E. and Hooper, Frank H. (Eds.), *Children's play in diverse cultures*. Albany: State University of New York Press, pp. 9–30.

Rosen, C.E. (1974). The effect of sociodramatic play on problem solving among culturally disadvantaged children. *Child Development* 45, 920–927.

Rossie, J. (1993a). Bibliography on play, games and toys in North Africa and the Sahara. *Ethnographica* [Greece] 9, 237–241.

Rossie, J. (1993b). Children's play, generations and gender with special reference to the Ghrib (Tunisian Sahara). *Ethnographica* [Greece] 9, 193–201.

Rossie, J.P. (1999a). *Toys, culture and society: An anthropological approach with reference to North Africa and the Sahara*. NCFL–Nordic Center for Research on Toys and Educational Media. Sweden: University of Halmstad. HTML version: http://www.hh.se/ide/ncfl/Publications.html; jprossie@hotmail.com.

Rossie, J.P. (1999b). *Saharan and North African Ludic heritages: Children's dolls and doll play*. NCFL–Nordic Center for Research on Toys and Educational Media,

Sweden: University of Halmstad. HTML version: http://www.hh.se/ide/ncfl/
Publications.html; jprossie@hotmail.com.

Rossie, J.P. (2000). *Saharan and North African Ludic heritages: Commented bibliography on play, games and toys.* NCFL–Nordic Center for Research on Toys and Educational Media, Sweden: University of Halmstad. HTML version: http://www.hh.se/ide/ncfl/Publications.html; jprossie@hotmail.com.

Rossie, J.P. (forthcoming) *Saharan and North African Ludic heritage: The animal in play, games and toys.* NCFL–Nordic Center for Research on Toys and Educational Media, Sweden: University of Halmstad. HTML version: http://www.hh.se/ide/ncfl/Publications.html; jprossie@hotmail.com.

Rubin, K.H., Maloni, T. and Hornung, M. (1976). Free play behaviors in middle- and lower-class preschoolers. Parten and Piaget revisited. *Child Development* 47, 414–419.

Rubin, K.H. and Pepler, D.J. (1980). The relationship of child's play to social-cognitive development. In Foot, H.C., Chapman, A.J. and Smith, J.R. (Eds.), *Friendship and childhood relationships.* London: Wiley.

Rubin, K.H., Watson, K.S. and Jambour, T.W. (1978). Free play behaviors in preschool and kindergarten children. *Child Development* 49, 534–546.

Russ, S. and Grossman-McKee, A. (1990). Affective expression in children's fantasy play, primary process thinking on the Rorschach and divergent thinking. *Journal of Personality Assessment* 54, 756–771.

Ryan, V. (1999). Developmental delay, symbolic play and non-directive play therapy. *Clinical Child Psychology and Psychiatry* 4, (2), 167–185.

Sachs, J., Goldman, J. and Chaillé, C. (1985). Narratives in preschoolers' sociodramatic play: The role of knowledge and communicative competence. In Galda, L. and Pellegrini, A. (Eds.), *Play, language and stories: The development of children's literature behavior.* Norwood, NJ: Ablex, pp. 45–61.

Salamone, F.A (1989). Anthropology and play: A bibliography. *Play and Culture* 2, 158–181.

Salamone, F.A. and Salamone, V.A. (1991). Children's games in Nigeria Redux: A consideration of the "uses" of play. *Play and Culture* 4, 129–138.

Salter, M.A. (Ed.) (1977). *Play: Anthropological perspectives.* West Point, NY: Leisure Press.

Saltz, E. and Brodie, J. (1982). Pretend play in childhood. A review and critique. *Contributions to Human Development* 6, 1–158.

Saltz, E., Dixon, D. and Johnson, J. (1977). Training disadvantaged preschoolers on various fantasy activities: Effects on cognitive functioning and impulse control. *Child Development* 48, 367–368.

Sandler, J., Kennedy, S. and Tyson, R.L. (1980). *The technique of child psychoanalysis. Discussions with Anna Freud.* Cambridge, MA: Harvard University Press.

Saracho, O.N., Spodek, B. et al. (Eds.) (1998). *Multiple perspectives on play in early childhood education.* SUNY Series, Early Childhood Education: Inquiries and Insights. Albany: State University of New York Press.

Saussure, F. de (1972). *Cours de linguistique generale* [originally published in 1916]. Paris: Payot.

Sawada, H. and Minami, H. (1997). Peer group play and co-childrearing in Japan: A historical ethnography of a fishing community. *Journal of Applied Developmental Psychology* 18, 513–526.

Sawyer, K. (1996). *Pretend play as improvisation: Conversation in the preschool classroom*. Hillsdale, NJ: Lawrence Erlbaum.

Scales, B. and Almy, M., (Eds.) (1991). *Play and the social context of development in early care and education*. Early Childhood Education Series. New York: Teachers College Press

Schaefer, C.E. (1974). *Therapeutic use of child's play*. New York: Jason Aronson.

Schaefer, C. and O'Connor, K. (Eds.) (1983) *Handbook of play therapy*. New York: Norton.

Schlosberg, H. (1947). The concept of play. *Psychological review* 54, 229–231.

Schultz, T.R. (1979). Play as arousal modulation. In Sutton-Smith, B. (Ed.), *Play and learning*. New York: Gardner Press.

Schwartz, U.V. (1991). *Young children's dyadic pretend play: A communicational analysis of plot structure and plot generative strategies*. Philadelphia, PA: John Benjamins.

Schwartzman, H.B. (1978). *Transformations: The anthropology of children's play*. New York: Plenum Press.

Schwartzman, H.B. (Ed.) (1980). *Play and culture*. West Point, NY: Leisure Press.

Schwartzman, H.B. and Barbera, L. (1976). Children's play in Africa and South America: A review of the ethnographic literature. In Lancy, D.F. and Tindall, B.A. (Eds.), *The anthropological study of play: Problems and prospects*. Cornwall, NY: Leisure Press., pp. 11–21.

Scott, E. (1999). Are the children playing quietly? Integrating child psychotherapy and family therapy. *Australian and New Zealand Journal of Family Therapy* 20, 88–93.

Scott, M.E. (1998). Play and therapeutic action: Multiple perspectives. *Psychoanalytic Study of the Child* 53, 94–101.

Seagoe, M.Y. (1970). An instrument for the analyis of children's play in an index of degree of socialization. *Journal of School Psychology* 8, 139–144.

Seagoe, M.Y. (1971). A comparison of children's play in six modern cultures. *Journal of School Psychology* 9, 61–72.

Sears, J.R. (1951). Doll play aggression in normal young children. *Psychological Monographs* 65, 6.

Sever, Irene (1980). *Conflict resolution and social control among preschoolers, Jews, Arabs and Bedouins*. M.A. Dissertation, Department of Sociology and Anthropology, Haifa University, Israel.

Sever, Irene (1984). *Arguments et argumentations des enfants juifs, Arabes et Bedouins*. These pour le doctorat, Universite de la Sorbonne Nouvelle, Paris.

Shmukler, D. (1984). Imaginative play: Its implication for the process of education. In Sheik Anees (Ed.), *Imagery and the Educational Process*. New York: Baywood.

Simon, T. and Smith, P.K. (1985). Play and problem solving: A paradigm questioned. *Merrill-Palmer Quarterly* 31, 265–277.

Singer, D. and Singer, J.L. (1977). *Partners in play*. New York: Random House.

Singer, D. and Singer, J.L. (1981). *Television, imagination and aggression*. Hillsdale, NJ: Lawrence Erlbaum.

Singer, D. and Singer, J.L. (1985). *Make-believe: Games and activities to foster imaginative play in young children*. Glenview, IL: Scott, Foresman.

Singer, D. and Singer, J.L. (1990). *The house of make-believe*. Cambridge, MA: Harvard University Press.

Singer, J.L. (1961). Imagination and waiting ability in young children. *Journal of Personality* 29, 396–413.

Singer, J.L. (1973). *The child's world of make-believe.* New York: Academic Press.

Singer, J.L. (1998). Imaginative play in early childhood: A foundation for adaptive emotional and cognitive development. *International Medical Journal* 5, 93–100.

Slade, A. and Wolf, D.P. (1994). *Children at play: Clinical and developmental approaches to meaning and representation.* Oxford: Oxford University Press.

Slobodkin, L.B. (1993).*Simplicity and complexity in games of the intellect.* Cambridge, MA: Harvard University Press.

Smilansky, S. (1968). *The effects of sociodramatic play on disadvantaged preschool children.* New York: Wiley.

Smith, P.K. (Ed.) (1986). Children's play: *Research developments and practical applications.* London: Gordon and Breach.

Smith, P.K. and Connoly, K.J. (1980). *The ecology of pre-school behavior.* Cambridge: Cambridge University Press.

Smith, P.K. and Dutton, S. (1978). Play and training in direct and innovative problem solving. *Child Development* 50, 830–836.

Smith, P.K. and Sydall, S. (1978). Play and non-play tutoring in preschool children: It is play or tutoring which matters? *British Journal of Educational Psychology* 48, 315–325.

Smith, P.K. and Vollstedt, R. (1985). On defining play: An empirical study of the relationship between play and various play criteria. *Child Development* 56, 1042–1050.

Solnit, A.J., Cohen, D.J. and Neubauer, P.B. (1993). *The many meanings of play.* New Haven, CT: Yale University Press.

Solomon, J. (2000). Social disorder and school order: Children's play and educational practices (1830–1913) [Greek text]. In Gougoulis, C. and Kouria, A. (Eds.), *Children's play in modern Greek society: 19th and 20th centuries.* Athens: Kastaniotis Publishers and Foundation for Research in Childhood "Spyros Doxiadis," pp. 173–252.

Stevens, P. (Ed.) (1977). *Studies in the anthropology of play: Papers in memory of B. Allan Tindall.* West Point, NY: Leisure Press.

Stocking, G.W. (1988). *Functionalism historicized: Essays on British social anthropology* (History of Anthropology, vol. 2). Madison: University of Wisconsin Press.

Storey, K.S. (1976). Field study: children's play in Bali. In Lancy, D.F. and Tindall, B.A. (Eds.), *The anthropological study of play: Problems and prospects.* Cornwall, NY: Leisure Press, pp. 66–72.

Strauss, C. and Quinn, N. (1998). *A cognitive theory of cultural meaning.* Publications of the society for Psychological Anthropology, no 9. Cambridge: Cambridge University Press.

Stromquist, S. (1984). *Make-believe through words: A linguistic study of children's play with a doll's house.* Goeteborg, Sweden: Department of Linguistics, University of Goeteborg.

Sutton-Smith, B. (1966a). Piaget on play: A critique. *Psychological Review* 73, 104–110.

Sutton-Smith, B. (1966b). Role replication and role-reversal in play. *Merrill-Palmer Quarterly* 12, 285–298.

Sutton-Smith, B. (1967). The role of play in cognitive development. *Young Children* 6, 361–370.

Sutton-Smith, B. (1971). The playful modes of knowing. In *Play: The child strives toward self-realization*. Special Monograph. Washington, DC: National Association for the Education of Young Children.

Sutton-Smith, B. (1972). Research in play. *Leisure Today* 1, 6–7.

Sutton-Smith, B. (Ed.). (1979). *Play and learning*. New York: Gardner Press.

Sutton-Smith, B. (1981). *The Folkstories of children*. Philadelphia: University of Pennsylvania Press.

Sutton-Smith, B. (1982a). One hundred years of change in play research. *Newsletter of TAASP* 9, 13–17.

Sutton-Smith, B. (1982b). A performance theory of peer relationships. In Borman, K.M. (Ed.), *The social life of children in a changing society*. Hillsdale, NJ: Laurence Erlbaum.

Sutton-Smith, B. (1984). Text and context in imaginative play. In Kessel, F. and Goencu, A. (Eds.), *Analyzing children's play dialogues: New directions for child development*. San Francisco: Jossey-Bass.

Sutton-Smith, B. (1985). Play research: State of the art. In Frost, J.L. and Sunderlin, S. (Eds.), *When children play*. Washington, DC: Association for Childhood Education International.

Sutton-Smith, B. (1989). Introduction to play as performance, rhetoric and metaphor. *Play and Culture* 2, 189–192.

Sutton-Smith, B. (1997). *The ambiguity of play*. Cambridge, MA: Harvard University Press.

Sutton-Smith, B. and Rosenberg, B.G. (1960). Manifest anxiety and game preference in children. *Child Development* 31, 307–311.

Sutton-Smith, B. and Sutton-Smith, S. (1974). *How to play with your children*. New York: Hawthorne.

Sweeney, D.S. and Homeyer, L.E. (Eds.) (1999). *The handbook of group play therapy: How to do it, how it works, whom it's best for*. San Francisco, Jossey-Bass.

Sweeney, D.S. and Rocha, Sh. L. (2000). Using play therapy to assess family dynamics. In Watts, R.E. et al. (Eds.), *Techniques in marriage and family counseling*, The Family Psychology and Counseling Series, vol. 1. Alexandria, VA: American Counseling Association, pp. 33–47.

Takahama, Y. (1995). Developmental changes in negotiations in self-assertive children's play. *Japanese Journal of Developmental Psychology* 6, 155–163.

Takahashi, T. (1985). Verbal and non-verbal communication in mother-child relationship. *Hiyoshi Report* 12, 11–24

Takeuchi, M. (1994). Children's play in Japan. In Roopnarine, J.L., Johnson, J.E. et al. (Eds.), *Children's play in diverse cultures*. SUNY series, children's play in society. Albany: State University of New York Press, pp. 51–72.

Tamaru, N. (1991). Understanding role relations as demonstrated in children's play: A developmental observation in Japanese tag game (ONIGOKKO). *Japanese Journal of Education Psychology* 39, 341–347.

Tomkins, S.S. (1962). *Affect, imagery, consciousness*. New York: Springer.

Turner, V. (1988). *The anthropology of performance*. Performing Arts Journal Publications.

Tyndal-Lynd, A. (1999). Revictimization of children from violent families: Child-centered theoretical formulation and play therapy treatment implications. *International Journal of Play Therapy* 8, 9–25.

Udwin, O. and Shmukler, D. (1981). The influence of sociocultural, economic and home background factors on children's ability to engage in imaginative play. *Developmental Psychology* 17, 66–72.

UNESCO (1978). *Jeux et jouets des enfants du monde. Cataloge de l'expression.* Paris: UNESCO.

UNESCO (1979). *L'enfant et le jeu. Approches theoriques et applications pedagogiques.* Etudes et documents d'Education, nouvelle serie, no 34. Paris: UNESCO.

Vaihinger, H. (1924). *The philosophy of "as if."* London: C.K. Ogden.

Vanfleet, R., Lilly J.P. and Kaduson, H. (1999). Play therapy for children exposed to violence: Individual, family and community interventions. *International Journal of Play Therapy* 8, 27–42.

Verba, M. (1993). Cooperative formats in pretend play among young children. *Cognition and Instruction* 11, 265–280.

Vespo, J.E. and Caplan, M. (1993). Preschoolers' differential conflict behavior with friends and acquaintances. *Early Education and Development* 4, 45–53.

Vygotsky, L.S. (1966). Play and its role in the mental development of the child. *Soviet Psychology* 12, 62–67.

Waelder, R. (1933). The psychoanalytic theory of play. *Psychoanalysis Quarterly* 2, 208–224.

Walton, K. (1990). *Mimesis as make-believe*, Cambridge, MA: Harvard University Press.

Warren, S.L., Oppenheim, D. and Emde, R.N. (1997). Can emotions and themes in children's play predict behavior problems? *Journal of the American Academy of Child and Adolescent Psychiatry* 35, 1331–1337.

West. M.I. (1988). *Children's culture and controversy.* Hamden, CT: Archon Books.

White, J., Flynt, M. and Jones, N.P. (1999). Kinder Therapy: An adlerian approach to training teachers to be therapeutic agents through play. *Journal of Individual Psychology* 3, 365–382.

Whiting, B.B. and Edwards, C.P. (1988). *Children of different worlds.* Cambridge, MA: Harvard University Press.

Whiting, B. B. and Whiting, J.W.M. (1975). *Children of six cultures.* Cambridge, MA: Harvard University Press.

Winnicott, D.W. (1971). *Playing and reality.* London: Tavistock Publishers.

Wooley, J. (1995). The fictional mind: Young children's understanding of imagination, pretense and dreams. *Developmental Review* 15, 172–211.

Yawkley, D.T. and Johnson, J.E. (Eds). (1988). *Integrative processes and socialization.* Hillsdale, NJ: Lawrence Erlbaum.

Yawkley, T.D. and Pellegrini, A.D. (1984). *Child's play: Developmental and applied.* Hillsdale, NJ: Lawrence Erlbaum.

Zhang, R. (1998). Sand play therapy. *Psychological Science China* 21, 544–547.

Index

access rights to play territories, 44
adults' attitude toward children's play, ix,
x, 2, 111; in different cultures, 92–93
awareness of pretending, 8

child rearing, as related to make-believe
play, 111, 113
clinical play diagnosis, 144–145
cognitive development and make-believe
play, xi, xiv, 71–88, 149; creative
thinking and problem solving, 78, 83–
84, 105, 119; insight, introspection and
self-awareness, 78, 84; knowledge and
understanding of the world, 80–82, 85,
105; memory, 76–78, 83; organization
and planning, 78–79, 85; scientific research, 86; sense perception and attention, 76, 83
cognitive science as a framework for an
integrative theory of make-believe
play, 150
context-dependent componential analysis,
23, 170–180; as a method for revealing
the cognitive-affective regulating mechanism underlying make-believe play,

65–67; as facilitating the formulation
of rules, 178; validity of, 66–67
core conflicts, 61
cultural relativity of make-believe play,
xi, 89–116, 149; approaches to socialization research, 91; collectivistic vs.
individualistic make-believe play, 97–
98, 104, 106, 110; cross-cultural comparisons of the level of make-believe
play, 100–105, 114; cultural stereotypes and cliches in make-believe play
contents, 98–100; ethnographic research on make-believe play, 89–90;
the exotic appeal of modern technology
for traditional children, 103; functionalistic vs. constructivistic approaches, 90–
91, 94; is make-believe play universal?
94–95; modern vs. traditional cultures,
91–92; play and work in different cultures, 94; traditional vs. modern
formats for make-believe play, 98–100,
114

deep structure, 23, 39–40, 76
definition of the concept "make-believe
play," 5–8, 140, 149

delusions, as distinct from make-believe play, 5, 12, 13

developmental stages of make-believe play, 71–76; developmental parameters, 71–72, 83–85; for cross–cultural comparisons of make-believe play, 101–102; the beginning of make-believe play; 72–73, the middle stage—the third and fourth years, 73–76; the latest stage, 76–82; the waning of make-believe play, 82

"diplomatic" uses of make-believe play, 33, 34, 39, 41

distinctions between make-believe play and other forms of play, 8–9, 13, 119

distinctive features of the language of make-believe play, 24–30; absurd compounds designed to solve emotional difficulties, 29, 36, 59, 60, 61, 67; "absurd expressions" in make-believe play, 27–29; ad hoc combinations of different signifiers, 25, 73; attributing unconventional signifieds to signifiers, 25; transformations, 25

drama, as distinct from make-believe play, 5, 11, 13

duality of time, place and person in make-believe play, 28–29

education through make-believe play, 2, 117–126, 149; achieving specific educational goals through playing with the children, 123–125; the centrality of play and toys in early childhood education, 117–118; educational play diagnosis, 118–119; training in make-believe play skills, 119–122

egocentricity, 74–75

emotional concerns, 61,129

emotional regulation through make-believe play, xii, xiv, 2, 40, 57–69, 129; the cognitive-affective homeostatic feedback system regulating make-believe play, 57, 59, 61, 62–65; cultural differences, 98, 105; emotional regulation in integrative play therapy, 140–142

emotions and cognition, 62

emotives, 62–64, 130, 142; as motivational power regulating all cognitive processes, 63–64; association network surrounding emotives, 63; stimuli closer to the focal point or periphery of, 63

evoking mental images in make-believe play, 7

family structure, as related to make-believe play, 110, 112

family's values, as related to make-believe play, 111, 113

fantasy and imagination, as distinct from make-believe play, 10, 13

free associations and dreams and their similarity to play, 129

Freudian view of play, x, 127–129

games with rules, 8, 13

heuristic techniques for revealing covert dimensions and rules, 22, 153

imitation, as distinct from make-believe play, 5, 9, 13

in-play, meta-play and out-of-play expressions, 18, 21, 25–26, 43, 60, 168–169; types of out-of-play expressions, 26–27

Integrative Play Therapy, 134–144; as a "debugging" instrument, 139; indications for referral, 145–146; therapeutic properties of play ("bug-busters"), 139–142; types of moves in, 139, 143

internalization, 82

interpersonal goals and plans (strategies), 24, 35, 36–37, 40–41; cultural differences, 98, 105

leadership of sociodramatic play, 44, 114

learning through make-believe play, 2, 71, 78

"legal" negotiation skills, 52

linguistics, 22; anthropological, 22; general, 22

make-believe play as a language, xi, xiv, 1, 2, 15–16; animating by identifying,

6–8, 9, 10, 11, 13, 25, 28, 73; animating verbally, 6–8, 9, 10, 11, 12, 13, 28, 73; disclaiming seriousness, 6–8, 9, 10, 11, 12, 13, 28, 73; in integrative play therapy, 140–141; mental operations involved in make-believe play, 6–7

metaphors, 37

mimesis (imitation of adults' behavior) in make-believe play, 90; in different cultures, 95–97

"mini-legal systems" regulating sociodramatic play, xi, 43–55; and adult rules, 54–55; as different from rules imposed by adults, 44, 54–55; cultural specificity of, 44, 105–110; inequality and segregation–values underlying mini-legal systems, 54; interrelations among laws, 51; leadership laws, 44–45; the nature of legal negotiations, 52–53; participation laws, 45; possession laws, 50; in preschool education, 119; principles on which mini-legal systems are based, 106, 114; sanctions against law-breakers, 51; and territory laws, 48–49

moving in and out of make-believe play, xiii

participation in play groups, 44, 45

past tense as a designator of imaginary or hypothetical time, 28

Piaget's theory of play, 8, 72, 74

play therapy, xiv, 2, 127–148, 149; main play therapy methods: Adlerian,131–132; child-centered, 132–133; cognitive-behavioral, 133; ecosystemic, 133–134; integrative, 134–144; Jungian, 130–131; psychoanalytic, 127–130

plot structure of make-believe play, 21

possession of play objects, 44

power struggles through make-believe play, ix, xi, xii, 33–41, 40–41; cultural differences, 105–106; in integrative play therapy, 140–141, 143; negotiations for proximity and control, 32, 34, 38; tactics, 32, 33, 34, 40–41, 43

practice play, 8, 13

presuppositions and purposes, 23–24, 40–41, 165–169, 182–184

pretending, as distinct from make-believe play 5, 10, 13

proximity and control in interpersonal relations, 33, 37–39, 40–41, 55

relations between social structure, socialization and the nature of sociodramatic play, 107–115

representation, 6

rituals, as distinct from make-believe play, 5, 12, 13

Saussure, Ferdinand de, 25

scripts, 35

semiotic analysis of make-believe play texts, 15–30, 153–184, analysis by expressive media across time units, 22–23, 118, 162–164; classifying features into minimal signifier-signified units, 23, 37, 118, 162–165; constructing underlying patterns and rules, 179–180; revealing the players' interpersonal goals and their plans or strategies, 24, 37–39, 119, 183–184; revealing underlying dimensions by context-dependent componential analysis, 23, 118–119, 170–179; semiotic systems, 15, 149; underlying rules describing structures and their users' presuppositions and purposes, 23–24, 118–119, 166–169, 180–184

semantics, 23

semiotics, 22, 135, 150

signifier and signified, 8, 9, 10, 12, 13, 14, 20, 21, 23, 25, 62, 64, 73–74, 75, 178; arbitrariness of signifier, 25; categories of, 22; dimensions defining categories, 22; patterns of correspondence between signifiers and signified, 178

simplicity, 136–137; as a property of information-processing systems, 136; debugging and restoring simplicity as the goal of integrative play therapy 139; dysfunctional, "bugging" attempts to restore lost simplicity, 137–138; lost in situations of change, 136

social-communicational functions of play, 1

social development and make-believe play, 82, 85

socialization, as reflected in play, xi

standard of living, as related to make-believe play, 110, 112–113

storytelling, as distinct from make-believe play, 11, 13

structural (syntactic) rules of make-believe play, 21, 22

structure of make-believe play, 21

structures as syntactic units, 23

symbolic representation, as distinct from make-believe play, 5, 9, 13

synonyms of the term "make-believe play," 5, 8, 9

systematic interrelations among various components of the integrative theory of make-believe play, 150–151

theoretical integration of theories and findings about make-believe play, 149

verbal and nonverbal make-believe play, 7

About the Author

SHLOMO ARIEL is Co-Director of the Integrative Psychotherapy Center in Ramat Gan, Israel. He is the author of *Culturally Competent Family Therapy* (Greenwood, 1999).